The Book of
Codford

From the Bronze Age to the Bypass

ROMY WYETH

First published in Great Britain in 2005

British Library Cataloguing-in-Publication Data.
A CIP record for this title is available from the British Library.

ISBN 1 84114 464 9

HALSGROVE

Halsgrove House
Lower Moor Way
Tiverton, Devon EX16 6SS
Tel: 01884 243242
Fax: 01884 243325
E-mail: sales@halsgrove.com
Website: www.halsgrove.com

Title page photograph: *The Lodge, once the gatehouse to Stockton estate, in the snow. This photograph was taken prior to 1989 when the bypass construction began.*

Printed and bound in Great Britain by CPI Bath.

Whilst every care has been taken to ensure the accuracy of the information contained in this book, the publisher disclaims responsibility for any mistakes which may have been inadvertently included.

A Timeline of Codford

4000–2500BC	Neolithic
2500–800BC	Bronze Age – Codford Circle/Barrows
800BC – AD43	Iron Age
43–410	Romano-British settlements
901	Saxon – Codan ford/shaft/burial
1086	Normans – Domesday
1252	Charter for Market
1317	Charter for Hermit
1500	Medieval Chalice
1597	Baptism Records
1620	Marriage Records
1679	Burial Records
1778	Congregational Chapel founded
1801	First census
1808	Harry Biggs, lord of the manor
1810	St Peter's enclosure
1815	Ashton Giffard enclosure
1820s	'Rural Rides'
1840s	Water meadows
1841	St Peter's School opened
1844	St Mary's enclosure
1875	St Mary's School opened
1914	First World War
1916	New Zealand General Hospital/Australian Badge
1922	First radio broadcast
1924	Woman's Institute formed
1926/28	Parishes united
1934	First Parish Council
1937	Foot and Mouth outbreak
1939	Second World War
1941	6th Guards Armoured Brigade
1943	British 11th Armoured /US 3rd Armored Division
1944	3rd Armored leave after D-Day
1949	Playing-field conveyed to village
1951	First piped water
1956	Railway station closed for passengers
1960	Railway station closed for freight
1963	Theatre Club purchased Woolstore
1987	Public inquiry for Codford bypass
1990	Bypass opened
1993	New village hall opened

Acknowledgements

It has taken ten years from the initial desire to write this book to the publication date – looking at the important events in the history of Codford from the Bronze Age to the bypass. During the past decade I have consulted many people and my research has taken me to diverse sources of information. Without the following contributions *The Book of Codford* would never have been possible:

Photos and illustrations: Brian Marshall, David Wiltshire, Mike Elcomb, Janet Hill, David Mason, Ken and Doreen Axtell, Alan Nash, Sally Thomson, Rosamund Willoughby, Antony Barrington-Brown, Richard Carr-Gomm, Maurice Cole, Martyn Lock, Joan Dredge, Gordon Norris, Mike Read, Ron Sutton, Chris Jones, Nigel Lampard, Christopher Crooks (Head Verger of Salisbury Cathedral), Dr Paul Robinson (Wiltshire Heritage Museum at Devizes), Wiltshire Constabulary, H.T. Construction, and Kitchenham Ltd of Bournemouth.

Research: Maurice and Godfrey Cole, the late Paul and Harry Cole, John Chandler, Gordon Norris, Sally Thomson, Rosamund Willoughby, Kate Forbes, Dr Mike Allen, Dr Julie Gardiner, Janet Hill, Steve Davis, Bert Doughty, Fred Read, John and Will Collins, Ken and Doreen Axtell, Euan Hutchings, Nick Claypoole, Christine Bradley, Anne Willis, Terry Crawford, Christopher Green, Richard Carr-Gomm, Nigel Lampard, Simon Firth, Steven Pope, David Falcke, Josh Stratton, Joan Dredge, Charlie Cotton, Greg Puddy, Ken Lowe, George Russell, Karen Johnstone, Ann Jessey, Dr Ann Williams, Dr Rosemary Cramp (Durham University), Prof. Michael Swanton (Southampton University), Bruce Purvis (Salisbury Library Local Studies), Alwyn Hardy (curator Warminster Dewey Museum), *Wiltshire Archaeology and Natural History Magazine*, R. Haynes (Wiltshire County Council), Nicholas Pearson Associates, the Highways Agency, Martin Wright (Salisbury and South Wilts Museum), the *Warminster Journal,* Warminster History Society, and the Commonwealth War Graves Commission.

Source Materials
A.D. Mills, *A Dictionary of English Place Names*, Oxford University Press, 1991.
Sir Richard Colt-Hoare, *The Ancient History of South Wiltshire*, 1812.
Sir Richard Colt-Hoare, *The History of Modern Wiltshire*, 1824.
Nikolaus Pevsner, *The Buildings of England – Wiltshire*, Penguin Books, 1963.
Prof. Michael Swanton (translated and edited by), *The Anglo-Saxon Chronicles*, new edition, Phoenix Press, 2000.
Caroline and Frank Thorn (ed), *Domesday Book – Wiltshire*, Phillimore, 1979.
John Laffin, *Brassey's Battles*, Brassey's, London, 1995.
Revd John Ingram, *Memorials of the Parish of Codford St Mary*, 1844.
J.E. Nightingale, *Church Plate of the Country of Wilts*, 1891.
Douglas Palmer, *The Atlas of the Pre-Historic World*, Marshall Publishing Ltd, 2000.
W.J. Arkell and S.I. Tomkieff, *English Rock Terms*, Oxford University Press, 1953.
Henry Beauchamp Walter, *The Church Bells of Wiltshire*, Wiltshire Archaeology Magazine, 1927.
Anne Willis, *Warminster Bellfounders*, Warminster History Society and Dewey Museum of Warminster.
Romy Wyeth, *Warriors for the Working Day – Codford During Two World Wars*, Hobnob Press, 2002.
William Cobbett, *Rural Rides*, 1830.
R. Haynes, *Wiltshire Milestones, Leisure in Wiltshire*, Wiltshire County Council, c.1968.
Charles Thomas Perfect, *Hornchurch During The Great War*, 1920.
Bernard Grun, *Timetables of History – the New Third Revised Edition*, Simon & Schuster, 1991.
Chris Scarre, *Chronicle of the Roman Emperors – The Reign by Reign Record of the Rulers of Imperial Rome*, Thames & Hudson, 1995.
Arthur Shuttlewood, *The Warminster Mystery*, Tandem, 1967.
Karen Johnstone, *The History of a Country Theatre*.
A36 Codford to Heytesbury Improvement- Environmental Statement Additional Information Appendix 7, prepared by Nicholas Pearson Associates, c.2003–4.
Country Railway Routes, *Salisbury to Westbury*, Middleton Press.
Kelly's Directory, 1927.
Wiltshire Inquisitions Post Mortem
Parish Register Codford St Peter
Burial Register Codford St Mary
Wiltshire Sites and Monuments Records
Anglo-Saxon Studies article by Prof. Michael Swanton

Introduction

The Codford of the twenty-first century was once three settlements – Codford St Mary, Codford St Peter and Ashton Gifford. The two Grade I listed churches of St Mary and St Peter, after which the villages were named, are still regularly used as part of a team ministry that includes Boyton, Sherrington, Upton Lovell, Sutton Veny, Knook, Heytesbury, Tytherington and Norton Bavant.

The village is very much a 'chalk and cheese' settlement; to the south the tranquil and beautiful Wylye Valley with its lush meadows and ethereal morning mists, and to the north the vast open landscape of Salisbury Plain, endless tracts of green sward with vast expanses of sky. East and west, protectively encircling the community, are the rolling downs, partially covered with trees, offering shelter to the deer, badgers, foxes, rabbits and all manner of birds.

Codford has Bronze Age and Romano-British settlements, Saxon origins, was recorded in Domesday, is documented through the medieval period and was turned into a military encampment during both world wars. The Army and agriculture are the joint threads that run throughout the recent and the distant past.

Certain names in this book will not be consistent throughout. I have done my best to be historically accurate and to use the spelling as in the source material. Names have evolved. For example, Ashton Giffard has been referred to through time as Schetone, Aiston, Ayston, Ashton and Ashton Gifford/Giffard. Similarly, Humphrey de L'Isle is also called Humphrey D'Lisle and Humfridi de Insula, and the Giffard family is also referred to as Gifford. In various incarnations the George public house has been called the George Hotel, the George Inn and sometimes just The George. As the woollen industry in the Wylye Valley declined the old wool store building was divided to become the Woolstore with the annex now known as the Woolstore Theatre, and where once an ancient ox barn stood there is now a cottage called Oxbarn. The Commonwealth War Graves are more commonly known as the ANZAC Cemetery.

This book tells the story of one Plain village using valley voices, offering glimpses of brief moments in time and bringing together the threads of history in a vivid Codford kaleidoscope.

Romy Wyeth.
2005

Church Lane, Anzac War Graves, St Mary's Cottage and St Mary's churchyard.

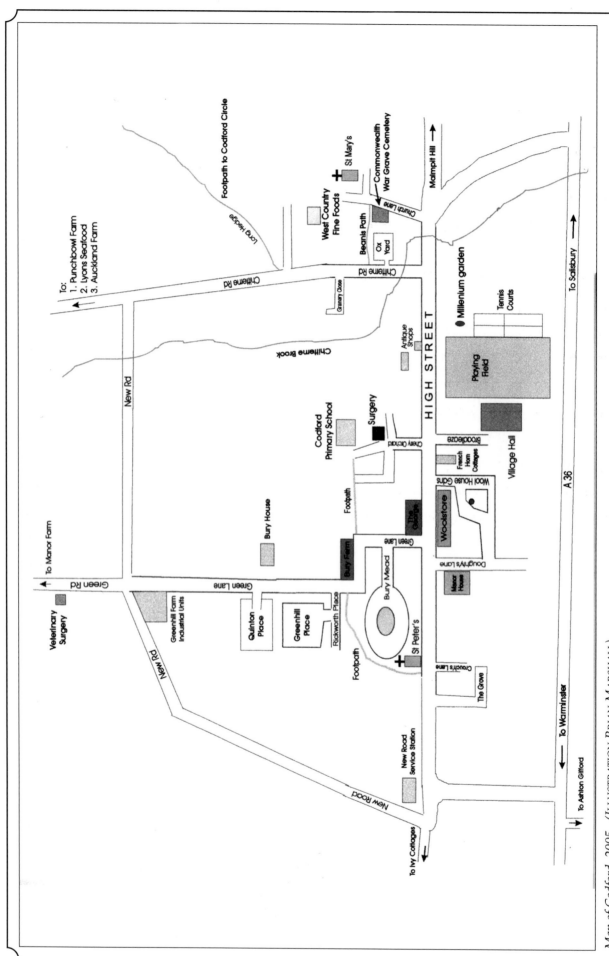

Map of Codford, 2005. (Illustration Brian Marshall)

Contents

Codford Circle, 2005.

Above: *Bronze Age urn from Codford.* (COPYRIGHT PERMISSION WILTSHIRE HERITAGE MUSEUM, DEVIZES)

Right: *The Saxon shaft, which originates from c.AD900.* (PHOTO BY B.G. MORGAN FOR KATE FORBES, C.1960S)

Chapter 1

From Prehistory to Domesday

Worshipping Upon High Places

The first three sections of this chapter show the nineteenth-century perspective as understood by the antiquarians of the time. Codford Circle is seen through the eyes of the men who did the first investigations as well as the twenty-first-century archaeologists.

Codford Circle

William Cunningham of Heytesbury first recorded Codford Circle in 1804. While out riding Cunningham discovered the site, consisting of a low bank and infilled ditch forming an almost perfectly circular enclosure on the crest of the hill above Codford. Despite numerous notable antiquarians living and working within the area, such as Sir Richard Colt-Hoare at Stourhead, William Cunningham and Aylwn Lambert at Boyton, all of whom visited Codford Circle, no archaeological fieldwork was recorded on the site until the beginning of 2001.

In 1812 William Miller of Albemarle Street, London, published Sir Richard Colt-Hoare's *The Ancient History of South Wiltshire*. Colt-Hoare wrote:

... but the one [earthen works] *on Codford Hill so far exceeds all these in symmetry of form, and beauty of situation, that I have purposely reserved my description of similar antiquities for the present occasion.*

This earthen work is situated on the summit of a hill commanding a most extensive and interesting prospect. It forms a complete circle, the area of which contains above nine acres, and the circuit amounts to three furlongs and one hundred and ten yards. It is surrounded by neatly formed vallum [a wall rampart of earth] *and foss* [an excavation outside ramparts or outer wall of a fort], *which, together with the area, have been much defaced by the plough. It is vulgarly called OLDBURY CAMP, but the smallness of the enclosure, as well as the slightness of the ramparts, evidently contradict the idea of it having been made or used for military purposes; it has no signs of any entrance, nor is the ditch within, as we frequently find the case in the earthen works appropriated to religious purposes. That this work was dedicated to some juridical or religious ceremonies, the nature of its plan, its size and elevated situation seem to indicate.*

In the summer of 2000, two local archaeologists living in Codford, Dr Julie Gardiner and Dr Mike Allen made a discovery which is likely to have national importance. They were working in their spare time, augering a long barrow in Corton as part of the village's millennium project. While sitting around a kitchen table looking at an aerial photograph from the 1970s, owned by Thomas and Caroline Wheatley Hubbard, they spotted what looked like a soil mark indicating a possible pit and ditch, an oval enclosure inside the Iron Age enclosure of Codford Circle. This inner enclosure had never been noticed before and had not been recorded by the County Archaeologists, the Royal Commission for Historical Monuments Survey nor English Heritage. Drs Allen and Gardiner felt that this was possibly evidence of a much earlier and totally unknown prehistoric site inside Codford Circle. Its form could indicate a Neolithic (New Stone Age) Henge (2400BC) or even a Neolithic causewayed enclosure (3500BC).

Little is known about the site, a scheduled ancient monument, and the bank and ditch that were visible in the nineteenth century led Colt-Hoare to the conclusion that this was not a defensive site, but a place of meeting, of ritual or of community activity. Since then nothing has been done. English Heritage, which categorises it as an Iron Age hill-fort, has scheduled it. However, Codford Circle could be a late Bronze Age (around 1000BC), hilltop enclosure, possibly used for stock. Mike Allen described the site thus:

The bank and ditch may be a late Bronze Age enclosure site, of which there are many across Southern England. What is exciting is that in the centre of Codford Circle we think there are a series of hidden pits which have never ever been known before, English Heritage nor the Royal Commission were aware of the pits, and no other archaeologists have picked them up.

The archaeologists were determined to find answers to the burning questions: 'Is there something there, what is it, how old is it, what type of site is it?' They had to apply to the English Heritage and the Secretary of State for permission to excavate, and scheduled-monument consent to undertake a limited programme of archaeological investigation was obtained after a six-month wait at the beginning of 2001. As the site is in the middle of farmland, which was due to be ploughed and drilled in March, Julie Gardiner and Mike Allen had just a couple of weekends in which to begin work with a team of volunteers. Farmer Josh Stratton was very helpful in allowing the archaeological

Above: *Dr Mike Allen at Codford Circle.*
Above, middle: *Dr Mike Allen with local visitors to Codford Circle, 2001.*
Above, right: *Dig at Codford Circle, 2001.*
Below left: *In a trench at Codford Circle.*
Below right: *Excavations at Codford Circle.*

team on site, and four trenches were put in as the first stage of the ongoing investigation. Farm machinery was used to strip the topsoil and reveal hidden archaeology, and Alan Nash skilfully stripped the trenches, saving many days of removing plough soil by hand.

On a freezing Saturday morning, with the wind whistling across the hilltop, and a snowy afternoon on Sunday (24 and 25 February 2001), nearly 50 local residents visited Codford Circle and were taken on a tour of the dig. The monument was carefully sited to give commanding views in all directions, especially towards the Wylye Valley and Yarnbury. To the north there is a view to the Marlborough Downs and on a clear day the Bristol Channel can be seen to the west. Codford Circle fitted into the gently undulating chalkland valley with its clear stream that has flooded regularly for generations, and has been farmed for at least 5,000 years. The river and the landscape offered vast resources for the early farmers – materials for coppicing and thatching, pannage for the pigs and slopes to accommodate agriculture and sheep. During this period the cattle were smaller and the sheep more woolly; Iron Age sheep were most like the Soay breed, hardy and able to jump six feet from standing. Their wool was plucked rather than shorn, but they were used for meat rather than wool.

The river we now call the Wylye and its tributary, the Chitterne Brook, provided a regular supply of

fresh food from fish traps, as well as from birds and all manner of wild game as they congregated by the water. The major function of the rivers was as communication routes – stone was a commodity moved all over the country: pottery, amber, jet and possibly women were also transported from place to place.

The thick virgin soils were ideal for the early farmers – by 2000BC the rich soil was beginning to degrade and break down, and there were changes in the way farming was practiced. It became more intensive. The field systems dividing the landscape that allowed this intensification can still be seen in the low light. By 1500BC conditions were similar to those in the twenty-first century.

The long barrows of the New Stone Age were placed in prominent positions, often on false crests, perhaps as territorial markers; they may also have been sited close to ancient drove ways.

Initially it was hoped that Codford Circle might have Neolithic origins. Mike Allen explained:

From the valley the site is not visible, so it was not here as a statement of defence. On the skyline across the Wylye Valley there are some Romano-British sites, a number of Iron Age enclosure sites and Neolithic long barrows. Those Neolithic long barrows are sited precisely so that when you are in the river valley they were visible, so one of our possibilities was that this could be Neolithic but our excavations have disproved our hopes.

The new monument is inside the bank and ditch of Codford Circle; a series of very deep (2.5m) pits hewn out of solid chalk defining an important ritual site. From the pottery found in the bottom organic dark layers, the archaeologists know that this probably dates to the early Iron Age. At the bottom of the pit a large Sarsen boulder was carefully placed as a symbolic gesture over 2,500 years ago. Sarsen

is a very hard sandstone of the same type as the large stones at Stonehenge, which originated from the Avebury landscape of the Marlborough Downs. Digging through the chalk rubble near the bottom of the pit, they discovered evidence of cooking – burnt charcoal, bone and flint dating from approximately 700BC. The amount of burnt chopped bone indicated to the archaeologists that there had been ritual feasting, the communal sharing of food, in the area.

Soils paint a picture to the expert eye. The grass turf line of the bank was where the feet of prehistoric man walked – it was not ploughed in the past and soil analysis shows a thicker soil that can still be found on the hilltop today.

A large V-shaped ditch marked the inside area clearly; the ditch was put on a natural bank. In prehistory chalk was hewn out. Microscopic land snails tell the story of the landscape – some live in woodland, some on pasture. From their evidence this land seemed to have been open and farmed. There are freshwater snails all across the site, very likely brought from the rivers by humans.

After its construction, the newly discovered site contained an inner area marked by a series of pits, clearly marking off the central area as sacred, special and important. It is not defensive, nor is there any evidence of settlement and people living there, and it looks like a ceremonial site of some importance. As yet there is no known similar site in southern England, indicating that the new site within Codford Circle is unique and significant.

Ashton Valley

This area was described by Colt-Hoare as 'a little secluded vale called ASHTON VALLEY, in which is a group of eleven barrows.' There is a large bowl barrow about 80 feet in diameter and 6 feet in elevation. When it was opened by Cunningham in 1801, five urns were discovered, containing burned human bones, immediately under the turf. Later he found four more urns and a skeleton lying on his face with the head to the north and his legs gathered up, deposited 3 feet 4 inches from the surface. In 1803 he again excavated the barrow and found a cist containing a simple interment of burned bones. In January 1812 Cunningham and Colt-Hoare sectioned part of the south side and found the skeleton of an infant, less than 12 months old, in a cist. A section on the north of the mound uncovered the remains of a large urn with burned bones scattered in a cist. Colt-Hoare described this as:

... one of the most remarkable barrows we have ever opened, and may be denominated as a family mausoleum, as it seems to have contained eleven internments [sic] of burnt bones and two skeletons.

In the second mound fragments of a coarse urn, more burned bones and a circular cist were found. The third mound contained two pieces of fine Roman pottery and, at a depth of 11 feet, earth and chalk had been excavated to form a room, in the centre of which was a human skeleton angled nearly south and north, fully extended and laying on its back, contrary to general custom. While excavating the workmen found pieces of charred wood and iron nails from half an inch to 5 inches long. The mode of burial and the artefacts suggested an interment of a much later date than the others.

Mound number four was circular and flat with a floor covered with black ashes, charred wood and half-burned human bones. Nothing was found in mound number five. Number six was a bell barrow, 63 feet in diameter and 8 feet in elevation. At a depth of 8 feet they discovered a large sepulchral urn inverted over an interment of burned bones and a fine black stone celt or battleaxe. The ashes were placed in a pile near the urn.

The seventh mound was a circular barrow containing a skeleton interred from south-west to north-east at a depth of 3 feet 9 inches. The position inclined the antiquarians to suppose this was the remains of a warrior. The head was reclined on the breast, one of the arms thrown backwards and some of the fingers were scattered about, yet there were no indications it had been disturbed. Colt-Hoare recorded:

We found part of the shield of the deceased lying by its side; it had been made of fur, and was strengthened by slips of brass riveted through, and though not thicker than a quarter of an inch, was quite firm, and had splinters remaining at the end where it had broken off. By the right side of the skeleton lay a considerable quantity of corroded iron, which was probably once a sword or spear of the warrior and with it some small bits of cloth, so well preserved we can distinguish clearly the size of the spinning and that it was what we now term a kersey cloth. The circumstances suggest this was a subsequent rather than a primary burial as there were burned bones in a cist near the bottom.

No 8 contained more burned bones, a fine stone hatchet and a bone arrowhead. Nos 9, 10 and 11 were very small and each contained an urn with human bones deposited close to the surface and thus crushed by the cattle.

From hence I crossed the vale leading from Chittern to Codford, to a clump of trees, which is conspicuous on this eminence. Near it are some quarries, which are singular in their produce; for here, as well as upon most of the high points of land on the chalky stratum, we find a strange assemblage of sand, gravel, clay and pebbles; and all these articles have been deposited within the compass of a few yards. From hence probably came the pebbles mentioned in my account of Bratton Camp as found there, and used by the Britons of former times for slings.

At a short distance to the south of this clump of trees, are the remains of a very extensive British town, covering several acres of ground, in which on digging, we have found the usual and undoubted indicia of ancient population. On a high point of the same hill, but nearer to the vale of Wily, is a very interesting monument of antiquity, and by far the most complete of any we have yet met with Codford Circle etc.

Lamb Down

After describing Codford Circle in his *History of Ancient Wiltshire*, Colt-Hoare continued with his sacred theme:

We learn from the highest authority, that a very general and ancient custom prevailed in worshipping upon high places, which originated from the very natural idea of approaching as near as possible to the Deity on these holy occasions. In the Book of Kings, *we are told, 'nevertheless the high places were not taken away, for the people offered and burned incense yet in the high places'; upon which passage a modern writer has made the following note: 'Many of old worshipped upon the hills and the tops of high mountains; imagining that they thereby obtained a nearer communication with heaven.'*

Referring to Codford Hill, Colt-Hoare continued:

This Down is connected with another called Lamb Down [where Codford's First World War badge is in 2005], on which are several barrows, the greater part of which appear to have been opened in former times. One small tumulus had been overlooked, and produced a fine sepulchral urn inverted over a pile of burned bones in a cist.

Through A Glass Darkly – The Settlements

The period of settlement for the Codford environs can be traced from archaeological finds in a timeline that begins in the New Stone Age (5000–2400BC) and concludes in the First World War. During the Neolithic period pottery, flint flakes and part of a stone axe were discovered at the eastern boundary of the present village. A single find at Starveall, the cutting edge of a stone axe, was unearthed in a remote pasture beyond the present village site. The source of this stone has been identified as Cornwall. On the arable land of Lamb Down 14 flint flakes were found in the filling of a Bronze Age bowl barrow, and three sherds of Windmill Hill pottery were discovered on the level of the old land surface in another bowl barrow during excavation.

The Bronze Age heralded a period of intensive ritual activity on Salisbury Plain. The Beaker people constructed the great megalithic circle of Stonehenge over a period of approximately 800 years, and the immediate area around the site became the British Valley of the Kings. During the Neolithic period 15 long barrows were constructed within 3 miles of Stonehenge, and in the Bronze Age almost 500 round barrows, the last resting place of the elite of pre-history, were added to the sacred landscape. The Bronze Age tribes frequently chose the high places for their important burials. Codford has 25 identified Bronze Age and three undated round barrows, consisting of a group of six barrows on Codford Down, and there are 11 more listed as Codford Down/Ashton Valley and a further eight on Lamb Down.

Beyond Lamb Down the enigmatic remains of Codford Circle, also known as Oldbury Camp, is in the midst of arable land. This was a site that faced the direction of the Stonehenge landscape. Eight barrows are in the immediate vicinity, with unidentified finds, and fragments of pottery from Faith Vatcher's excavations in 1958. One of the low mounds excavated at this time was recorded as probably being a throw-out from a First World War trench and may never have been a burial mound at all.

One of the other seven mounds is listed in the Wiltshire Sites and Monuments Records as an undated round-barrow site opened by Colt-Hoare, who found a primary cremation beneath a middle Bronze Age collared urn. The site was destroyed, levelled during the First World War and excavated again in 1958, at which time there were no finds listed. This site appears to have been listed more than once – it lists a Bronze Age bowl being excavated twice, but notes that Faith Vatcher doubted the site had been subject to earlier investigation – there was no sign of previous digging. In this instance she uncovered a pyre site. When visited by an Ordnance Survey (OS) field researcher on 10 January 1976, the site had been re-ploughed.

One small ditched bowl barrow was also the subject of a later excavation in 1963, when traces of a primary cremation of a child with a collared urn, Beaker sherds of stabbed and lattice decoration and a small cup fragment were discovered. This mound had also been destroyed and when visited by the OS on 17 February 1975 there was no longer any trace of the site.

Another ditched bowl barrow had apparently been robbed of its primary inhumation, likely a Beaker burial. The barrow still contained an intrusive inhumation and two secondary cremations, together with middle and late Bronze Age sherds. A second site close by yielded a contracted child inhumation and a Beaker sherd plus two secondary cremations. In all Faith Vatcher excavated six mounds on Lamb Down in 1958, one of which was likely to be the result of trench digging in the First World War. One more damaged and undated bowl barrow, with a central mutilation, was recorded as having the ditch present but being ploughed to the north in early 1975.

The Ashton Valley group of mounds on Codford Down, at Manor Farm, are the best recorded of the Codford barrows. Sir Richard Colt-Hoare of Stourhead excavated them all, and he wrote about them in his first volume of *The Ancient History of Wiltshire*, published in 1812. The first Bronze Age barrow, either a bell or a bowl, was excavated at the turn of the nineteenth century by both Colt-Hoare and Cunningham, and again by Revd Steele in 1952. The 2-metre high mound contained a primary cremation with a large urn and subsidiary interments. Nine more late Bronze Age urns containing burnt bones and secondary interments were discovered by Revd Steele before 1952.

The second mound, a mutilated 1-metre high bowl barrow on the west side by the trackway, contained a primary cremation, the bones half burned and mixed with wood ashes, and a third damaged and undated bowl barrow nearby was found to be unproductive. Revd Steele, who found a flexed skeleton in 1957, also excavated mound number four; farmer John Collins discovered a human bone on the site. The nineteenth-century excavation unearthed a primary cremation south of the centre, with a granodiorite battleaxe and a bone point. The fifth mound is a damaged bell barrow, opened by Colt-Hoare who found a primary cremation with a dolerite perforated axe hammer beneath an urn from the middle Bronze Age with a pile of ashes nearby.

The sixth barrow was to yield an exciting and unexpected discovery – when Colt-Hoare opened the mound, a bowl barrow, inside he found a primary cremation. He also unearthed a Saxon skeleton, obviously an intrusive burial added somewhere in the early medieval period between the fifth century and the Norman Conquest. Although the widely accepted understanding is that round barrows date to the Bronze Age (2500BC–800BC), during the Roman occupation and the age of the Saxons round barrows were also in use.

There is another bowl barrow, small with a circular shaft 5 feet deep, by which there was a secondary cremation in a cist, and another barrow with fragments of an urn. The eighth burial mound held a primary extended skeleton together with pieces of wood and iron nails in 'room' 11 feet deep. The ninth mound was a bowl barrow 24 feet in diameter and 9 inches high. When it was opened in the nineteenth century the primary cremation in an urn was crushed to pieces. Sir John Willoughby visited the site in 1975; two years later Revd Steele found a decorated late Bronze Age urn with applied cordons. Barrow number ten, again a bowl barrow, had contained a primary cremation in an urn; Revd Steele found evidence of two urned burials which had been discovered by Hoare.

The final barrow in the Ashton Valley group was a bowl barrow. Revd Steele discovered much burnt bone and many sherds in 1957; Colt-Hoare had found a primary cremation in an urn. Neither one of the latter two barrows had been visible when Sir John Willoughby visited the sites in 1975.

Also from Manor Farm land a single find, the handle of a Bronze Age socketed axe, with a battleaxe from an unlocated site in Codford St Peter, are now in the keeping of the Salisbury and South Wilts Museum. The Lamb Down and Ashton Valley finds are in Devizes Museum – the most important of these are the pair of axes discovered by Colt-Hoare at the beginning of the nineteenth century.

In pastureland east of the Chitterne Brook two undated circular mounds, possibly bowl barrows, remain into the third millennium, as evidence of the burial practices that began 4,500 years ago in a world where the ancestors, the earth goddess and the sky god were venerated and worshipped. The Bronze Age people, the early farmers, would have lifted up their eyes to the hills, with their chosen sites generally close to the canopy of the heavens. The barrows would have been stripped of vegetation, the white chalk mounds clearly visible against the green sward of the rolling downland.

The Iron Age dawned in the seventh century BC, and the farmers learned how to store grain and cereals, the population increased, and there was a growth of trade between the tribes and waves of invasions from across the sea. At the time of the Roman invasion the Wylye Valley was the land of the Durotriges. On Manor Farm a silver coin, a Durotrigian stater, together with a La Tène III brooch, was found with a metal detector. Two more coins were discovered south-east of Ashton Giffard Lodge – another Durotrigian stater made of bronze but with traces of silver on the surface, and a bronze coin of Carthage, 30mm in diameter, dated to 146BC. The fourth find was on Lamb Down – a skeleton with an iron penannular brooch on its shoulder was found in one of the barrows.

The Emperor Claudius sent the Roman Legions to Britain in AD43; the next 400 years saw the settlements of the Romano-British flourish within the present village environs. The majority of the finds have been to the south-east in the St Mary's end of the village, along the bypass route, and at Malmpit Hill, Lamb Down, Clay Pit Clump, Chitterne Road, with one find each at Punchbowl Bottom, Manor Farm and close to the river, and two finds at St Peter's. Like a giant sickle the evidence of settlement cuts a broad swathe from its zenith at Lamb Down, across the hillside to the east and the north, then arcing and narrowing as it reaches the nadir point towards the sunset at the western end of the village, at St Peter's.

When the new bypass route to the south was being investigated in the late 1980s there was a find of two Romano-British brooches and a coin. One brooch was a tapering bow, another in the shape of a Dolphin, and the coin was a third-century Antoninianus.

Habitation evidence, presumably pottery, was found by Nan Kivell on the north-west and the south-east slopes of Malmpit Hill, but in 1974 and 1976 OS researchers found nothing there. On Lamb Down, during Faith Vatcher's excavation of 1958, many sherds were discovered, along with two fragments of Romano-British moratorium, chips and sherds of Samian ware (glossy red pottery). An unidentifiable piece of Samian ware was found in the mound, which was possibly the result of the digging of trenches during the First World War. A coin of AD364–67, a bronze brooch component and three iron studs or rivets were located in the same area as modern horse and dog burials. Behind Lamb Down to the south of Clay Pit Clump a C-shaped enclosure was plotted in arable pastureland in 1995 from aerial photography, while south-west of Punchbowl Bottom a silver coin of Flavius Claudius Julianus was discovered. To the east of the settlement an iron sickle was found, and to the south-east there was evidence of an industrial site; a hypocaust or a possible corn-drying oven was discovered with sherds and a brooch.

In the wetlands by the Chitterne road two Romano-British brooches of 'type K' and a 'type M' fibula were found, while on Manor Farm the Codford Down Barrow group yielded two sherds of Romano-British coarse pottery from Revd Steele's excavations, and a metal detectorist discovered many Romano-British coins and brooches during 1992 and 1993. Near the river (Chitterne Brook?) a Constantinian coin dated AD332–33 is a reminder of the first Emperor to promote Christianity, Constantine the Great, who died in AD337.

It appears that during the Romano-British period of our history the settlements were on the hills with vantage points across the valley and the Plain. Malmpit Hill, Lamb Down and Clay Pit Clump have been identified as being places of habitation, pottery sherds being frequent finds on all three sites. Brooches and coins were scattered around the arc of the Romano-British occupation, with the St Peter's end of the village, further from the water, having only one registered find of this period – a fourth-century radiate coin (a coin with a picture of the emperor on it, wearing a 'sunburst' crown) was found at St Peter's Church while drainage work was being carried out in 1999.

The early medieval period, the time of the Saxons, appears to pinpoint two buried sites, one close to St Peter's Church, the other between the river and St Mary's Church. The present village site has Saxon origins, it's name originating from AD901 – 'Codan Ford', the ford of a man called Cod(d)a, or 'the wooded ford'. Certainly at the St Mary's end of the village the ford was in use until after the Second World War, and there are some surviving unsurveyed earthworks to the south of the church. In St Peter's Church one of the treasures of Saxon England was discovered in 1864 during restoration work – a carved tapering shaft about 4 feet tall, showing a man wearing a crown or fillet, with his head thrown back at an acute angle with a branch above his head. This is believed to be a cross shaft dating from around AD900.

Manor Farm has been a treasure trove of artefacts from the Bronze Age to the Second World War – many of the twentieth-century discoveries were the result of the Collins family's commitment to the past, especially the late John Collins whose private farm museum houses a wealth of fascinating memorabilia. The early medieval finds include a late Saxon eleventh-century stirrup mount, a silver sceat, porquipine series (a coin with a 'prickle' effect on it), and two sherds of fine Saxon pottery fragments, which were discovered by Cunningham and Colt-Hoare during the opening of a barrow on Codford Down in 1800. These fragments were incorrectly identified by the excavators as being Romano-British. In the Bronze Age barrow the Saxon inhumation, mentioned earlier, was found with the remains of a bronze mounted wooden bucket, corroded iron and bits of cloth.

In the late medieval period, which spanned the years between the Norman Conquest in 1066 to 1600, on arable land in Codford St Mary a stirrup was lost, to be rediscovered in the twentieth century. Between 1992–3 coins, buckles, a brooch, a weight, a purse frame, a stud, a jetton and other objects were found on Manor Farm with the aid of a metal detector. These finds are in Salisbury Museum at the time of writing.

Ansty Hill is recorded in the Wiltshire Sites and Monuments Records as the possible site of a deserted medieval village with no visible remains. Another buried settlement with medieval origins is also listed as being at Ashton Giffard. Ashton, the 'farmstead where ash trees grow' (see *A Dictionary of English Place Names*, by A.D. Mills), is mentioned in the Domesday Survey of 1086 as the manor of Schetone and was held by Humfridi De Insula (Humphrey de L'Isle), and in 1242 Elias Giffard held the manor of Aiston.

In 1291 the records mentioned Codeford Sancte Marie and Codeford Sancti Petri – the late Major General Sir John Willoughby was the source of information that coarseware sherds were found 50 metres south-west of St Peter's Church. Five medieval pottery fragments resurfaced when the new bypass was being constructed in 1989/90.

For finds dating from 1600 the term used is 'post medieval' – in 1999 a late-sixteenth-century copper alloy Nuremburg token or jetton was found at St Peter's Church in an unstratified backfill of a soakaway pit.

A number of undated field systems were discovered from aerial photographs and plotted in 1995. The sites are north and south-west of Codford Circle, north of Wraxworthy Barn and north of Ashton Giffard. Faint traces of a field system around barrows on Lamb Down were noted by Faith Vatcher, and in 1966 they were under the plough. An undated enclosure with internal features visible from the air can be found on arable land to the north of Ashton Giffard. It is impossible to date any of these features as they could have been in use any time between the Iron Age and the medieval periods, or even later. North of Codford Station an undated ditch aligned north–south, 1.2 metres wide and 0.7 metres deep, was revealed in a water pipeline during an evaluation excavation in 1991.

The *Sites and Monuments Records* for Codford take us back in time to the Neolithic period, with Codford Circle/Oldbury Camp as the oldest site, dating from the Bronze Age, through to the First World War Australian Commonwealth Military Badge cut into the hillside of Lamb Down in 1916. From the Beaker people to the Australian and New Zealand Army Corps (ANZAC), on the hilltops and in the valley, beneath the slopes and beside the rivers, brief glimpses of evidence of habitation have surfaced. The Bronze Age burials and the Romano-British settlements have left the most indelible marks on the landscape. The Saxon origins echo in the earliest known name, Codan ford, and from Domesday the written records follow the evolution of the settlements to the present day.

Saxon Origins

The origin of the name Codford can be traced back to 901. Consisting of a personal name and a location, it was known as Codan ford, the ford of a man named Cod(d)a. In Anglo-Saxon times the settlement was in the land of the West Saxons – Wessex. It was an independent kingdom, outside the Danelaw during the time of the Scandinavian settlements, between 875 and 950, when the Danes and the Norsemen came to England. Wessex was free from the invaders from across the sea, thanks to Alfred the Great, who beat the Vikings at the Battle of Ethandun in May 878. The site of the decisive victory is approximately 14 miles from Codford, at Edington outside Westbury.

In the ninth century Codford was in the Bishopric of Winchester, and by 1040 the religious responsibility for the area came under the Bishopric of Sherborne. Earl Godwin of Wessex held the furthermost reaches of south-west England at this time and on the powerful Earl's death in 1053, the territory was under the control of Godwin's elder son, Harold. When Edward the Confessor died without issue on 5 January 1066, Harold Godwinsson was crowned in Westminster Abbey. Codan ford/Coteford was, for a brief spell, part of the personal domain of the King of England.

The Saxon Shaft

St Peter's Church houses one of the treasures of Saxon England – a cross shaft, thought to be of early ninth century origin. The shaft is all that remains of what was possibly a Saxon preaching cross. Itinerant preachers would travel through the countryside and gather the villagers around the cross to hear the word of God or the latest news. The crosses were usually placed at the highest point in a village – in this instance probably The Bury close to the site of St Peter's Church.

The cross was obviously not exposed to the elements for any length of time as there is no evidence of weathering. Only one half of the upright has survived, and it has been cut in half lengthways.

Nikolaus Pevsner described the shaft in his *The Buildings of England – Wiltshire* thus: 'Wiltshire is poor in Anglo-Saxon remains, but what there is, is in valley-villages and valley towns.' He described the architecture of various churches, then parts of graves and cross shafts:

> *But the great age of sculpture in this part of England was the Ninth Century... the mysterious slab at Codford St Peter with the agile figure of a man bending backwards and holding up a branch. What does it represent? The figure is not at all small, and the piece is in every aspect unique in Europe. Its date cannot be regarded as finally settled.*

The extreme importance of the shaft is without question, however experts are divided as to its age and the significance of the carved male figure. To some it represents an archer while others see a semblance of a dancer on the stone.

In *Anglo-Saxon Studies* Michael Swanton BA, Reader in Medieval English Studies at the University of Exeter, presented an intriguing argument that the figure is an archer. He commented on the 'unquestionable artistry of the sculptured cross-shaft' and noted that the fruiting branch clutched in the up-raised right hand above the man's head has significance, that the figure is recognisable through the documentation of Christian art as 'that of an archer in the vine', generally accepted as 'a symbol of Christ in union with the church and the co-existence of the transformed nature of the living God.'

Michael Swanton compares the Codford carving with other archer figures, at Ruthwell, Halton, Sheffield and Bishop Auckland. He suggests the twisted neck of the Halton figure may have more to do with the proportions which 'he is now obliged to aim vertically and unrealistically upwards, his head craned at an awkward angle, his body contorted into a posture which seems almost to resemble a dance.' He says the Codford shaft is a:

> *... particularly cramped and narrowly converging panel. The figure adopts the traditional archer's pose: one leg*

The Saxon shaft, c.2004.

slightly raised, bent at the knee, an arm reaching directly over the head to clutch a bowed member; the head is bent conventionally as at Bishop Auckland, and drawn curled with fillet and fringe in a fashion that seems customary with these figures, when sculpted in sufficient detail to allow it to be seen. A hunter's seax [accoutrement] is slung round the neck. The figure's left hand holds what is apparently, fruit plucked from the tree above.

Local historian Kate Forbes differs in her opinion – she believes that, unquestionably, the man is a dancer. The following article appeared in the *Wiltshire Archaeological and Natural History Magazine* in the late 1960s/early 1970s:

The Codford Saxon Carving, by Kate Forbes

In 1864 the Church of St Peter, Codford, was extensively altered and modernised under the direction of T.A. Wyatt. In the course of removing the Norman chancel arch[1] the Saxon carving was found built into the nave side of the north wall of the arch about two feet from the floor.

In 1878 the Reverend J. Baron[2] thought that it might represent 'some religious incident, e.g. Noah as the builder of the ark, and as a husbandman, or the return of one of the spies from the promised land.' He described it as a 'figure of a man holding in his right hand, over his head, a branch of an apple or other fruit tree, and looking up at it in a very awkward manner; in his left hand he holds a mallet, or it may be a wallet,' and commented that 'His short smock and slipper-shaped shoes agree with Anglo-Saxon costume. The bamboo-formed moulding or leaning pillars with which the figure is enclosed appear also to belong to the same period, i.e. the tenth or eleventh century, say about A.D. 1,000.' Mr Baron added that he hoped the subject of the sculpture might be identified sooner or later and that 'it is possible that the design, which now appears grotesque and unintelligible, may, in its own time, have been well understood as the received and orthodox expression of some point in Scriptural or legendary lore...'

C.E. Ponting[3] quotes J. Baron and notes a few extra details; T.D. Kendrick[4], D. Talbot Rice[5] and L. Stone[6] have studied it more recently, chiefly to try to determine its date, but this will be more easily discussed after a full description of the carving.

As a resident in the parish of Codford St Peter I have had plenty of opportunity to study the stone and I would like to draw attention to details not mentioned by other writers and to put forward an interpretation of its meaning, for I think that this carving gives a most interesting picture of life in Wiltshire at a time when little was recorded in writing.

It is made of Bath stone and still has a dusting of Norman mortar on it. It is just over four feet high. It has apparently been split in half lengthways, as on the right-hand side near the top is about half of a cross of Maltese type which suggests that when the stone was

complete the top was probably square. It now stands in the chancel with what is known to be the uncarved face against the north wall. The top has been plastered to make a neat finish.

The front of the stone shows a young man dressed in the usual Saxon style in a full smock and a short cloak, which is fastened with a long pin. He has a luxuriant moustache. But for the band around his hair he could have been a model for the English on the Bayeux tapestry. He has the handle of a knife in his belt under his left hand. The object in his left hand could well be a rattle. He has his head thrown back to look at the branch he is waving in his right hand, but it is also turned to one side so that all may recognise him, for he surely has paid for this elaborate carving.

He looks as if he is taking part in a dance or procession similar to those held in the nearby village of Wishford[7] on Oak Apple Day[8]. There is one big difference, for the branch has certainly not got oak leaves on it. The leaves are relatively small, appear pointed, with deeply cut veins, and grow on long stalks. Low down on the branch is a drupe or cone, again on a long stalk. At the top of the branch is a spray of bobbles, also on a long stalk.

This is an alder twig magnified to about two and a half times its normal size. The leaves are rather too pointed, but this may be an attempt to show that they are not fully expanded. The bobbles at the top are the young female cones and the drupe or cone the remains of a previous years cone, which may hang on the tree all summer. The twig must represent a whole branch, the carver's chief concern being that it should be recognisable as alder. Alder trees grow by streams and in marshes. There was very extensive marshland in Codford until the seventeenth century when it was drained.

On either side of the dancer are banded pillars [J. Baron's bamboos] which may be at attempt to copy the end-posts of hurdles; note the double band at the third down on the left-hand side which looks like a split withy. The band around the top of the stone could be an imitation of hurdling or basketwork.

The stepped imposts above the pillars appear to be typical of early Saxon buildings[10]. These details give an idea of the kind of buildings the carver was familiar with and that would have been in Codford then. The little bits of twirly scroll above the stepped imposts on the front and also the left-hand side seem to be just space fillers. Under the dancer's feet is a panel with vertical parallel grooves of differing depths cut into it, this might be an unfinished inscription.

Round on the right-hand side is more evidence that this stone is concerned with water and wet places. Below the cross and beside the impost is a bobble similar to those on the front of the stone. Underneath it the stone has been levelled off at the back, but the detail at the edge is not damaged. Going down beside the pillar are first a possible leaf, then two eels with rather over large fins at each side of their head. Next there is a creature with short legs, a long swishing tail and a long neck. *This is probably intended to be an otter, but the carver has made its neck much too thin which gives its head a leaf-like appearance. Below this animal is a tangle of branches with another bobble just discernible and finally there are two fish with crossed tails. The upper one has one dorsal fin so it might be a dace, which are common in the Wylye. By the lower fish are apparently large stones, presumably on the bed of the river. As there seems to be an alder cone at the top and another with branches lower down, the defaced portion may have shown an alder tree growing beside the river.*

On the left-hand side of the stone there are what T.D. Kendrick describes as 'thick and luscious foliate scrolls' and he compares them to the scrolls in Britford church[11]. But this design is not repetitive as it is at Britford. Below the impost are three sprays. The first one suggests leaves unfolding from a bud, perhaps willow leaves, much magnified. The second one looks like a head of honeysuckle flower buds which spring from an oddly-shaped centre and there is one open flower hanging down with its long stamens falling to the lowest spray. This last suggests a comfrey plant with three flowers dangling down not inappropriately to the stones of the riverbed at the bottom.

Modern authorities on Saxon art do not agree as to the date of the carving. Professor D. Talbot Rice thinks it belongs to the reign of King Alfred at the end of the ninth century[12]. He does not think Wiltshire was a region of sufficient importance for work of this outstanding excellence to have been produced here before that date, but he gives no reasons for this opinion. He can see details which resemble tenth century work and notes that on the Foundation Charter of the new Minster at Winchester, dated A.D. 966[13], King Edgar holds his head in a similar position to that of the dancer. But he does not mention the mid-eighth-century archer at St Andrew Cross at Auckland, County Durham, who has his head at the same angle[14].

T.D. Kendrick[15] and L. Stone[16] consider that the Codford carving dates from the early ninth century. There seem to be features which resemble eighth century work, especially in the way the folds of the smock are carved in deep parallel grooves as they are on the slab at Wirksworth, Derbyshire, and on the cross at Rothbury, Northumberland. Also the headband was a Carolingian fashion[17] and is seen again on the Rothbury cross. As these details do not seem to appear on later work, the arguments for a date around A.D. 800 seem very convincing.

On considering all the evidence it may be inferred that in Saxon times [and perhaps before] the people of the Codford district claimed rights of fishing, trapping eels and otters[18] cutting stakes and withies for house building and hurdles as the people of Wishford and Barford St Martin once could[19], also gathering herbs[20] and no doubt anything else worth having in the marshes and streams of their neighbourhood, and that they confirmed their rights with an annual ceremony in late June[21] when they cut alder branches and held some sort of dance, or possibly beat the bounds of their territories, waving branches and rattles.

It may also be deduced that about A.D. 800, which is less than 100 years after the death of St Aldhelm, the donor of the carving [and the owner of the estate was probably the only man who could have afforded it] decided that the best way to lead the local population to Christianity was to blend their customs with Christian teaching. He therefore hired a first-class mason to carve this cross[22] with the annual ceremony of the alders which brought everyone together as a theme.

Three hundred years later the men of Codford may have been using the dancer as evidence to prove their traditional rights in the marshes. In that case it is quite easy to understand why the Norman lords of the manors of Codford and Schetone[23] [now Ashton Gifford] made sure that when the chancel was built the stone was hidden out of sight, no doubt with the blessing of the clergy who may have found very pagan sides to the festivities.

There seems to be no record of what happened to the other half of the cross. It might have shown some Christian figure [perhaps St Peter, the Fisher of Men] whom the Normans would have approved of and placed in their new church. If so it has been removed by Reformers at a later date.

Kate Forbes's interpretation of the carving is masterly and she makes a very strong case for the dancer theory. It has echoes of a very old tradition; on 29 May each year the villagers of Great Wishford, in the Wylye Valley, still celebrate Oak Apple Day. Initially this was a ceremony in which villagers reasserted their age-old forest rights, to collect firewood from the ancient forest of Grovely. The present date has Restoration connections – Charles II arrived in Dover to claim his throne on 25 May 1660. Four days later, on his thirtieth birthday, he rode into his capitol city to the rapturous acclaim of his people.

Nine years earlier in 1651, after the final battle of the Civil War, the Battle of Worcester, Charles was making his way to the coast in order to escape the Roundhead Army. Travelling through the Midlands he hid in a large pollarded oak tree, safely obscured from the eyes of the enemy soldiers. After the Restoration, 29 May was declared a public holiday, Oak Apple Day. Great Wishford is thought to be unique in still celebrating this day. The villagers rise early and noisily make their way to the forest, collect wood boughs and greenery, processing through the village streets. A small group of villagers in costume then travel to Salisbury Cathedral, dancing and waving their boughs above their heads, singing 'Grovely, Grovely and all Grovely'. They then enter the cathedral and their rights are confirmed from the Charter of 1603.

Kate's feeling is that perhaps the flowering of the honeysuckle indicates a mid-June ceremony such as St Peter's Day on 29 June. However, it seems likely that if the aim were to encourage the people of the ninth century to embrace Christianity and forsake the old ways, a logical date would be the time of the summer solstice which falls on 21 June. The Christian Church appropriated many of the Pagan celebration days, including the festival of Samhain, rededicated in AD835 as All Saints' Day, and Christmas Day named by Pope Julius in the fourth century as 25 December, the Roman festival of *Die Natalis Invicti Solis*, the birthday of the Unconquered Sun.

However, several experts on Saxon art stress that realistic carving dates from a period later than the Codford Cross and that the flowers and foliage would not have been indicative of a specific season, but rather decorative or symbolic.

A new theory emerged during 2001. Professor Rosemary Cramp of Durham University, one of the leading experts on Saxon England, is looking at the Wessex area for a new national survey researching Saxon sculpture, of which perhaps 4,000 pieces, mainly incomplete, are in existence across Britain. Professor Cramp wondered if the carved figure could represent David dancing before the Lord. She said:

I feel that the figure on the Codford Cross must have more significance than just a figure from a vintage scene, as some have said. I do think that the carver has tried to show a figure dancing in the way that dancers are shown around King David in the Vespasian Psalter. A lot depends on how one interprets what is in his hand – some think that it is an implement, but I wonder if it is a long-necked flask. I cannot find a good iconographic parallel for this figure but David is the only biblical figure that I know who got drunk and danced before the Lord.

Whatever the truth, approximately 1,200 years ago a skilled mason was commissioned to carve a cross by a Saxon of great importance. The Saxon shaft was dressed and worked by a master craftsman; its design was likely to be recognisably symbolic to the worshippers of the settlement by the wooded ford. It is wonderful that, despite the religious and military turmoil that occurred at intervals throughout the history of the West Country, the shaft remains where it was surely intended to be, in a small village church in Wiltshire, almost one and a quarter millennium after its creation.

Kate Forbes's article reproduced with permission of the Wiltshire Archaeological and Natural History Society.

Kate Forbes's sources:

1] In the library of Devizes Museum there is a drawing of this arch made in AD1804 by Buckler. It was a typical Norman arch carved in a similar style to the font which still survives. It was only 6 foot 2 inches high and 5 feet nine inches wide. Judging by the description given by Sir Stephen Glynne when he saw it in AD1863 the Norman arch must have been partly destroyed in the intervening years.

2] J. Baron, *Sculptured Stone at Codford St Peter*, 1882.

3] C.E. Ponting, *Notes on the Churches in the Neighbourhood of Warminster*, 1894.

4] T.D. Kendrick, *Anglo Saxon Art to AD900*, 1938.

5] D. Talbot Rice, *English Art 871 to 1100*, 1952.

6] L. Stone, *Anglo Saxon Art*, 1955.

7] Codford lies outside the Hundred of Branch which included Wishford and the lower Wylye Valley. Surely the name Branch was connected somehow with the customs of the local inhabitants.

8] Chr. Wordsworth, *Customs of Wishford and Barford in Grovely Forest*, 1907–08. (Once held on Ascension Day at Wishford and Whit Monday at Barford St Martin.)

9] T.D. Kendrick.

10] Ibid

11] Ibid

12] D. Talbot Rice

13] Ibid

14] T.D. Kendrick

15] Ibid

16] L. Stone

17] Charlemagne was born in AD742 and died in 814.

18] Otter skins are quite valuable.

19] Chr. Wordsworth 'The custom is to fetch Speeke [spike] Rods and Breeding [braiding] Rods for their houses, also Fould Shoars [hurdle stakes] and Wrethers.'

20] *Bulletin No.76 of the Ministry of Agriculture and Fisheries*, 1938. Comfrey tea used for colds, sprains and bronchitis.

21] Wild honeysuckle begins to flower in the second half of June. Mr Harry Ross suggests that this points to a midsummer ceremony. St Peter's Day is 29 June.

22] T.D. Kendrick. An early cross was a stone with a cross carved on it. Although this is much smaller than most, there is no reason why it should not be one.

23] Abstracts of the *Inquisitions Post Mortem* relating to Wiltshire from the reign of Edward III published by the *Wiltshire Archaeology and Natural History Society*, 13. The advowson of St Peter's, Codford, was held by the lord of the manor of Ashton in the early-thirteenth century, although not in his manor. As the manors were held by different Norman families until that time, this arrangement was probably very ancient.

Domesday 1086

In 1085, according to the Worcester Manuscript in *The Anglo-Saxon Chronicles*:

Then at midwinter the King was at Gloucester with his council, and held his court there for five days; and afterwards the archbishop and ordained men had a synod for three days.

After this the king had great thought and very deep conversation with his council about this land, how it was occupied, or with which men. Then he sent his men all over England into every shire, and had them ascertain how many hundreds of hides there were in the shire, or what land and livestock the king himself had in the land, or what dues he had to have in twelve months from the shire. Also he had it recorded how much land his archbishops had, and his diocesan bishops, and his abbots and his earls, and – though I tell it at too great length – what and how much each man had who was occupying land here in England, in land or in livestock, and how much money it was worth. He had it investigated so very narrowly that there was not one single hide, not one yard of land, not even [it is shameful to tell – but it seemed no shame to him to do it] one ox, not one cow, not one pig was left out, that was not set down in his record. And all the records were brought to him afterwards.

(Taken from *The Anglo-Saxon Chronicles, New Edition* translated and edited by Michael Swanton, published by Phoenix Press, London, 2000.)

Twenty years after the Norman Conquest, William the Conqueror received the Domesday Book, possibly just 14 miles from Coteford at Sarisberie, the place at which he disbanded his victorious army in 1070. This was the original city of Salisbury, also known as Old Sarum, built atop an Iron Age hill-fort in a prominent position at the junction of four Roman trade routes. The medieval city, with its beautiful cathedral, was built in the valley at the confluence of five rivers in the early-thirteenth century.

Of the 335 Wiltshire settlements recorded in the Domesday Survey only 29 churches and 197 mills are mentioned. Coteford (Codford) and Schetone (Ashton Gifford) account for two mills. During the period before 1066, and at the time of the Domesday Book in 1086, present-day Codford was comprised of four settlements. The first survey of the people, the property and the livestock of Norman England lists the landholders (in Wiltshire 68), together with the men of the feudal society, the Freemen, cottagers, villagers and slaves, makes no mention of the women or children. Figures need to be multiplied by four or five in order to get a realistic indication of the population.

The country was divided into districts within a shire – these districts were known as Hundreds. Wiltshire had 40 Hundreds, and Codford fell in the Hundred of Heytesbury. Each Hundred had an assembly of notables and village representatives who usually met once a month.

The first local reference is to Humphrey De L'Isle who appears to have held no land outside Wiltshire under that name in 1086 (according to Dr Ann Willliams). It was Robert who held Ashton (Gifford) from Humphrey. Prior to 1066 it was held by Kenwin, who paid tax for six hides (approx. 720 acres). There is recorded land for four ploughs, of which three hides (360 acres) are in lordship; two ploughs (a plough included a number of oxen, normally eight, in this case suggesting 16 oxen), three slaves, four villagers and three cottagers with two ploughs. The book also recorded half a mill which paid 6s.3d.; meadow, 12 acres; pasture six furlongs long and as wide. The value is recorded as 'was £4; now £6'.

It appears the settlement was made up of about 50 people with 32 oxen. The half mill at 6s.3d. is completed by the third and fourth parts at 3s. and 3s.1$^1/_2$d. at Codford. Saxon mills were often shared between neighbouring settlements.

Humphrey De L'Isle proved elusive – he may also have been known as Humphrey d'Insula, while Robert is a common name impossible to identify without further information – however, thanks to Dr Ann Williams, I have been able to establish the identities of other landowners from this period. 'Kenwin' is the name the *Phillimore Translation of Domesday* gives the landholder before 1066 – Dr Williams identified this Englishman as 'Cynewig', an unusual name. In Domesday the name is found only in Wiltshire, Somerset, Gloucestershire and Oxfordshire. The presumption is that all the entries relate to one man, who held, apart from Ashton Gifford, two hides of land worth £2 at Ash (unidentified) in Oxon; 10 hides worth £12 at Saintbury, Gloucs; and one hide and one virgate (a quarter hide) worth 10s. at Thorne, Somerset. In Gloucestershire he is called 'Cynewig chelle', and he was in the King's service; he was the reeve in charge of the royal estate at Arlington (assessed at five hides) in the entry for which he is described as a thegn of King Edward. Since the name elements '–wig' and '–wine' are often confused in Domesday, he may also be the 'Cynewine' who held five hides (600 acres) worth £8 at Chitterne. The only other 'Cynewine' in Domesday held land in Staffordshire. Whether or not 'Cynewine' and 'Cynewig' are the same person, it is certain that the man who held the manor of Coteford prior to 1066 held 19 hides one virgate (3,210 acres) worth £18.10s., plus the manor of Arlington in the reign of King Edward.

The first Coteford reference is to land of William de (of) Eu (Owe):

Bernard holds Coteford from William. Before 1066 it paid tax for one and a half hides [180 acres]. *Land for 2 ploughs, of which 1 hide is in lordship; 1 plough there, with 1 slave; 2 cottagers with 1 plough. Meadow 10 acres; the fourth part of a mill which pays 3s* [the mill is shared with Ashton Gifford suggesting that the nearest Codford was St Peter]; *pasture 4 furlongs long and 2 furlongs wide. The value was £4; now £3.*

This was obviously a small settlement with about the same number of people as oxen, possibly 16 of each! It was also the only place that had decreased in value, being worth £1 more in King Edward's time.

Alstan of Boscombe held the above lands of William de Eu. Bernard is another common name but Alstan has been identified by Dr Williams. William de Eu's predecessor in most of the eight counties is Aelfstan of Boscombe, with 230 hides (approx. 27,600 acres) worth £289. Aelfstan ranks as one of the five richest thegns below the rank of earl in pre-Conquest England. Sevington in Wiltshire was given to him by Edward the Confessor in 1043. A total of 14 of the 17 of William's Wiltshire landholdings had been the inheritance of Aelfstan of Boscombe, possibly the result of successive generations within one family.

William de Eu (family name sometimes styled de Auco) was the son and heir of Robert, Count of Eu (d.1090), whose father, another William, is said to have been the illegitimate son of Richard I, Duke of Normandy. The elder William married a woman named Lesceline and had three sons, Robert, William Busac and Hugh, Bishop of Lisieux (1049–77). Robert's wife (name unknown) may have been a kinswoman of Ralph de Limesey, whose lands in Dorset and Gloucestershire belonged to William de Eu at the time of Domesday.

In 1086 William de Eu held 336 hides (40,320 acres) of land in eight shires – Wiltshire, Dorset, Somerset, Gloucestershire, Hampshire, Berkshire, Bedfordshire and Hertfordshire, with the bulk of it in Wiltshire and Dorset. His father Robert (Robertus de Ewe), Count of Eu, whose lands in England included the rape of Hastings, was chief councillor to William of Normandy before the Conquest, from whom he received great honours and revenues.

In 1088 father and son were on opposite sides in the disputed succession. Robert supported William Rufus (William II) and William was allied to Duke Robert of Normandy. Despite being on the losing side William was nevertheless allowed to inherit his father's lands and title. In 1094 he was again conspiring against William II. According to *The Anglo-Saxon Chronicles*, on 13 January 1096 William de Eu was accused of treachery, and took part in a trial by combat with his accuser Geoffrey Bainard. William was defeated and convicted of treason, deprived of his property, blinded and castrated at Salisbury during the time the King was holding a great council there, probably dying shortly afterwards. Henry, William's son by his second wife Helisende, the sister of Hugh de Avranches, Earl of Chester was allowed to inherit the county of Eu. Henry died in 1140.

The second Coteford entry is for land held from the King by Waleran Venatoris (Hunter) in 1086 and Erlebald held it prior to the Norman Conquest when he had paid tax, usually an equal number of pence to each hide of land, for six hides (approx. 720 acres).

In the Domesday Book there was recorded:

... land for 6 ploughs [48 oxen], of which 3 hides [360 acres] are in lordship; 2 ploughs there; 3 slaves; 7 villagers and 6 smallholders with 3 ploughs. A mill which pays 10s; meadow, 10 acres; pasture half a league [³/₄ mile] long and five furlongs wide. The value was £10; now £12.

This landholding probably refers to Codford St Mary, held as East Codford by Oliver de Ingham, a descendent of Waleran. The settlement was the most substantial both in value and in size – it had its own mill and perhaps 80 inhabitants with 88 oxen.

Erlebald is not an English name – Erlebald was one of the many Frenchmen to be found in England prior to 1066. There is only one other reference in Domesday to an Erlebald holding land before the Conquest; this is in Somerset, where he held two hides at Witham (Friary), worth 20 shillings. The rarity of the name and the distribution suggests that he is the same man that held Coteford. The suggested context of Erlebald's tenure is that the tenement of Witham belonged to the manor of Brewham, held by Robert fitzWymarc, one of King Edward's French adherents, in all probability a Norman. Erlebald held from Robert and 'could not be separated from the manor,' indicating he was one of Robert fitzWymarc's men, holding for his lord. Presumably he had come to England from Normandy in Robert's company.

Waleran Venator (the huntsman) is listed in the Hundred of Branch and Dole. The head of his barony appears to have been Grimsted in the Hundred of Alderbury. He is recorded as having 40 hides (4,800 acres) in Wiltshire and extensive domains in Hampshire and Dorset. From her research Dr Williams believes that, given the position of his lands, Waleran may have been responsible for the New Forest, and that he is presumably the ancestor of Waleran fitzWilliam, who accounted dues for the New Forest at the Exchequer in 1130, and Walter Waleran [sic], who accounted for the same dues in 1167–70. Walter Waleran died in 1200 or 1201, and his lands were divided between his three daughters, Cicely, Albreda and Isabella.

The third mention of Coteford in Domesday with an estimated population of 27 people with 16 oxen, is land of Osbern Giffard. It records that Osbern himself held Coteford. Aelfric held it before 1066; it paid tax for one and a half hides (180 acres). There was land for two ploughs, of which one hide is in the lordship:

... one and a half ploughs there; 2 slaves; 6 cottagers and 1 cottager with half a plough. The fourth part of a mill which pays 3s. and 3 halfpence; meadow 10 acres; pasture 4 furlongs long and 1 furlong wide. The value was 50s; now 60s.

Codford St Peter is the probable location for the land in question. Given that Aelfric is the commonest name in pre-Conquest English, without more information there is no way to identify individuals. However, Osbern Giffard's lands lay in Wiltshire and Dorset (one manor only) and he is assumed to be the elder brother of Berengar Giffard, who also held land in Wiltshire and Dorset, and whose descendants were tenants of Shaftesbury Abbey, Dorset.

William the Conqueror, King of England and Duke of Normandy, reigned for 21 years after the Battle of Hastings. He died, aged 60, in France on 9 September 1087 and was buried at Caen. The Domesday Survey offers an accurate record of life in diverse communities across England, not just as it was under the first of the Norman kings, but also during the final period of Saxon rule, in King Edward's time.

Chapter 2

Medieval Codford

The Medieval Lord of the Manor
Kate Forbes

The lord of the manor was a Crown appointment that administered the manor. It is not known how old this systems is, but it certainly went back to early Saxon times. The lord of the manor was not paid, because in early days there was no money anyway, but he also had the best farm, the Manor Farm, which could be called the demesne farm. He also had 'ownership' of the other people who lived on the property, commonly called the villeins. They paid customary dues – as there was no money they worked or gave produce, say half a dozen eggs. Every landowner very often gave one day's work a week, every day at harvest time – the man who had the land either had to go himself or send someone else, maybe a family member, to represent him. This due could not be increased and was always the same – if the lord of the manor wanted more money he had to think up other ways of making it.

The lord of the manor had to pay a knight's fee, or a percentage of a knight's fee. He either held land from the Crown or from someone else, perhaps from the Earl of Salisbury (Boyton was held from the Earl of Salisbury). When the king wanted troops, a knight was sent with a squire and men at arms with their horses, food and certainly a cook – this was a unit that went into the army. Landowners were only liable for so many days in the year, so if you went overseas the king had to pay. These troops were mainly for local use. They relied on the lords of the manor to provide knights. At Boyton there is a knight in armour memorial in the church. He was the eldest son of Hugh Gifford who was a younger brother of Elias Gifford, and he had to go instead of his father with the Count of Salisbury to the Middle East. He went to a battle called the Battle on Mensourah[1] where the Earl of Salisbury was killed[2] – young Gifford came home, where he died. His brother, who was also the Archbishop of Canterbury, inherited and built a side chapel at Boyton, where he made a memorial to his brother.

The lords of the manor did not own the manors, they held them, they were hereditary; but if a lord wanted to swap a field with another manor he had to refer to the Crown.

Notes:

1] The Battle of Mensourah, Egypt, occurred in the reign of Henry III during the Fifth Crusade. According to *Brassey's Battles* by John Laffin, Mensourah was fought in 1249, while Roy Spring, in *Salisbury Cathedral*, gives the date as February 1250. Salisbury Cathedral contains the effigy of the earl whose remains were buried at Acre in the Church of the Holy Cross.

2] The Earl of Salisbury who was killed was William Longspee (Longsword) the Younger. His mother was Ela, the heiress of William, Earl of Salisbury. His father, William Longspee the Elder, was the illegitimate son of Henry II and one of his mistresses; unconfirmed tradition suggests Rosamund Clifford.

The Hermit
Sally Thomson

From the early days of Christianity in this country until the Reformation in the 1530s, it was common for certain individuals to desire a solitary life, devoted to prayer and contemplation. These were the ascetics, anchorites and hermits. Usually, although not invariably, they were already members of a religious community, but desired more solitude than the convent or monastery could afford them.

Sometimes they would live completely isolated, living meagrely on wild plants and berries – the true ascetics. Anchorites had themselves sealed in a tiny room adjacent to a parish church, as Julian of Norwich did. She received offerings of food from parishioners and in return blessed them, prayed for them or gave them spiritual guidance. Still others,

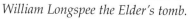

William Longspee the Elder's tomb.

although they might have lived alone, gave service to the local community – these were the hermits. They lived, for instance, in chapels on bridges, or by the roadside, often in conjunction with a shrine, and the offerings they received had to be used for the maintenance of the shrine or the bridge. Or they were allotted a certain work to perform. Henry de Mareys was such a hermit.

Although he lived in Codford St Mary, his name has nothing to do with St Mary's, but is derived from the Latin 'mariscus', a 'marsh' – Henry Marsh; an apt name in those days of uncontrolled flooding in the river valley.

We know little of Henry, only that a Royal Charter was issued in 1317 by King Edward II, granting Oliver de Ingham, the lord of the manor of Codford St Mary, permission to assign two acres of land, called Crouchland, to:

... our beloved brother in Christ, Henry de Mareys, chaplain and hermit, to construct anew in that place a chapel in honour of the Holy Cross, and houses fit for habitation, in order to celebrate therein divine service... for the souls of our predecessors and the souls of the predecessors of the said Oliver.

Where Henry hailed from, or how long he remained in Codford, we do not know. There are no other documents to tell us. But his hermitage has been the subject of discussion for many years. Malmpit Hill was known as Hermitage Hill in the seventeenth and eighteenth centuries, and possibly earlier. Both Sir Richard Colt-Hoare, the nineteenth-century archaeologist, and Dr John Ingram, vicar of St Mary's, spoke of the site being marked by ancient yew trees. However, Dr Ingram placed the site of the hermitage on part of East Codford farmhouse itself, with the two acres of land around it called Crouchland ('cross land'). Colt-Hoare referred to a site on the promontory of down above the farm, somewhere around OS ST 978398. There are still yews to be seen in this part of the hillside, but it must be sheer speculation today as to where Henry Marsh's little hermitage stood.

Poll Tax Records

In 1379 Codford was the centre of an emerging specialised cloth-making area. Poll tax records show that in a 4-mile stretch of the Wylye there appear to have been nine fullers and six weavers. According to *The Victorian County History* Codford had two fullers, as did Boyton and Heytesbury, while Knook, Corton, and Upton had one each.

The Codford Chalice

In the dying days of the brief reign of the boy king, Edward VI, on 3 March 1553, three knights were commissioned to make an inventory of all Church goods – all the plate, *juels, bellis* and ornaments in Wiltshire were to be counted. The 13 churches in the Heytesbury Hundred are listed in Colt-Hoare's *The History of Modern Wiltshire*: Heitesburye, Chitterne S'ci Maris, Horningsham Magna, Tytherington, Imber, Knoke, Upton Lovell, Chittorne Om'um Sanctorum, Orcheston S'ci Georij, Brighteston Deverelle, Boyton and the two Codford churches, Weste Codford and Codfforde S'ci Marye.

At Codfforde S'ci Marye delivered to Will'm Minbe and Phillipe Stevens 1 cup or challis, by indentuer of x ouz di. and iiij bells x ounce di. Bells iiij in plate of Kings use. At Weste Codford delivered to William Crouch and to William Longe one cuppe or challis by indentuer of iij ounces di and iij bell x ounces belle iij In plate to Kings use ij ounce di.

From this we see that St Mary's Church contained a chalice weighing 7 ounces, a 3-ounce plate and four bells. At West Codford St Peter's Church chalice was 10 ounces, the plate 2 ounces and the church had three bells. 'For the King's use' in an England under Protestant rule, was in fact the confiscation of Church property for the royal coffers.

It is obvious that the church bells were of little use either in themselves or to be melted down, whereas plates, cups, chalices and jewels were commercial commodities. The indenture was an agreement drawn up with two copies on one piece of parchment or paper to ensure that the goods were not forgeries. The copies were severed with jagged edges, a copy of each kept by the Commissioners and the churchwardens. In order to prove authenticity the two copies would be brought together – if they lined up and the edges fitted the goods were genuine.

The chalice retained by St Mary's Church for the purpose of the ministration of the Holy Communion was not handed to the clerics, Willielmus Stephyns or Willielmus Warde, but to Will'm Minbe and Phillipe Stevens, most likely the contemporary churchwardens. In 1843 the chalice was still in use. In Dr Ingram's *Memorials of the Parish of Codford St Mary*, published in 1844, the year of his death at the age of 70, he wrote:

The belfry now contains only THREE bells; though it appears from the return made to the Commissioners of Edward the Sixth, respecting church goods, that at that time there were FOUR. The cup or chalice of eight ounces, there mentioned, has been preserved to this day; though much worn, and in bad condition. It appears to have been as old as the reign of Henry the Sixth. The stem is elegantly formed, as well as the cup itself, and it appears to have been partly gilt.

In 1891 the Diocese of Salisbury published a record of the *Church Plate of Wiltshire*. Under Codford St Mary the chalice is described:

This parish retains its medieval Chalice. It corresponds very nearly, both in size and details, with the fine Dorset example at Coombe Keynes, with the important difference that the original shallow bowl has been replaced, in modern times, by one of a much larger size, thus destroying the proportions of what must originally have been a very beautiful object. The present dimensions are: Height, 7³/₈ in.; depth of bowl, 3³/₈ in.; diameter of foot, 5¹/₈in. by 3¹/₄ in. The stem is plain and hexagonal, with an elaborate knot of considerable projection formed of six lobes having facets of human heads, and between the lobes are open compartments of flowing Gothic tracery; the foot is plain with the exception of one space filled with an engraved representation of the Crucifixion. The outline of the base is a curved hexagon, the moulding relieved by a vertically reeded band; the points of the mullet foot are crescent-shaped, and seem to correspond with the description of a similar chalice given in an inventory of church goods belonging to the parish of St. Margaret Pattens, London, drawn up in 1526, and described as 'half mones, other wise called knappes.' The parcel guilding has been applied with good artistic effect. No trace of any hall mark is found; if it ever had one it probably disappeared with the old bowl. The date is perhaps somewhat earlier than A.D. 1500. The knot alone shows signs of wear, the heads having now become a little indistinct on the outer surface, but this is not remarkable after a continuous use of some 400 years.

The Codford medieval chalice. (COPYRIGHT PERMISSION SALISBURY CATHEDRAL)

The chalice remained in St Mary's Church for little short of half a millennium. On 7 April 1983 it was loaned to Salisbury Cathedral, where it remains to the time of writing, two decades later. The Codford chalice stands in a glass case within the Chapter House of one of the world's most perfect cathedrals, close to Salisbury's copy of the *Magna Carta*. Whether it is of late-fifteenth or early-sixteenth century origin, with a bowl disproportionate to the expert eye, the Codford chalice is a medieval treasure, in the perfect setting to display its stunning beauty.

Note:
The St Peter's Chalice mentioned in the 1553 inventory was part of the plate either stolen or lost, presumably sometime in the eighteenth century. In Nightingale's *The Church Plate of Wiltshire*, published in 1891, it is stated:

The plate now consists of a service given by a Rector in the middle of the last century. A Chalice, 9¹/₈ in height, with its Paten cover; the bowl is of bell shape resting on a plain baluster stem. A Flagon, 13in in height, of tankard form; an Alms-dish, 9ins diam. All these pieces bear the hallmark of 1761, and the maker's mark F.W. for Fuller White. They are also inscribed, 'The Gift of the Rev. Mr. Thos. Kellow Senr., late Rector of Codford St Peter, Wilts, Oct 26, 1764'. Thomas Kellow was the rector from 1730 to 1761; he died in 1767, at 67.

Additional sources:
Archaeological Journal, vol.xlii. p.326.
Special thanks for information about the chalice to Christopher Crooks, the head verger of Salisbury Cathedral, and to Doreen Axtell, churchwarden of St Mary's Church, Codford; for help with medieval terms thanks to Bruce Purvis, Local Studies Librarian, Salisbury Library, and to Sally Thomson BA.

Wiltshire Inquisitions Post Mortem

After the death of a landed person an inquisition was held to decide what feudal dues were held that could accrue to the Crown. A writ was issued by the Court of Chancery, usually to the escheator or feodary (an officer responsible for enforcing the obligations of Crown tenants) of the deceased's county, who was ordered to hold an inquest and to appoint a jury to see:

Of what lands the deceased had died possessed.
Of whom and by what services he held these lands.
The date of death.
The age and name of the heir at law.

The documents went to the Chancery, who then sent a copy to the Exchequer, which in turn collected the feudal dues. Under Henry VIII complaints about abuses grew so the Court of Wards and Liveries was set up and duplicate documents were sent there. Thereafter, three sets of these documents were in existence. Knight Sergeantry was abolished in practice in 1645 and in law in 1660.

In Domesday it is recorded that three Giffards held

land in Wiltshire. Nothing is known of Berenger who held the manors of Fonthill and Barford St Martin. Walter, Duke of Buckingham, held Maiden Bradley. Osbern, Baron of Brimsfield near Gloucester, held manors at Sherrington, Tytherington, Middleton (Middle Hill near Warminster), Winterbourne, Orcheston, Ugford, Stanton, one of the Deverills and a small manor in Codford, which appears to have included St Peter's Church.

Five generations later, in about 1230, Elias Giffard, the fourth of that name, was a widower with three daughters – Maud, Isobel and Mabel. He later married his second wife, Alice, the sister of John Mautravers, who sub-let the manor of Ashton as a dowry. John held it of the Dunstanville family, the heirs of Humphrey de Insula.

In 1249 an inquisition was held on Elias Giffard, lately deceased. In 1298 his son John, who had inherited at the age of 16, died. He had been married three times, first to Maud Longspee, the widow of his liege lord for the manor of Boyton, by whom he had two daughters, Katherine and Eleanor. His second wife, Alicia Mautravers, was childless. His son John was the issue of his third marriage, to Margaret Neville, a cousin of the Inghams who had succeeded to the manor of East Codford.

Margaret's son John, known as 'the Rich', was beheaded in March 1322 for taking part in the Baron's Revolt against Edward II. The lands of the King's opponents were redistributed to his supporters – John Giffard held land in South Wales, and had come into conflict with the Marcher Lords, father and son, the elder and the younger Hugh Despenser. John Giffard had forfeited the lordship of Iskennin; Hugh the younger was the beneficiary of this, while his father certainly held Codford for a short period of time. Five years later, in 1327, after the death of Edward II, there were several detailed enquiries into his manors and his rightful heirs. At an inquisition held at Warminster the jury said that John had held the manor of Sherntone (Sherrington) worth £20 per annum from the King in chief as part of the barony. He also held Aschtone (Ashton Giffard) worth £10. John Giffard, the jury concluded, had died in possession of his lands as fee of all the manor of Aschtone, which he held as the heir of William Maltravers by fealty for all service and which was worth £10 per annum. However, he was not seised of any other lands. John de Caylewe was the cousin and heir to the said John. There were six claimants all told to this estate – its eventual distribution has not been discovered.

On the death of John Cayllewe, an inquisition at Chippenham in 1336 recorded that the deceased held no land in Wiltshire or elsewhere of the King, but only one messuage and one carrucate from Sir Maurice de Berkele by rent of 1lb pepper at Michaelmas.

John Giffard seised of his demesne as the fee of the manors of Sherntone, Aschtone and West Codeford (Codford). He also had the advowsons (the gift of the living – the right to select the clergyman) for Sherntone and Codeford churches. Sherntone was the chief manor of the barony, held for one Knight's fee worth £26.12.8d. per annum. It consisted of chief messuage (the most important house in the village) with garden worth 5s., 12 acres of meadow at 6d. an acre, and $349^1/_5$ acres of arable land – 75s. (55 acres were worth 6d. per acre, 94 at 4d. per acre and 200 at 1d. an acre). There were 100 acres of wood, the sale of undergrowth was worth 40s. a year while the pasture of the wood was common and worth 20s. 'Le Shipecroft' pasture was worth 12d. per year, common pasture for sheep 20s., a water-mill worth 36s.8d. per year, fishery of the millpond 6s.8d. per year, fishery of fish-pond 12d. per year, issues of dovecote $^3/_4$d. per year. Free tenants' rents accounted for £4.2s.8d., customary tenants, each holding $^1/_2$ a virgate of land, and other customary tenants and cottars there and at Boyton generated £7.11.7d. Gifts to the larder at Michaelmas 33s.4d., pleas and perquisites of the courts 40s. and advowson of the church 10s. The church was taxed at 10 marks.

Aschtone was held by Giffard from the heirs of John Maltravers, by fealty for all service. It was worth £17.4.11d. per annum. There was one messuage and garden – 6s.8d.; 18 acres of meadow – 3s. an acre; pasture for sheep in common pasture 4s.4d.; water-mills and fisheries worth 31s.11d. Of the $208^1/_2$ acres of arable land, valued at 53s.6d., $44^1/_2$ acres were worth 8d. per acre, 14 acres were worth 4d. per acre and the remaining 150 acres worth 1d. an acre. Rents from two free tenants brought in 31s.11d., rents and customs of eight 'virgatars' and four 'half-virgatars' equalled 119s.1d. A certain gift to the larder at Michaelmas was valued at 42s.1d., and pleas and perquisites to the courts worth 6s.8d.

West Codeford was held of the King, as was Sherneton, which also had the advowson of the church and was worth £12.4s.0d. per year. Of the 112 acres of arable land six acres were worth 6d. an acre, 58 were worth 4d. an acre and 48 worth 1d. an acre. Nine acres of meadows were worth 3s.4d. an acre, pasture in the marsh 3s.4d., pasture of 200 sheep in the common pasture 3s.4d. and 10 acres of underwood. Rents of the free tenants there and at Orchestone were valued at £4.13s.4d.; rents and services of one 'virgatar, five 'half virgatars' and three cottars were worth 68s.8d. Church shot were worth 2s.8d., pleas and requisites to the court 3s. with advowson worth 10s. per year, and the church was taxed at 10 marks.

There was a problem with the Giffard estates. On 13 July 1327 there was a writ about Aschtone to inquire about the manor, which was said to be held by fealty to the heirs of William Maltravers. In an attempt to prove that two wards of the King were the heirs of John Giffard, it was shown on behalf of James Daudele and John Lestraunge that John Mautravers had by charter granted the manor and advowson of Codeford (St Peter's) Church to Elias Giffard 'in free marriage with Alice, sister of the same John

Mautravers.' Kate Forbes noted that the advowson of St Peter's Church, Codford, went with the manor of Ashton Giffard, suggesting that the parish of St Peter was once one manor, despite having been three manors in the reign of Edward the Confessor.

On 16 September 1327 the writ was subject to an inquisition at New Sarum. Sir John Strug was one of the jury – he was also a juror at John Giffard's inquisition. The result of the inquiry was that the manor and advowson had indeed been given at the marriage, and should go to Daudele and Lestaunge. In December that same year another writ about these lands, directed to Simon de Bereford 'the King's escheator this side of the Trent' queried 'did John Giffard die seised of them?' The writ was subject to an inquisition on 15 January 1328 at Devizes. The jury said that Oliver de Ingham granted the manor of Codeford to Robert le Boor for his life. Later it was granted to John, the son of John Giffard, 'so that said John was not seised thereof in his demesne as of fee.'

Oliver de Ingham, Baron Ingham, was the son of Sir John de Ingham of Norfolk and his wife Mercy or Maroya. He served with the military in Scotland in 1310 and 1314, raised forces for Edward II during the conflict with Thomas of Lancaster in 1322, and five years later became one of the 12 councillors appointed to guide the 14-year-old King, Edward III. In Colt-Hoare's *History of Wiltshire* it is recorded that:

This last Sir Oliver de Ingham is frequently mentioned by Speed, Stow, and our earlier chroniclers, for his warlike exploits in France. He was Governor of Aquitaine; and in 19 [1325] Edward II he reduced the whole Province of Anjou, which the King of France unjustly withheld to the English power. But his boldest and most celebrated action was the total defeat of the French army at Bordeaux, by a ruse de guerre, which, I believe, has seldom been adopted. The French, in 13 [1339] Edward III had appeared before the town in great force: it was then in possession of the English, and Sir Oliver was Captain and Lord Warden there for King Edward. Instead of putting the town in a state to sustain a siege, he ordered the gates to be thrown open, and the French flag to be on the walls and citadel. Thus deceived, the enemy entered with confidence, and were received with tremendous slaughter, few escaping to report the fatal effect of their own incredulity.

Sir Oliver was Governor of the Castles of Marlborough and Devizes and Chief Justice of Chester. Oliver de Ingham had owned land up and down the Wylye Valley, and he was seised of the manor of Codeford worth £32.16s.1^1/$_2$d. per annum. Capital messuage and curtilage was worth 13s.4d., 360 acres arable land £11.10s.0d., 16 acres meadowland at 2s.6d. per acre, and pasture for 800 sheep at 66s.8d. per year. One water-mill was farmed by the year at 106s.8d. Rents of assize were worth £9.9s.10d., with 'larder of bond tenants and capoitage of bond tenants of menials.' This phrase is not well understood by the translator, the suggestion being that a guess is being made or implied! Pleas and perquisites of the courts amounted to 10s. per year.

Oliver de Ingham died on 'the Thursday before Purification' in 1344, leaving a widow and one living daughter, Joan. Their other daughter, Elizabeth, and Oliver's only son, John, possibly from a previous marriage, both predeceased him. Elizabeth left a husband, John Curson (Curzon) and, a nine-year-old daughter, Mary. Joan was the wife of 24-year-old Roger le Estraunge (le Strange) at the time of her father's death.

The story is taken up in the *History of Wiltshire*:

It was found by the inquisition after his death, that he died seised, inter alia, of the manor of Codford in Wilts; that John, his son, had died during his life without issue; that Elizabeth, his daughter, was also dead, having left an only daughter, Mary, by her husband, Sir John Curson, of the age of nine years; and that Joan, the younger daughter, was still living: and it was of course returned, that the said Joan, and Mary, the daughter of Elizabeth, were coheirs to Sir Oliver. This Mary was married to Stephen de Tumby, but died without issue at 23, Edward III being then only 14 years of age, so her property devolved to Joan, her aunt, who thus became the sole heir. She married, (1) Sir Roger le Strange, of Knokyn, by whom no issue appears; and (2) Sir Miles de Stapleton, of Bedal.

At this time Katherine, the widow of Oliver's son, John, had the manor and advowson of the church, granted by Oliver, with the King's license, for the term of her life. By her charter she granted both ('in seisin thereof, by her charter') to John, son of Sir Robert de Thorpe Kt, Robert de Marcham, and John, son of Robert de Ingham. Codeford was held *in capite* of the King.

According to the *History of Wiltshire*, Joan de Ingham appears to have outlived her second husband, Sir Miles Stapleton – when she died she left her son, his namesake, another Miles, as her heir. Joan was buried with her husband in the church at Ingham, Norfolk; a brass on her tomb, lost at the time of writing, 'had represented her as rather a tall and interesting figure, by no means advanced in years.'

Oliver de Ingham's grandson, the second Sir Miles Stapleton, was presented to the church of St Mary at East Codford in 1403 – the cleric at the time being one Thomas Day. He died in 1417, the fifth year of the reign of Henry V, leaving the manor to his son Brian, one of the patrons of the church, who died in 1438. His son and heir, another Sir Miles held the lordship until his demise in 1466, leaving his daughters Elizabeth and Joan as co-heirs. Elizabeth married Sir William Calthorp, while Joan was married twice, first to Christopher Harcourt Esq., and then to Sir John Huddlestone of Millum Castle in Cumberland. Both men are shown as patrons of the church, Calthorp in 1487 and Huddlestone in 1495 and 1507.

Sir Miles's second wife Catherine, in 1455, had been jointly enfeoffed in the manor of East Codford. After Miles's death she married Sir Richard Harcourt of Ellanhale, Staffordshire, whose son Christopher married the younger co-heir, Joan. In 1468 Sir William and Elizabeth Calthorp and Christopher and Joan Harcourt are returned as holding the manor of Codford and the advowson of St Mary's Church.

Sir William Calthorp presented to this living in 1487; afterwards the patronage of the living descended to the line of Harcourt. Sir Simon Harcourt, the eldest surviving son of Christopher, was knighted during the reign of Henry VIII for bravery in the Anglo-French Wars after the Battle of the Spurs at Guinegate on 16 August 1513. The English Army with German reinforcements attacked French cavalry who threatened them while they were besieging the city of Therouanne. The force of the English/German attack was such that the French hastily retreated without a fight – hence the name, The Battle of the Spurs. In 1539 Sir Simon was summoned to show what right he had to the manor of Codford. When he died in 1547, the manor passed to his son John, who then died in 1565. The manor was inherited by his son, Simon.

Sir Simon Harcourt was patron of the church in 1572, and died in July 1577, leaving his eldest son Walter as his heir.

West Codford

On 12 February 1347 Maurice, son of Maurice de Berkele Kt, died seised of the manors of Sharrenton, West Codeford and of Sharrenton advowson. He held them by barony *in capite*. On the death of his father, 13-year-old Thomas de Berkele was the heir.

At this time West Codeford consisted of one toft (a homestead or land occupied by it) worth 40d. per annum; one carrucate (80 acres) worth 6d. an acre; and eight acres of meadow at 18d. an acre. Rents of assize of free and bond servants totalled £4.3s.4d., payable at Michaelmas and Feast of the Annunciation. Church shot was 2s.13d., payable at Martinmas.

The church shot or scot was a tax, sometimes extremely high, which varied from place to place. It was a very old tax, levied on all free men in proportion to the amount of each man's holding, and was a payment in kind, dating back to the laws of Ine, which said that the tax should be paid at Martinmas. It is often confused with the tithe, but although it was often in a measure of grain, it was not the same tax.

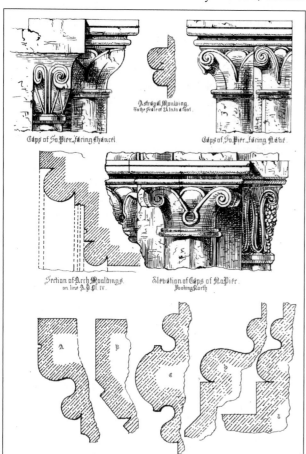

Fragments found in St Mary's Church, taken from Revd John Ingram's Memorials of the Parish of Codford St Mary, *published in 1844.*

Chapter 3

The Sixteenth and Seventeenth Centuries

'An Obstinate and Ignorant Fanatic' Parish Registers Uncovered

The Parish Register for Codford St Peter begins in the last days of Elizabethan England, just five years and four months before the death of the Virgin Queen. An *[sic]* Hibbert, the daughter of John Hibbert was listed as the first baptism on 27 November 1597.

The first marriage listed seems to have been towards the end of the reign of Elizabeth's successor, the first of the Stuart Kings, James I, when Thomas fferris, otherwise called Stokes, and Alice Turner wed on the XXV (25) May 1620. There were periods when no one in Codford St Peter married at all – in 1673, 1678, during the four years from 1683 to 1686 and between 24 February 1660 and 19 April 1664, no one in the village entered into holy wedlock. The Parish Register for Codford St Peter is said to date from 1680, but the register in the Wiltshire County Archives runs from 1716 until 1812.

While the baptisms and marriages catalogue the bare facts – names, dates, origins – some of the entries in the burial register record small details, which enable us to catch just a glimpse of the living person and an insight into the mind of the recorder. In the Burial Register for Codford St Mary a picture emerges. The records begin in 1679. Codford St Mary lost a barber and a carpenter in 1680, the shoemaker died in 1681, and in both 1882 and 1883 the village mourned the death of a shepherd.

There is one entry in particular, which grabs the imagination. It is for 18 April 1684, when Henry Knight was recorded as 'an obstinate and ignorant fanatic – not excommunicated.' John Wyatt, interred on 26 June 1684, was a 'vagrant whose father, he said, lives in Taunton,' and John Hood, buried in September of 1685, was 'an idiot'.

In the five months between September 1781 and February 1782 the village lost a blacksmith and a shoemaker. Buried in May 1787, Christopher Oliver was described as 'an old bachelor', while John Oliver, aged 87 and buried in July, was listed as a 'pauper' residing in Stockton Almshouse. In 1788 James Baverstock, many years the clerk of the parish, died aged 77; the following year, on 27 March 1789, Giles Withers, 'a poor labouring man' was 'buried by the Parish'.

The Sparey family appeared to have had an unlucky tendency to disaster: in January 1785 Richard Sparey died of 'a decline'. In October 1793 11-year-old James, the son of James and Ann Sparey, was 'killed by the falling in of a pit'. In February 1811 William Sparey's 32-year-old wife Ruth died in childbed. James and Ann Sparey's daughter Sarah was only 20 in October 1812 when she went into a decline and died, just 11 days short of 19 years from her brother's tragic accident.

A 68-year-old journeyman, a saddler at Mr Bendall's, William Richardson died in February 1793; the cordwainer's wife died in the autumn of 1794; and the collarmaker became a widower in 1795. In August 1796, 68-year-old Elias Weeks died of a seemingly isolated case of 'smallpox'; the following May John and Ann Yates's eight-month-old son John died 'from inoculation'.

Life could be very hard. A local barn in winter was the last resting place of 'a poor sailor unknown name who died in Coopers Barn' in November 1798, and in February 1804 'a poor man name unknown' also died there. In 1801 on 27 January Christopher King who 'had worked on the road until his death' was buried.

In July 1800 Abraham and Betty Cooper lost a son and a daughter just ten days apart, when John aged three and two-year-old Jane succumbed to a fever. In 1805 another of their children died – he was also named John, also aged three and died on the last day of July of 'scarlet fever'. At the beginning of 1802 William and Ann Whatley's 13-week-old baby William died of 'fits', and in August 1807 Daniel and Mary Dewe's eight-year-old daughter Ann was 'dragged and trod to death by a cow'.

Thomas Morgan, the landlord of the George Inn, was 82 when he died; although he lived at St Peter's he is listed in the St Mary's burial records.

The St Peter's burial register was less of a treasure trove of the absurd and the tragic. Common causes of death in Codford St Peter appear to have been dropsy, decline, consumption, natural decay and whooping cough. In April 1789 Jacob, the 25-year-old son of William and Elizabeth Grey, was killed by a cart. In 1794 the poignant entry for 5 October is 'a four day old soldiers child – no parents'. James Dredge, aged 20, died of a 'fever after a chill' in September 1797. Between 16 December 1801 and 10 February 1803 three boys, six weeks, three weeks and five months old respectively, and an 11-month-old girl died of 'hooping cough'. Measles claimed three lives between 22 March and 5 April 1807, the victims were two, five and 26 years old.

Meanwhile among the older generation, Jane Banger (aged 51) died in March 1798, 'suddenly, back from Upton', and in 1811 two men in their early

Above: *Malmpit Hill in the early-twentieth century.*

Left: *Sixteenth- and seventeenth-century graffiti in St Peter's Church.*

sixties were listed as succumbing to 'evil' and 'inflammation of the bowels'.

The Manor in the Sixteenth and Seventeenth Centuries
Sally Thomson

The two parishes of Codford St Mary and Codford St Peter lie side by side and by the sixteenth century covered roughly the same areas as their manors. Ashton Gifford, although a separate tithing, and for many centuries a separate manor, was included within the manor of Codford St Peter by this date.

Geographically, the two manors were endowed with very similar features. They shared the valley of the Chitterne Brook, which runs north–south between them, and both had access to extensive chalk down-land for the grazing of their sheep. They both had a southern boundary formed by the River Wylye, although St Mary's had a more extensive coverage here. Why, then, when these two manors were contiguous and geographically similar, did they prove to be so different? There seems to be no one answer to this, but a multiplicity of reasons. It is necessary to examine the ways in which these two manors were run and how they differed, and in which ways they were similar.

If one looks at the end of the story, Codford St Peter was enclosed by a Parliamentary Act in 1810, with 697 acres enclosed out of a total of some 1,668 acres in all – less than half the acreage of the parish. Codford St Mary, on the other hand, was enclosed as late as 1844. The area for enclosure was given as 2,123 acres out of a total of 2,129 acres, but the actual area enclosed amounted to 1,267 acres. Codford St Mary still operated an open-field system in 1844, as can be seen on the Tithe Award map of 1839. The

field divisions are the same as they were on the 1771 map of the manor, made for Thomas Walker, the then lord of the manor.

This difference in what were two obviously differently run manors may be accounted for by the lordship. In 1582, the earliest date of records in the period under study, the manor of Codford St Peter was owned by Sir Walter Hungerford, whose ancestral seat was Heytesbury, where an ancient house stood on the site of the present Heytesbury House, just 3 miles north-west of Codford. Sir Walter's other Wiltshire manors included Heytesbury itself, Tytherington, Knook, Sutton Veny, Norton Bavant, Bishopstrow, Warminster, Upton Scudamore, Leigh, Imber, Horningsham, Maiden Bradley, Fonthill and Teffont Evias, all within an easy day's walk of Codford and mostly situated near the upper Wylye Valley. There were a number of other Wiltshire properties, further afield.

By 1597, the manor was in the hands of Sir Edward Hungerford, Sir Walter's son. Until 1521 the Hungerfords were all buried at Heytesbury, in the collegiate church there. However, at some date after this, the family removed to their other seat at Farleigh Castle some 16 miles away in Somerset, and most of the ancestral tombs were removed to the castle chapel. Sir Edward Hungerford, who played an active part in the Civil War, had his seat at Corsham, in the north of the county. So, for much of the period covered by the Codford St Peter manorial records, the lordship was based some distance from the manor.

By the time of the Court of Survey in 1609, which produced a Rent Roll for the manor, the lord was a Sir Walter again. But the court was held by Francis, Earl of Rutland, and Lady Cicely, his wife. This seems strange, since Sir Walter died in 1596 and his half-

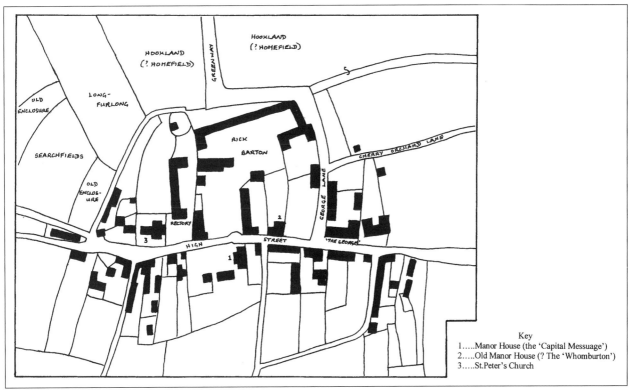

A map of Codford St Peter, based on the 1810 Enclosure Award map, showing the positions of the two manor-houses and the presumed demesne farmyard at Rick Barton. (SALLY THOMSON)

brother, Sir Edward, inherited the estates from him. Sir Edward died in 1607 and left his estates to his nephew Sir Edward Hungerford of Corsham, the son of Sir Anthony of Black Bourton. The Court of Survey still bore the title of the last Sir Walter.

The second of these Sir Edwards (1596–1648) commanded the Parliamentary forces and held Codford manor through most of the Civil War. He was succeeded by his nephew Sir Edward, a royalist (1632–1711), who sold the manor, among others, to Sir Stephen Fox in the 1670s. He became known as 'Spendthrift Hungerford'. In her book, *Wiltshire Forefather's*, Countess June Badeni stated that in 1682 Sir Edward Hungerford was dispersing all his family's fortune and estates and sold some of his Wiltshire property to Sir Stephen Fox, later Lord Ilchester, although the earliest documents in the Fox family papers relating to Codford date from 1678 (deeds) and 1679 (customs of the manor).

Sir Stephen Fox was born in Farley, in east Wiltshire, and purchased a number of 'spendthrift Hungerford's' manors. Codford St Peter was one of these and in due course it passed to his heirs. The Wiltshire Record Office documents show the lords of the manor of the eighteenth century to have been:

Sir Stephen Fox	*1709–15*
Stephen Fox	*1716*
Christian Fox	*1717–18*
John War and Henry Fenn	*1719–25*
Stephen Fox (after 1741 Lord Ilchester)	*1726–64*

Stephen Fox, Lord Ilchester	*1765–72*
Henry Thomas Fox, Lord Ilchester, Lord Stavordale	*1773–93*

The manor remained with Lord Ilchester until 1812, when it was sold, by auction, to Harry Biggs, lord of the manor of Stockton and of Codford St Mary, effectively putting Codford St Mary and Codford St Peter under one lordship. How this affected the running of the manor is not clear, especially since one half was enclosed in 1810 and the other not until 1844.

Codford St Mary's lordship is not quite so easy to follow. In early-medieval times it belonged to the Stapletons (Stapeldon) of Bedale, Yorkshire, but through marriage it passed to the Harcourt family who came form Staffordshire. By the mid-sixteenth century a branch of this family was established in Oxfordshire, and the manor remained with the family until 1612, when Sir Richard Mompesson became lord. It is not known where the family lived, although there are records of many Mompessons in Wiltshire, but Thomas Mompesson, who was lord in 1623, was based at Pewsey. Giles Mompesson, lord from 1640–51, lived at Bathampton, a bare 4 miles east of Codford St Mary. The manor continued in the hands of the Mompessons, the last being Elizabeth, who was lady of the manor from 1715–44. She lived in London. She devised her estates to Thomas Walker, her husband's grand-nephew, who lived in Soho, and it was he who had the map of the estate drawn up by William Wapshire. In 1771 he sold the manor to William Bennett; the Bennetts had been in the upper Wylye Valley for centuries and one of their main seats was at Norton Bavant. They were united through marriage with the Fanes of Pythouse. By 1791, William Parry was lord and he was followed in 1808 by Harry Biggs, the lord of Stockton manor. Thereafter, it remained with the Biggs family, together with Codford St Peter, until the twentieth century. The Yeatman-Biggs family still live in the village of Stockton in 2005.

Ashton Gifford's history is very obscure – there are very few extant records for the manor and for the purposes of this study is best included with Codford St Peter. It had variously belonged to the Gifford, Mautravers and Lestraunge families and, until the nineteenth century, the Earl of Shrewsbury. But it shared the advowson of St Peter's, having no church of its own, and the manorial records of St Peter's frequently refer to tenants in Ashton Gifford.

Manorial Records
Sally Thomson

By the sixteenth century, the 'manor' had come to mean the unit of administration for an estate, which included all the land and property belonging to its lord. There was not necessarily a manor-house within the manor, or, if there was, the lord did not always live there. The great landlords, such as the Hungerfords, who owned many manors including Codford St Peter, usually resided at one seat, often the family seat, or a large property. His tenants came under his final jurisdiction and their rents went to him, although his work was sometimes carried out by his steward. Nearly all of Codford's lords of the manor were absentees and there is no evidence of manor-houses, as such. Of the two buildings called 'Manor House' in Codford St Peter, one is a composite building based on the remains of a cottage; the other, a substantial sixteenth-century stone building, almost certainly on older foundations, which may have been the steward's abode. Codford St Mary has a stone-built, late-eighteenth-century farmhouse close to the church, which may well stand on the site of an original manor-house, but which has almost certainly been a farmhouse from at least the seventeenth century onwards.

Manorial jurisdiction took the form of Courts Baron and Courts Leet. The former court was the lord's right and was usually held every three weeks. Codford's Courts Baron seem to have been held only twice, or at most three times a year. This, on the face of it, would appear to have been the same interval as for a Court Leet. However, local customs with regard to manors varied enormously and by the period under study, the two forms of court were often merged. This appears to have been the case in Codford – the proceedings are mainly those of the Court Baron, while the sessions are held with the same regularity as Courts Leet. This implies two

possibilities: either there was no need for a regular court of jurisdiction by this time, or that the steward, in whose presence the courts were usually held, was, like his lord, not resident and had to make regular rounds of the manors on his lord's behalf. This latter is most likely for Codford St Peter, whose lord owned a number of manors in Wiltshire.

The main items which came up as presentments at the courts held in Codford St Peter in the first half of the seventeenth century deal with tenements falling into disrepair, encroachments on others' land, breaking the manorial laws of common pasturing, and misuse of waste. Nothing here indicates crimes of violence or moral misdemeanour; they were merely petty nuisances, which were serious enough to those concerned with obtaining a living from the land, and were dealt with as such by fining.

There is a complete custumal for Codford St Peter attached to a survey of the manor of 1623, listing eight customs. In the same document, however, are several 'memoranda' which are in fact customs and probably formed part of a much earlier, longer custumal. In a document of 1679 these memoranda are combined with the customs to form a 'Comons and Customs' of the manor. These cover the stints of the marsh and downs, the patronage, woods, copyhold, widows, heriot, licence, claim, surrender, distress and executors.

Land Tenure
Sally Thomson

The information on the holding of land in Codford comes mainly from the Manorial Court records of Codford St Peter. The relevant documents date from 1582–1761 and include proceedings of the court, surveys, rent rolls, custumals and bargains. There are also Glebe Terriers for 1588, 1608 and 1671. For Codford St Mary, the court records, which deal only with court business, date from 1640–1741. There are Glebe Terriers for 1609, 1672, 1705 and 1783. But the only rent roll, in the form of a 'particular' is for 1790.

The main form of tenure throughout the sixteenth and seventeenth centuries was that of copyhold, where a tenant held land or property of the lord of the manor by virtue of a copy of the agreement made in court at a given date. The court retained a record of the agreement and the tenant received a copy as his receipt or proof. A typical example is:

John Coxe & Maud Snelgar the daughter of John Snelgar holden for term of their lyves successivelie by Copie dated primo Aprilis Anno xxvij Elizabeth Regine [1 April 1585] of the graunte of Walter Hungerford knighte one Cotage with a backside adioyning late in the tenure of Robert Prior.
iij acres of land in the com[m]en feildes of Codforde and payeth of rent at the said feasts by even porcyons, iiijs22.

Sometimes a heriot (due to the lord at the death of the

copyholder) was payable, in the form of the best beast, best goods or in money. The entry fine for the heir to the copyhold is often listed with the copyhold details.

Rents in Codford St Peter were paid usually half-yearly, at Lady Day (25 March) and at Michaelmas (25 September) and the tenants would have trooped to whichever house the steward allotted for collection of the rents. There is a strong indication in the records where this house was, at least during the seventeenth century.

It was first found in the 1582 survey which recites John Bright's (formerly John Prior's) property. In this survey there are two tenements and three yardlands recorded, together with a 'covenant' as follows:

... vpon condycon that euerie of the said tenants being tenant shall find the Steward Surveyor and Receaver of the lorde of the said Mannor aforesaid for courts to holde rents to receave or lands there to Survey twise in the yere And to their horses sufficyent and convenient by the space of too nyghtes and one day at eury tyme during the terme aforesaid And vpon condicon and covennt that the said John (Pryor) shall p[ro]vide during the terme of his life and a lyverie cote of the lorde and his heires as often and whensoev as the lorde and his heirs from tyme to tyme at his p[ro]per charge and expenses during the terme aforesaid.

Here, then, is the answer to how the tenants paid their rents. In return for the hefty rent of £6.4s., an entry fine of £15, two heriots and the use of two houses, stables, barns and land of some 75 acres, John Pryor, and later John Bright, had the privilege of accommodating the lord's steward, surveyor and/or receiver and their retinue twice a year. This property came to be called a 'capital messuage' in the manorial records, rather implying that it was a manorial demesne. Perhaps this is where the steward had originally lived before he became an absentee, although there is one other building in the village which may lay claim to that.

If we extend the resources a little to go beyond 1750, we can trace John Pryor's property into modern times. In the rent roll summary of 1679, Mrs Jane Bright, the widow of John Bright, was paying an annual rent of £5.17s.5d., still the highest rent of the copyholders. Then in the survey of 1776, the rent was £5.17s.0d., the value having risen to £65. By the time the manor was sold in 1812, this same property was the main manorial holding and was known as The Manor House; it is still known by that name at the time of writing, although undoubtedly it was never the home of the lord of the manor.

The other property which may have had a high status within the manor is known in 2005 as The Old Manor. This building dates from the sixteenth century but is obviously on older foundations. Its site is on what was originally the south side of the main demesne farmyard, called the Rick Barton. The Tropenell Cartullary (fourteenth to fifteenth century) mentioned the house and close called the Whomberton, garden and land of Thomas Tropenell to the west (*ad domos et clausam voc. the Whomberton, gardinum et terram Thome Tropenell versus west*) in a grant of 1469. 'Whom' is a commonly-recurring West Country word for 'home'; 'berton' is clearly 'barton', or farm; hence the Home Farm, or demesne farm, which Thomas Tropenell was farming, or at least leasing, at this time. This would have been an ideal building for the collection of rents and may have been the medieval forerunner of the later rent-collection house listed above. It stands on the opposite side of the road to The Manor House, although the latter used to have garden land in the vicinity of the Old Manor House and Rick Barton, which rather indicates the close connection between the two buildings.

Copyholders not only held property in the form of houses or cottages, but also land, which they worked or could rent out to others by a licence, depending on their status within the community. Yardlands, or virgates, were the most common units of land held during the medieval and post-medieval period. However, by the end of the sixteenth century in Codford St Peter, only nine copyholders held their land as yardlands. The yardland was never a constant quantity and could vary in size from 16 to 30 acres. The entry for Thomas Snelgar's copyhold in the 1582 survey records that his three yardlands contained half an acre of close, just over one and a half acres of mead and $74\frac{1}{2}$ acres of arable in the common fields – a total of about $76\frac{1}{2}$ acres. The Codford yardland, therefore, would seem to have been a rough 25 acres.

By 1621, Thomas Snelgar's son, William, was the only tenant recorded holding three yardlands, by this time equalling some 79 acres. There were still six half-yardlanders and one holding of one yardland. John Pryor, who held three yardlands in 1582, held only a half yardland in 1621, the bulk of the holding having passed to John Bright.

Wylye, another village in the Wylye Valley, only three miles south-east of Codford and under the lordship of the Earl of Pembroke at Wilton, has a survey of 1631, drawn up as part of the Earl's general survey of all his estates at that time. It has been published and makes a useful contrast to Codford. In 1631 Wylye had 11 tenants who held by indenture. There were 32 copyhold properties, although some of these were held by the same tenant, often with a different combination of lives. Again, the commonest holding was the half yardland, of which there were 17 in Wylye, six of which were held by two tenants with three half yardlands each; there were six yardlands and two two-yardlands. No one held more. Yardlands in Wylye measured anything from 22 to $24\frac{1}{2}$ acres. So the yardland in this part of Wiltshire can fairly safely be assumed to have been between 20 and 25 acres. J. Bettey says that tenements usually 'consisted of between twenty and forty acres of arable, together with rights to meadow land and access to the common grazing of the downs.' In this respect, at least, Codford was typical of the area.

While the copyhold tenant was the commonest type of tenant in Codford in early-modern times, in the century between 1679 and 1776 the numbers decreased, while leaseholds became the more common form of holding. By 1829 most tenants had bought their holdings outright and there were only three copyholds and five leaseholds left. This number altered slightly in the following year, when the only copyhold left was that of the George Inn and its lands, and there were three leaseholds. However, there were eight yearly tenancies, or 'Michaelmas Bargains'. By 1844, when the rent rolls end, there was one copyhold, five leaseholds and two yearly tenancies. Clearly, the old manorial hold on the village had all but expired.

Early Enclosure
Sally Thomson

In both Codfords there is evidence of early enclosure. This evidence is found in the Tropenell Cartullary, the 1770 map of Codford St Mary and the 1810 Enclosure Award for Codford St Peter. The Tropenell Cartullary holds evidence of, perhaps, some of the earliest enclosures of all. It covers the fourteenth and fifteenth centuries, but there is no mention of closes in the fourteenth-century entries, only curtilages, which were not truly enclosures. However, by 1458 Sir Miles Stapulton, the lord of the manor of Codford St Mary, made a grant of three closes lying in East and West Codford (respectively, St Mary's and St Peter's), one of which was named Grogans Close. In delineating the boundaries of these closes, others are mentioned: a tenement and close called Buxtons, one called Ballys and another known as Wattmans. None of these names exist today, although in the seventeenth-century surveys of Codford St Peter a cottage called Buckstones was recorded. In 1469, the same Cartullary names a close called Dodemanys, containing one acre of pasture. This is said to lie in East and West Codford and could be the close later known as Home Close, which lay in East Codford parish (St Mary's), but which belonged to West Codford (St Peter's) – this arrangement persisted until the twentieth century.

The maps of Codford show numerous closes stretching from the homesteads southwards towards the river. Those of Codford St Mary tended to be squarish or to run west–east, while those of Codford St Peter and Ashton Gifford are regular rectangles running north–south. The Enclosure Awards for Codford St Peter (1810) and Ashton Gifford (1815), when locating certain new enclosures, fixed boundaries by referring to 'old enclosures' or 'old enclosed meadows'.

The manorial records for Codford St Peter frequently referred to closes of pasture, usually of about an acre, but the process of enclosure was obviously still continuing. In 1609, John Bright, by copy of 1595, held a close of half an acre adjoining his 'Capitall Messuage', a half-acre close of pasture called Broad Close, a half-acre close of pasture called Davies Close, and another close of pasture containing one rood, called Follers Ham (also called Fellows Ham). This latter might well have been 'fullers ham' originally, and was perhaps sited near the mill, long since gone; but being a 'ham', it would certainly have been close to water.

In the same manor court, in 1630, William Snelgrove, the elder, held among many other lands 'near the west end of a certain Marsh there, recently enclosed out of the said marsh.'

Wylye, 3 miles east along the valley, had a number of enclosures around the homesteads – home closes – and a 10-acre pasture called the Moor, part of the demesne lands. The demesne lands of Codford St Peter were probably those immediately north of the complex around the Rick Barton and there were a number of small closes in the vicinity.

The manorial survey for Codford St Peter, of 1776, is full of entries concerning closes, mostly of pasture or meadow, but there are also references to closes of 'pasture inclosed out of the Common Marsh'. Clearly, there was piecemeal enclosure of the marshlands by the river, as more and more land was reclaimed, perhaps through the construction of water meadows, although there is no mention of them in these records.

Malmpit Hill

The Malmpit was a local source of chalk for building and also lime for acid soils. According to Douglas Palmer, in *The Atlas of the Prehistoric World* (Marshall Publishing Ltd, 2000):

Chalk is a soft limestone formed from the 'mud' of calcium carbonate, often made up of the shells of tiny marine organisms, as in the Cretaceous chalk deposits of Western Europe.

In *English Rock Terms*, by W.J. Arkell and S.I. Tomkieff (Oxford University Press, 1953) it is stated that the earliest record of 'Malm' for a variety of chalk dates from 1477.

In the seventeenth and eighteenth centuries Malmpit Hill was known as Hermitage Hill.

The Nine Bells of Codford

Saxon and Norman Codford are represented in the two churches – the Christian Saxons favoured St Peter as the holder of the keys of heaven, while the Normans preferred the Blessed Virgin St Mary. St

Peter's Church has records stretching to the thirteenth century, when a priest, John le Prestre of Codford, was accused of larceny in 1249; he was found guilty, exacted and outlawed. The discovery of the Saxon cross shaft during alterations in 1863–64 indicated that there may have been a place of worship on the site as early as the eighth century.

St Mary's Church has a Roll of Rectors dating from 1297, the font dates back to approximately 1180, and, given that Codford is recorded in a Saxon Charter of AD901, it is likely that there was an earlier church, prior to the Norman invasion.

According to Kate Forbes, the position of a tower in the church is an indication of its age. The earliest, over the door, held a room for the priest; towers located on the crossing in the floor plan were not designed to hold bells and date from the twelfth and thirteenth centuries, while towers located at the west end were intended to hold bells. Bell-ringing in England started in the 100 years before the Reformation.

Since the sixteenth century St Mary's Church appears to have lost one bell, while St Peter's has retained the number it had when King Edward VI commissioned an inventory of all Church goods in 1553; in 2005 there are three bells in St Mary's and six in St Peter's. Possibly some of the bells were recast using recycled metal, however, it does appear that those Codford bells cast by John Wallis were new as they are not prefixed by 'old' in his list of bells. Bells were often cast in pits in churchyards, frequently close to rivers for ease of transportation. The diameter of a bell dictates the note, while the thickness defines the tone.

The two oldest bells are in St Mary's with the earliest, the 7cwt tenor, inscribed 'GEVE THANKS TO GOD', dating from 1582, during the reign of Elizabeth I. The treble dates from 1602 and bell number two dates from 1615, the latter being cast when James I, the first of the Stewart kings, was on the throne. Both bells are inscribed 'PRAISE GOD', all three bells being made by founder John Wallis of Salisbury, who was also responsible for St Peter's oldest bell, which is dated 1608. This bell, number five, is the G# note and weighs 8cwt 0qtrs 22lbs and is inscribed 'LOVE GOD I.W.'

John Wallis's work spanned 45 years, from 1581–1624. During this period he cast 216 bells, which are still in existence in Wiltshire and neighbouring counties in 2005. In 1581 he made nine bells and a clock; the tenor at St Mary's was the second of three bells he made in 1582, the first was for Chute, and the third for St Martin's Church in Salisbury. It is likely that the foundry was located in Culver Street, also known as 'Bellfounders' Street', which was in St Martin's parish.

John Wallis was a founder of great skill; very little is known of his personal life, although his character may be implied by his inscriptions – brief and expressing simple faith. From St Edmund's parish accounts we know that John Wallis began work in

1580. It appears his last bells were made in 1624. According to the book *Warminster Bellfounders*, published by the Dewey Museum, he died that year. However, there are unsubstantiated claims elsewhere that the date of his death was 1630.

Warminster bellfounders, father and son, John Lott I and John Lott II, were responsible for two of St Peter's bells – the tenor F# note, weighing 10cwt 2qtrs 1lb, inscribed 'ANNO DOMINI *Philip Ingram Iohn Hobbs – Churchwardens*' and dated 1625, the year of the death of James I and the accession of the ill-fated Charles I. Number four, the A# note weighing 6cwt 3qtrs 15lbs with the inscription '*Henry Thring Iohn Sednum Church Wardens I(Bell) L'*, dated 1671.

The tenor bell was made the year after John Wallis's death, so it is feasible that, with the great Salisbury bellfounder gone, it was decided to use a more local man.

John Lott is an unknown entity – where he came from and where he learnt his trade cannot be established, but what is known is that by 1624 he was a skilled founder. Similarities in his decorations support the possibility that he may have been an apprentice to Richard Purdue, a member of the most famous family of West Country bellfounders who cast bells in various places including Bristol and Salisbury from 1570–1710.

Anne Willis, in her book *Warminster Bellfounders*, believes John Lott may have settled in Warminster because he was able to acquire the necessary fittings:

A bell requires fitting; a clapper; bearings [usually called brasses until the twenty-first century] *to mount it on a frame; iron straps to hang it from a headstock; a wheel and a rope. It also needs someone to help hang it. In Warminster there was a pewterer by the name of Richard Cockey who had cast brasses for Frome Church in 1620. John Lott could have struck up a friendship with him.*

A perfectly usual transaction between a founder and a church, an old bell being part changed for a new one, the founder charging a slightly higher price for any metal that needed to be added, with due allowance for waste.

John Lott married a local girl, Christian Lawrence, in 1626/27, and they had ten children, nine of whom survived childhood.

Up to around 1641 around thirty bells are known to have been cast by John Lott. There is a break for the next four years when presumably the foundry had more pressing business in the way of arms and equipment for the first stage of the Civil Wars. The next known bell is the tenor for Chippenham which John Lott recast in 1645, a most extraordinary time given the state of the country at this time.

Only one of his known output of 50 bells over 32 years was cast outside Wiltshire or Somerset; this would hardly have provided an adequate living, and it is possible that he had another occupation. John

Above: *One of St Mary's bells in a view from below.*

Above: *The bell wheel in St Mary's Church.*

Above and below: *Bells in St Peter's Church.*

Left: *The oldest bell in St Peter's Church, which was cast by John Wallis.*

The John Ingram inscription on the 'C#' number two bell in St Peter's Church, cast by William Cockey.

Ken Axtell in St Mary's bell tower.

Lott died in 1663 and is buried at St Denys in Warminster.

In 1685 two of John and Christian's sons joined the Monmouth Rebellion. They were tried at Wells and sentenced to hang. Thomas Lott was certainly hung in Frome, but it appears that his brother, Lawrence, was alive in 1710, so may have returned having been transported, thus cheating the gallows.

John Lott's bellfounding business passed to his eldest son of the same name. John Lott II made the bell for St Peter's eight years after the death of his father, but he did face strong competition from foundries in Salisbury and later from Lewis Cockey of Frome.

The cost of a bell in 1686 appears to have been 20d. per lb. John Lott II was paid £14.14s.6d. for a seventeen hundred one quarter and ten pound bell.; £2.11s. for waste at four pounds to the hundred at nine pence the pound. It apparently cost 8s.6d. – 'Spent in beer in taking down the bell casting of him and putting him up'. (Bells were usually female in gender but in Wiltshire they appeared to be classed as male.)

John Lott II died inestate in April 1692; the business passed to his brother Richard, who left his son Edward 'my Bell house and all that belongs to the Art of Casting Bells and the bell mettle I have in my possession' when he died in 1710. In his will he referred to himself as a 'yeoman'; Richard was known to have cast only six bells, and Edward was credited with just three.

It is interesting that bell number three, the B# note, was cast by an itinerant journeyman founder Nathanial Bolter; the 5cwt 1qtr 3lb bell, inscribed with the name of the founder followed by the capitals 'C.P.' was founded in the time of Cromwell, during 1655.

Nathanial Bolter can be traced to Buckinghamshire in 1628, moving to the Bristol area. His letters and marks indicate that he possibly worked with Roger Purdue. This lettering appears with his name in 1631 on an old 1st at Tickenham in Somerset, and again in 1638 at Sutton Benger in Wiltshire on a 1st. Three more bells cast in 1632, one in Tickenham, another at Dauntsey and a third at Lynham, the latter two in

Wiltshire, contain the lettering but not his name.

For 16 years there is no trace of him in the records:

... he re-appears in 1654, using the Salisbury lettering and stamps of the period, and evidently working for William Purdue and his associates there. In 1655 he is similarily associated with John Lott of Warminster at Stapleford. But in any case he now loses his professional individuality, and his subsequent career can only be considered in connexion with that of his contemporaries.

In 1725 the C# number two bell, weighing 4cwt 1qtr 9lbs, was cast by Frome founder William Cockey; the inscription reads 'Mr Iohn Wise Mr Iohn Ingram - Church Wardens'. In 1928 the compiler of the *Frome Guide*, T.D. Lewis, wrote:

An old Frome family named Cockey previously resided in Warminster as Brass founders, Bell makers, and also I believe Clock Makers. Our Churchwardens in 1620 paid Richard Cockey 'pewterer' 37s for casting 8 brasses for our bells.

William Cockey succeeded Lewis Cockey II who died in 1703 – the relationship between the two men is not known. Lewis had a younger brother, born in 1663, and son born in about 1682, both called William. William Cockey cast over 50 bells just in Somerset, but none of the bells appear to have been of great worth and some were particularly bad. The question is, was the fault with the founder or the metal? Despite this William became wealthy, retiring as a bellfounder in 1751, 11 years before his death.

From the late-sixteenth to the early-eighteenth centuries the Codford bells came into being, whether they were reincarnations of earlier bells or newly cast. In 2005 the oldest bell has existed in its present form for more than 420 years, from the reign of the first Elizabeth into and no doubt far beyond the reign of the second queen of that name.

The last bell, the treble, is the Victory Bell, cast by Mears & Stainbank of Whitechapel in 1946, in

Ben Sheppard's grave.

Tom Stacey's grave in St Mary's churchyard.

St Peter's mechanism.

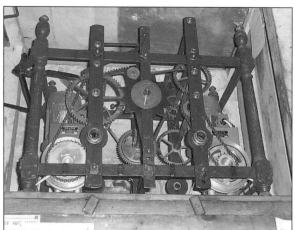
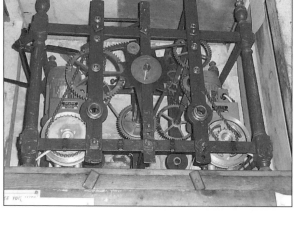

In St Peter's bell tower.

From inside St Mary's tower.

Droppings in St Mary's tower.

memory of the Codford men killed in the Second World War. Weighing 4cwt 1qtr 9lbs, with the inscription *'Ad piam memoriam virorum Codfordiensim qui pro patria sua vitas suas dederunt in bello mango MCMXXXIX – MCMXCV'*. The other bells were rehung at the same time. In 1946 a fête in the grounds of the Manor House raised £600 towards the costs.

The bells of St Mary's and St Peter's have pealed and tolled across the generations; their voices have heralded glad tidings and announced disasters and deaths; cast anew or reborn in the fires of their founders, they are reminders of the passage of time, of our mortality and of our continuity. The world moves on; the population is transient; but the bells remain!

The Men Remembered by the Victory Bell

The men who died in the Second World War and who have a memorial plaque in St Peter's Church are:

Charles Homer Bosworth. 1888–17 September 1939. Killed in action when the first aircraft carrier to be sunk in the war, HMS Courageous, *was torpedoed in the Atlantic.*

Percy Conduit. 1920–11 September 1943. Percy had survived Dunkirk, was posted to the Far East and was captured at the fall of Singapore. He was sent to work on the Thai–Burma Railway and died at Chungkai Base Hospital from pellegra – malnutrition.

Ben Sheppard died 11 March 1944 aged 20. Ben was wounded in the shoulder at Anzio, his wound turned gangrenous. He died in Cambridge Military Hospital and is buried in St Mary's Churchyard, Codford.

Guy Westley. 1919–6 June 1044. Killed in action off Jig Green Beach [Gold Beach West].

Anthony Hancock. 1923–26 April 1945. Survived the Bremen raid and was killed in the company carrier by a magnetic mine.

Tom Stacey. 1903–7 March 1945. Killed when a fire tender he was on overturned on a call out at RAF Charterhall. Tom is buried at St Mary's Church, Codford.

Alan Roney-Dougal. 1917–13 August 1945. Died in South Africa of an acute intestinal obstruction and congestive heart failure.

A Poor Widow's Tale – The Story of Dorothy Bassett
Sally Thomson

Widows often appear in manorial court records, since they continued to occupy their deceased husband's tenancy and to pay the rent to the lord of the manor. Dorothy Bassett's name appears among the Codford inventories and also in the manorial records. As she was probably one of the poorest members of the community, it is worth writing down what is known of her. Her husband, Roger, appears on the Codford St Peter Survey for 1582. The entry reads:

Roger Bassett & Thomas his sonne clayme to hold for t[er]me of their lyves successively of the graunt of Sir Walter Hungerford knighte by Copie dated viij Septembris Anno xxviij Eliz' Regine [1586] One Cotage w[i]th a p[ar]cell of grounde adioyning cont[aining] by est[imate] iij lugg sometyme in the tenure of John Randall and by him surrendered And payeth of rent yearly at the said feasts by even porc[i]ons iiijs.

A 'lugg' was a Wiltshire term for a rod, pole or perch, 40 of which made up a furlong. Three luggs, therefore, would have been a little under one tenth of a furlong – it seems an almost negligible amount of land.

It is not known what Roger did for a living and he left no will, but he was a member of the manorial jury in 1592 and 1597. From later entries we know that he must have been born in about 1559 and probably married Dorothy in about 1580.

Their son, Thomas, was born the following year and there were two daughters, Elizabeth and Katherine.

In the Rent Roll of 1609, Roger's holding consisted of the cottage and four parrocks of ground and the rent was then 2s. Like the lugg, a 'parrock' is the Wiltshire equivalent of a perch. Roger was said to have been 50 years old, Thomas 28. But the word 'mort' and a cross are written by each in a later hand and we know from the Parish Registers that Roger was buried on 9 July 1611 and Thomas on 14 January 1613. Following the recital of the property in the Rent Roll, is the following clause:

Vpon Surrender of the Widowes estate of dorothie Bassett widowe of Roger, a new estate is graunted to the said dorothee and to Elizabeth & Katherine her daughters by copie dated primo die octobris Anno xij Jacobi Regis [1 October 1615] Fyne £4.

In 1623 Katherine had married John Cosens, but she is erroneously recorded as Dorothy. Perhaps the clerk was confusing her with her mother. At some stage her sister, Elizabeth, married Thomas Wallis, but the marriage was not recorded in either Codford parish. John and Katherine had two sons, John and Thomas.

In the two surveys of 1621 and 1623 Dorothy was recorded as holding the cottage and four perches of ground for her life and those of her daughters, at a rent of 2s. per annum. But in October 1635, Katherine's husband, John Cosens, went to the manor court and claimed entry to the property in right of his wife. Dorothy was not yet dead, nor was Elizabeth, although Katherine may have been. There was no heriot to pay, as it was an unheriotable property, and John claimed the tenure for his life and the lives of his two sons, John and Thomas.

The customs of the manor of Codford St Peter had an item dealing specifically with widowhood. In the custumal of 1679 is the following:

Widowhood: Item that by the Custome of this Mannor the wife of euery ten[an]t being purchaser either in possession or reuercion and being admitted Ten[an]t and in possession at the tyme of his death shall have widdows Estate whether shee be named in the Coppy or not and whether she be first or last wife and not the wife of any other being named in the sayd Coppy.

Thus the widow on this manor was well protected; yet Dorothy seems to have been dealt a raw deal by her son-in-law. However, it may have been that Dorothy went to live with John and his family and that there was an amicable agreement between all of them that he should take over the holding. To add to the mystery, Dorothy made a will in 1623, the year of Katherine's marriage. She bequeathed a little table board and frame and 12d. to Elizabeth, the wife of Thomas Wallis, but the rest of her goods she left to

her 'sonne in lawe John Cossens whom I make my whole and sole Executor.'

There is no mention of Katherine. Dorothy was buried on 8 September 1636 and John Cosens made his appearance on the manorial jury of 1637 and 1639. Dorothy's inventory is a pathetic little document; it was made by Thomas Hibberd (who also witnessed her will), John Coombes and Thomas Crouch, on 4 October 1636:

In primis all her Wearing Apparrell   xs
Itm one Little Table Board and Frame one Cubberd two Coffers one Trendle one Cowell and one olde Boarden Beddsteed   xvs
Itm two keetles one skillett one brasse Crocke one brasse Candlesticke and two pewter Pottengers   xvs
Itm one Iron Chaine wth all other small implements   vijd

The Whole Summe is xljs [41s. or £2.1s.0d.]
[The corrected sum is 40s.7d. (£2.0s.7d.)]

The sum total is little enough and, when put in perspective with other inventories of the time, it is of very small value indeed. The total wealth of inventories for the decade 1630–39 for both Codfords was £1,013.3s.2d., covering 14 inventories. Dorothy's inventory was of the least value out of 142 inventories between 1552 and 1760. Her cottage may have been two roomed, but is just as likely to have been a one-roomed, cob and thatch edifice, with a bed in the corner. However, there is another possibility – that she was living in only part of a larger cottage, while her daughter and family lived in the rest. But since the rent charge was relatively small – 2s. per annum, when most tenants paid upwards of 4s. – and the value of the property was assessed (in 1621) as 6s.8d., it is unlikely to have been commodious. In the latter days of her life, Dorothy may have lived with one of her daughters' families, but in 1631 there was an entry in the manorial records which showed she was in her own home: 'A day is given for Widow Bassett to sufficiently repair her house in all necessaries and repairs before the next Court on pain of forfeit of 10s.' Ten shillings would have been an enormous sum to Dorothy; she must have got her son-in-law to help put the place to rights, since there is no further mention of her house being in a state of disrepair. One is left with the impression of something not much more than a leaky hovel.

Dorothy was undoubtedly one of the poorest people in Codford. Three other widows, from 1619–39, were worth little more than her at their deaths: Phillipa Skoser (1619) worth £3.10s.8d., Maude Coxe (1635) worth £4.7s.8d. and Joane Toms (1639) worth £3.16s.8d. The latter did not even have a bedstead listed, although she had linen, pewter and brass, a deal of wood and two bushels of wheat. Phillipa Skoser, on the other hand, had a detailed inventory made out, separating the goods in the hall from those in the chamber, where she had two bedsteads, although there is no mention of beds. At this time, the bed was the equivalent of today's mattress. The bedstead would be slatted (or of boards) or, in wealthy households, corded, to give some suspension to the bed. Beds themselves were of feather for the wealthy, flock for the less-wealthy and straw or even oat chaff for the poor.

She also held a cottage in 1609, 4 acres of arable land and common of pasture for two cows. Her holding was valued at 25s. (£1.5s.0d.) and she had a third of a land in wheat and 1 acre of barley, at her death.

Maude Coxe's clothes alone were valued at 20s. and she owned a flock bed. Her pots, pans, kettle and candlestick were all brass and the comforts of her bed included bolster, pillow, sheets, blankets and coverlet. On the manor she held a cottage with curtilage, 3 acres of land in the common fields, one rod of meadow and common of pasture for one beast, all for 4s. rent per annum. The holding was worth 30s. (£1.10s.0d.). Here, the tenancy was to pass to her two sons, John and Edmund, who may have farmed her land for her, but who probably had their own homes. John surrendered her holding in 1636, as is duly recorded in the manorial court proceedings for 4 October that year, and it was re-released to William Card and his brothers Christopher and Thomas, along with an enclosure of 120 perches recently made out of the common marsh. The value was £10, but the rent remained at 4s. per annum.

Kate Forbes at the Codford Bypass Party in 1990. (PHOTO DAVID WILTSHIRE)

Above: *Cheapside, Codford St Mary.*

Left: *Graffiti St Peter's Church, dating from the seventeenth, eighteenth and nineteenth centuries.*

Below: *Graffiti in St Peter's Church.*

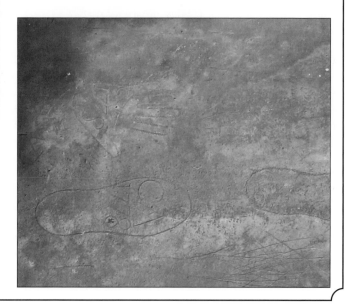

Chapter 4

The Nineteenth Century

The Parishes of Codford

Richard Colt-Hoare traces the evolution of the present village of Codford from a nineteenth-century perspective in a volume of *The History of Modern Wiltshire*, published in London in 1824. This was one of a series of books which recorded known information from the past covering each Hundred in the county. The foreword reads:

My Fellow Countrymen in Wilts.
To rescue from total oblivion the relics of ancient Britain;
To illustrate the remaining vestiges of its conquerors,
 the Romans;
To investigate the monastic and ecclesiastical history of
 our county;
To trace the genealogy of distinguished families, and the
 descent of property;
To record the monumental inscriptions, and the biography
 of celebrated characters;
And, above all, to endeavour by this example, to excite the
zeal of my fellow countrymen in the same desirable cause;
Is the sole purport of my humble undertaking
 Richard Colt-Hoare
 Stourhead June 1822.

Codford St Mary, Codford St Peter and Ashton Giffard lay within the Hundred of Heytesbury.

Codford St Peter, or West Codford, with the tything and hamlet of Ashton-Giffard, contains about 1720 acres of land. It is bounded on the North by Chitterne St Mary; East by Codford St Mary; West by Upton Lovell; and South by the Wily, which divides it from Sherrington and Boyton.

This parish is situated seven miles E.S.E. from Warminster; and its resident population in 1801 was, including Ashton Giffard, returned at 393; in 1811 the return makes it only 320; 1821 it was 347.

Of the two tythings, which constitute this parish, Codford St Peter contains about 700 acres and Ashton Giffard about 896 acres. They, however, seem to be both described in Domesday by the name of Coteford, and I confess myself unable to distinguish them. One of these two Cotefords, then, was granted to Osbern Giffard at the Conquest; and he most probably, obtained the other at the attainder and forfeiture of William de Ow, which happened shortly after the general survey. It is evident from the records that both Codford St Peter and Ashton Giffard descended to the heirs of this Osbern from a remote and undefined

period; and this, though not amounting to proof, yet considerably strengthens our conjecture.

In later times the family of Polden were respectable freeholders in this parish, and held also a good estate at Imber, under the Pawletts. They made several good matches, and were reckoned among the gentry of Wilts in the time of Charles II. Their house here was a small one, and is now nearly in ruins; and their estate has become, by purchase, the property of Mr... Slade.

Harry Biggs, Esq. is the lord of the manor, which he purchased of the Earl of Ilchester, but he does not possess much domain. James and John Slade are the chief proprietors in Codford St Peter, and William Hubbard and Bingham, of Dorset, Esq. are the principal landowners in Ashton Giffard. Both tythings have lately been divided and enclosed; and the tyth is taken in kind.

The church is dedicated to St Peter. It is a rectory, valued in the King's books at £17. 15s. The patronage was in the family of Kellow; but the reversion, after the present incumbent, is sold to Magdalen College, Oxford.

It is rather singular, that the patronage of the church did not descend with the lordship of the manor, but, as will be seen by references to the patrons, with that of Ashton Giffard. This seeming anomaly, may, however, be easily accounted for John Lord Giffard, of Brimfield, father of one who was attainted, had settled the manor of Ashton Giffard and the advowson of Codford on his first wife, Matilda Longspee, and his children by her, in perpetuity; consequently these properties did not escheat on the attainder of his son, but passed to his daughters by the said Matilda, and their heirs. Accordingly, we find these heirs enjoying the right of presentation alternately, till about the year 1608, when they sold it, and since which it has passed through various hands.

This rectory was in existence before the year 1291, when it was valued at £6.13s.4d.; and in the Inquisitiones Nonarum, 15 Edward III, its value was increased to £7.16s.8d.

Codford St Mary, or East Codford, is the next parish to Codford St Peter, and lies so closely adjoined to it, as to form in appearance, one continued village. These two Codford's were, however, totally distinct lordships long before the Norman Conquest.

Codford St Mary on the north by the Chitterns; on the east by the Hundred of Branch and Dole; on the south by the river Wily; and on the west by Codford St Peter. It contains 2080 acres of land; and its population in 1801 was 187; in 1811 it was 175; and in 1821, 258. It is distant eight miles E.S.E. from Warminster, and the road from that town to Salisbury passes through this village, as well as Codford St Peter. Harry Biggs, Esq.

is lord of the manor, which he purchased lately of Mrs Parry, who was the widow of T. Bennett, of Norton Bavant. The large farm and bulk of the property passed by this purchase. W. Bennett, Miss Hinton, and John and James Slade, are the other proprietors. There are copyholds in each parish.

Of the under-tenants, or possessors of the land within this manor, we find several at an early period. In 17 Edward II. We find Robert Russell and Elena his wife holding lands here; also John Serich is mentioned at the same time; and above all, our inexplicable knight Sir Robert le Bor had then obtained certain possessions in this place. In that and the following year he founded his chantry for four priests in the church of Hill Deverill, the care and patronage of which he gave to the priory of St. Radegund at Longlete, and endowed it, amongst other lands, with pasture in East Codford or two horses, eight oxen, twelve pigs, and two hundred and sixty sheep, in auxilium sustentationis quatuor capellanorum; and for which the prior, 17 Edward II paid a fine of twenty shillings for himself and convent. I suspect this Sir Robert le Bor to be an extraneus in our county, perhaps brought in by the Inghams, as the only other person of the name that I have been able to find was John le Bor, who in 1322 was presented by Sir Oliver de Ingham to the rectory of this parish. I am inclined to think, from the number of feoffments and other transactions in which Robert was engaged, that he was by profession a lawyer; and in a deed amongst the Longleat papers, 19 Edward II. He signs himself 'Robertus le Boor, Seneschallus D'ni Hugonis Dispenser, Comitis Wynton.'

The Hermitage

East of this village is an elevated and projected point of the Down, which is clothed with wood on the side towards Codford, round the outsides of which are eight venerable yew trees. These, from the situation which they occupy, would appear to have been planted by hand, and, by their age and size, to have long survived all their brethren of the forest. This projection is called, in old maps of Wilts, HERMITAGE HILL, and in the view from above the wood is fine, taking in the vale of the Wily from Codford to Warminster, with Cley Hill in the background. Favourable as these circumstances are, we should not, perhaps, have supposed that this spot had ever been devoted to religious seclusion, had not the registers of the See of Sarum afforded us undoubted evidence of the fact, as the name of the hermit is there mentioned.

A note at the bottom of the page comments: 'Mr Offer told me he had ascertained the name of the hermit, but on searching his numerous MS. Papers, I have not as yet been able to discover it.'

The church, as its name implies, is dedicated to St Mary. It is a Rectory in the Deanery of Wily, valued in

the King's books at £18. The patronage is in St John's Collage, Oxford, by purchase in the year 1640. This rectory was always in the patronage of the lords of the manor, who succeeded in uninterrupted descent from the Conquest to the year 1577, between which and 1645 it was purchased by St John's College, the present patrons. It was valued in 1291 at £6.13s.4d. per annum; in 15 Edward III at £6.18s.; and in the King's books, according to Ecton and Bacon, at £18. But I must here notice another disagreement between them and the Valor Ecclesiasticus, in which it is returned at only £14.11s.3d. This difference is so great, that I cannot account for it by any ordinary supposition; and therefore leave it as I find it.

The church is ancient and built of stone, with a low embattled turret, without aisles or chantry. The chancel is separated from the nave by a pointed arch springing from low circular columns with rudely ornamented capitals; the pulpit of wood, old, and neatly carved; and the font is entirely plain. Over the East window, without, is the date, 1622, and the letters I.M. These, most probably, are the initials of John Mompesson, who was then rector, and who either repaired or rebuilt the chancel.

South of the altar, within the rails, is a tomb with a canopy over it, supported by two arches and three columns in front, in what may be called the Italian styles, and of course not very ancient. On the tomb once lay two recumbent figures, now broken and gone; nor could I find any inscription; but from the time of its erection, and the shield sculptured on the tomb, I think must be attributed to the above John Mompesson, who died in 1645. The arms are, Mompesson, a lion rampant, charged on the shoulder with a martlet or pinzon, impaling the following coat: 1. a fesse between three... heads erased; 2. five lozenges in fesse; 3. three lions passant in pale; 4. as the first. The colours are not known.

Ashton Giffard is a tything and hamlet in the parish of Codford St Peter, containing within it about 600 acres of land, and was the manor of the family whose name it bears at a very remote period. It appears in the early records by the name of Aiston and Cliftune; sometimes with and sometimes without the adunct Giffard; but it does not appear in Domesday under either of these appellations.

The earliest distinct notice which we have of Ashton Giffard, by name, is in Liber Feodorum temp. Henry III.; where we read that Elias Giffard held in Aston one fee of John Matravers, who held it of Walter de Dunstanville, and Walter of the King in capite.

Extracts from *Rural Rides*
William Cobbett

William Cobbett (1763–1835) was a man of many parts; a journalist, civil-rights activist, political commentator, farmer and MP. Born in Farnham in Surrey he ran away from home when he was 10 or 11, enlisting in the 54th Regiment of Foot in 1784, and was posted to America as a sergeant. Returning to England eight years later he exposed military corruption, but was hounded from England to France and later America by the establishment.

In the New World Cobbett continued to speak out as a crusading political journalist. On his return to his native country he wrote for *The Political Register* newspaper, once again speaking out against government incompetence and corruption. His outspoken condemnation earned him support and popularity amongst the masses but the enmity of powerful figures, and he was sent to Newgate Prison for two years after being found guilty of seditious libel. After he was released he lived again in America, before taking up the cudgels once more, railing against the mismanagement of the economy.

Cobbett set himself up in the business of selling exotic seeds and saplings, while at the same time writing books for the education of the poor. In 1832 he became an MP for Oldham. His most famous work was *Rural Rides*, published in 1830. It contains a series of articles and essays from *The Political Register* columns of 1822–26.

Cobbett came to Wiltshire in the 1820s, travelling on horseback and by stagecoach. While in the county he visited Codford and the Wylye Valley, in *Rural Rides*, Volume II, he wrote:

Wylye Valley from Sarum to Heytesbury

In coming from Salisbury, I came up the road which runs nearly parallel with the river Wyly, which river rises at Warminster and in the neighbourhood. This river runs down a valley twenty-two miles long. It is not so pretty as the valley of the Avon; but it is very fine in its whole length from Salisbury to this place [Heytesbury]. Here are watered meadows nearest to the river on both sides; then the gardens, the houses and the cornfields. After the cornfields come the downs; but generally speaking the downs here are not so bold here as they are on the sides of the Avon. The Ah-ah! if I may so express it, is not so deep, and the sides of it not quite so steep, as in the case of the Avon; but the villages are as frequent; there is more than one church in every mile, and there has been a due proportion of mansion-houses demolished and defaced. The farms are very fine up this vale.

Cobbett was concerned about the 'decline of the population' and the 'beggary of the parsonage houses'. He observed that there were 24 parishes, 24 parish churches and that there should be as many parsonage houses:

And, indeed, the mansion-houses are gone, except in a very few instances. There are but five left that I could perceive all the way from Salisbury to Warminster, though the country is the most pleasant that can be imagined. Here is water, here are meadows; plenty of fresh water fish; hares and partridges in abundance, and it *is next to impossible to destroy them. Here are shooting, coursing, hunting; hills of every height, size and form; valleys the same; lofty trees and rookeries in every mile; roads always solid and good, always pleasant for exercise and the air must be the best in the world. It is impossible for the eyes of man to be fixed on a finer country than that between the village of Codford and the town of Warminster; and it is not very easy for the eyes of man to discover labouring people more miserable.*

The whole of the population of the twenty-four parishes down the vale amounts to only 11,195 souls, according to the official return to parliament; and, mind, I include the parish of Fisherton Anger [a suburb of Salisbury], which contains 893 of the number. I include the town of Heytesbury, with its 1,023 souls; and I further include this very good and large market town of Warminster, with its population of 5,000! So that I leave, in the other twenty-one parishes, only 4,170 souls, men, women and children! That is to say, a hundred and ninety-eight souls to each parish; or, reckoning five to a family, thirty-nine families to each parish. Above one half of the population could never be expected to be in the church at one time; so that there are one and twenty churches built for the purpose of holding 2,080 people! There are several of these churches, any one of which would conveniently contain the whole of these people, the 2,080! The church of Bishopstrow would contain the whole of the 2,080 very well indeed; and it is curious enough to observe that the churches of Fisherton Anger, Heytesbury, and Warminster, though quite sufficient to contain the people that go to church, are none of them nearly as big as several of the village churches. All these churches are built long and long before the reign of Richard II; that is to say, they were founded long before that time, and if the first churches were gone, theses others were built in their stead. There is hardly one of them that is not as old as the reign of Richard II; and yet that impudent Scotsman, George Chalmers, would make us believe that, in the reign of Richard II, the population of the country was hardly anything at all! He has the impudence, or the gross ignorance, to state the population of England and Wales at two millions, which, as I have shown in the last number of the Protestant Reformation, would allow only twelve able men to each parish church throughout the kingdom. What, I ask, for about the thousandth time I ask it, what were these twenty churches built for? Some of them stand within a quarter of a mile of each other. They are pretty nearly as close to each other as the churches in London and Westminster are.

What a monstrous thing to suppose that they were built without there being people to go to them; and built, too, without money and without hands! The whole of the population in these twenty-one parishes could stand, and without much crowding too, in the bottoms of the towers of the several churches. Nay, in three or four of the parishes, the whole people could stand in the church porches. Then the church-yards show you how numerous the population must have been. You see, in some cases, only here and there the mark of a grave, where the church-yard contains from half an acre to an acre of land, and sometimes more. In short, everything shows that here was once a great and opulent population; that there was an abundance to eat, to wear and to spare; that all the land that is now under cultivation, was under cultivation in former times. The Scotch beggars would make us believe we sprang from beggars. The impudent scribes would make us believe that England was formerly nothing at all until they come to enlighten it and fatten upon it. Let the beggars answer me this question; let the impudent, the brazen scribes, that impose upon the credulous and cowed down English; let them tell me why these twenty one churches were built; what were they built FOR; why the large churches of the two Codfords were stuck up within a few hundred yards of each other, if the whole population could then, as it can now be, crammed into the chancel of either of the two churches? Let them answer me this question, or shut their mouths upon this subject, on which they have told so many lies.

As to the produce of this valley, it must be at least ten times as great as its consumption even if we include the 3 towns that belong to it. I am sure I saw produce enough in five or six of the farm-yards, or rick-yards, to feed the whole of the population of the twenty-one parishes. But the infernal system causes it all to be carried away. Not a bit of good beef or mutton or veal and scarcely a bit of bacon is left for those who raise all this food and wool. The labourers here look as if they were half starved. They answer extremely well to the picture that Fortesque gave of the French in his day.

Talk of 'liberty', indeed; 'civil and religious liberty': the inquisition, with a belly full, is far preferable to a state of things like this. For my own part, I really am ashamed to ride a fat horse, to have a full belly, and to have a clean shirt on my back, while I look at theses wretched countrymen of mine; while I actually see them reeling with weakness; when I see their poor faces present me with nothing but skin and bone, while they are toiling to get the wheat and the meat ready to be carried away to be devoured by the tax-eaters. I am ashamed to look at these poor souls, and to reflect that we are descended from those amongst whom beef, pork, mutton and veal, were the food of the poorer sort of people.

Cheapside

Cheapside is a tiny unadopted lane off the Chitterne Road. At the end of the nineteenth century a sheep market was regularly held in Cheapside and locals say it used to be known as 'Sheepside'. However the old English word 'ceping' or 'ceiping' meant market, and it is possible the present name is derived from this.

Revd Ingram's *Memorials of the Parish of Codford St Mary in the County of Wilts*, published in 1844, states that:

In the 37th year of the reign of Henry III [1252], Albreda, the last heiress of the family of Waleran the huntsman, obtained a Charter for a weekly market in Codford Magna [Great Codford].

The records are preserved in the Tower of London and read as follows:

For Albreda de Botereus – The king to the archbishops, &c. – Know ye-that we are at the instance of Oliver de Ingham have granted and by this our charter confirm unto Albreda de Botereus, that she and her heirs for ever may have a weekly Market on Tuesdays at Great Codeford in the county of Wilts – Provided the said market be not injurious to other markets in the vicinity. And that she may have free warren [Sally Thomson defines free warren as a franchise to keep or kill game] in all her demesne lands of Great Codford – Providing the said lands be not within the limits of our royal forest – So that no person may enter the said lands for the pursuit of game in them, or to take anything therein which may belong to the said warren, without the license and consent of the said Albreda and her heirs, upon pain of forfeiting to us the sum of ten pounds – The following persons being witnesses hereof: Walter bishop of Worcester, and Peter bishop of Hereford: John Jefferson [or Fitz-Geoffrey] justiciary

Fred and Ron Sutton outside their cottage in Cheapside, c.1930s.

A cottage on the lane leading to Cheapside.

Fred Sutton with Ron as a child, c.1922.

Ron Sutton and Stan Bissell behind Cheapside cottages, c.1994. (PHOTO DAVID MASON)

of Ireland: Ralph Nicholson: Richard, John, and William de Grey (a), brothers: Roger de Montalt: Nicholas Seymour [or St Maur] *and others.*

(a) These are three of the five brothers of Walter de Grey, sometime archbishop of York, and lord high chancellor of all England; who gave name to the parish of Rotherford Greys in the county of Oxford &c. The names of several others among the subscribing witnesses are highly interesting: such as Walter de Cantilupe, bishop of Worcester from 1236–7 to 1266–7, a most eventful period. They all held some of the highest and most responsible offices in the appointment of the sovereign.

The family of Boterels, Botreaux, or Botereus, was of high repute in former times; and the title of Baron Botreaux is still retained in the family of the marquess of Hastings. William lord Botreaux, the last of the name who possessed the honour of the castle of Botreaux in Cornwall, fell in the second battle of St Albans in 1462, leaving an only daughter, who carried the estates by marriage into the family of Hungerford and Hastings.

Though the market above mentioned has been disused for centuries, yet the name of Cheapside, which still remains, seems to indicate that it used to be held on that side of the parish.

By an inquisition post mortem, taken at Wilton in 1282, 10 Edw.I, on the death of the first Oliver de Ingham above-mentioned, it appears that he left a son of the name of John his heir, then twenty-four years of age and upwards; that the manor of East Codford was then

annually worth, in rents and services of free tenants and copy holders, 100 shillings; 10 acres of meadow, at 16d per acre = 13s.4d.; Court Close with a curtilege and every convenience of building, of the annual value of 13s 4d, with a small dovecot out of repair; that the arable land in demesne consisted of 300 acres, at per acre 6d = 71.10s.

The advowson for the church of the Blessed Mary, belonged to the said Oliver, was then estimated at 20 shillings per annum. The pleas and perquisites of the manor were worth 6s 8d. All these things he held of the king in capite as a portion appurtenant to the barony of Deene on the eastern confines of the county, which he derived from his marriage with the aforesaid Albreda, or Aubrei, the heiress of the Walerans; one of whom in the preceding reign held the custody of the isle of Lundy, the castles of Salisbury, Bristol, &c., and died about the commencement of the reign of Edward I.

Ron Sutton was the longest resident of Cheapside. He lived at number 33 from his birth in 1921 until 2003. During the the First World War Ron's maternal grandparents, Edmond and Elizabeth Portingale, lived in the farm cottage, which at the time belonged to Bill Mizen. Two of his uncles were killed in action. The youngest, Archie Portingale, was 22, newly conscripted into 7th Battalion, Somerset Light Infantry, and he had been on the Western Front for only two or three weeks. He fell during the third battle of Ypres, on 16 August 1917. There had been a lull in the fighting through the first 15 days of August – due to heavy rainfall in July the battlefield had become a bog. Archie, the reluctant recruit who had never wanted to be a soldier, did not survive the day his Battalion engaged in the battle for Langemark. He has no known grave but is remembered on the Tyne Cot Memorial, Passchendale, Belgium and in the Golden Book of Remembrance in Wells Cathedral. His older brother George Portingale, a member of the 1st/4th Battalion Wiltshire Regiment, died in Palestine during the capture of El Tireh on 19 September 1918.

Ron's father, Fred Sutton, was a Canadian soldier who came to Salisbury Plain during the First World War. He met and married Elsie Portingale and remained in Wiltshire after demobilisation. The young couple set up home at 33 Cheapside, renting the cottage for 2s.6d. a week from farmer Mizen. They had two sons, Ron born in 1921 and Dennis who died of meningitis, aged 13. Elsie cleaned for the Stratton family and for Revd Meyrick at the rectory, for 6d. an hour. Fred worked at the army camps, then for farmer Stratton tending pigs on the site of the present Oxyard. He bought 33 Cheapside in either 1945 or 1946 for £150.

Ron worked for John Sparey, the owner of the Milk Bar at the bottom of Chitterne Road. He milked cows, made butter and delivered the milk for 13$\frac{1}{2}$ years. He moved to a farm in Fisherton for 18 months, before taking a job at Manor Farm, Codford, where he spent the next 35 years working for John and Will Collins.

During the Second World War Ron was a member of the Home Guard and remembers he was shot by a rubber bullet while 'invading Chitterne', a village 3 miles away. There was a great deal of friendly rivalry between the two villages and their Home Guard sections. He lived with his parents until their deaths – Fred in 1955 and Elsie in 1977. Ron's only periods away from Codford, until he was in his mid-seventies, were day-trips and a spell in hospital. In the late 1990s he spent a week at a holiday camp with his neighbours and later visited Wales, trips he thoroughly enjoyed.

In his early eighties Ron had health problems and moved into a retirement home – for eight decades he had remained in the cottage where he was born and

War graves in St Mary's churchyard.

still has a remarkable store of tales and memories of 'the old days'.

Sources:

Additional information on Archie Portingale supplied by Brigadier A.I.H. Fyfe DL, Regimental secretary Somerset Light Infantry; on George Portingale Major P.J. Ball (retired) on behalf of Royal Gloucestershire, Berkshire and Wiltshire Regiment Museum, The Wardrobe, Salisbury, Wilts.

Memorials of the Parish of Codford St Mary

Revd John Ingram's pamphlet was published in 1844. Although much of the information is published elsewhere and earlier, it is possible to glean nuggets of contemporary events and thinking from the pages. In this record it is stated that:

Part of the south wall of St Mary's church having fallen down from decay in June 1843, whilst a labourer was employed in removing the rubbish which had accumulated for ages, a liberal subscription was commenced to enable the parishioners to embrace this opportunity of enlarging it by an additional aisle, to meet the demands of an increasing population.

In carrying this plan into execution, under the able superintendence of Mr Wyatt, the diocesan architect, it was deemed necessary to take down the greater portion of the old structure to the foundation, with the exception of the tower, and a part of the chancel.

During the progress of the work, a considerable quantity of the earliest and most interesting Norman sculpture has been discovered; hitherto rendered invisible, either by being overwhelmed with successive coats of thick plaster and whitewash, or being embedded in the walls in an inverted position amidst other materials, in the ordinary repairs and alterations which had been made at various intervals in the several parts of the edifice.

The arch between the nave and the chancel had been converted from a circular to a pointed design. Dr Ingram commented on the method of the conversion, so skilfully conducted that they preserved most of the original work:

To the surprise of all, when a load of plaster and whitewash was removed, in the late alterations, the finely sculpted architrave of the present Norman arch was found almost entire.

On the removal of the whitewash it was also found that the flat surfaces of the archivolt had been sprinkled in fresco with a darkish red colour, and partially enriched with a kind of running scrollwork of the same or similar material. It is much regretted that the several grotesquely carved masques, or corbels, heads of dragons winged symbols of the evangelists, and other fragments of ancient sculpture, discovered in taking

The view from St Mary's tower, across the roof.

Ken Axtell oiling the clock in the bell tower at St Mary's.

Right: *The workings of St Mary's clock.*

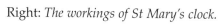

Above: *Cooper and Court graves in St Mary's churchyard.*

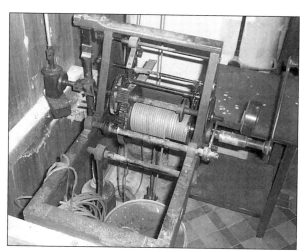

Sketch of the interior of St Mary's Church.

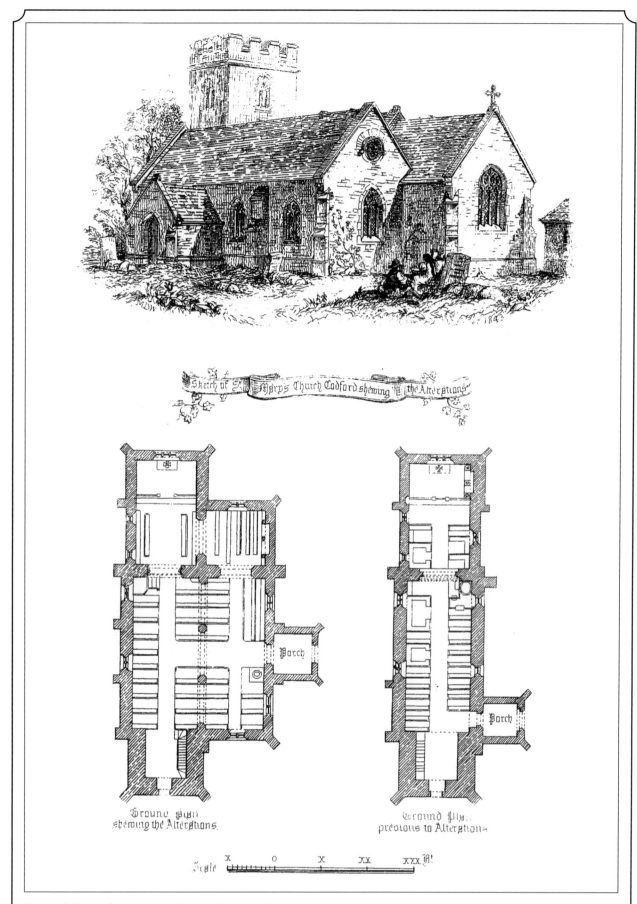

Ground plans of St Mary's Church, showing the alterations.

Codford celebrates the silver jubilee of George V, 6 May 1935. Pictured are: *Joan Simper* (page boy), *Mrs Sarnway* (Henry VIII) *and Hilda Stacey* (Katherine Parr). *The costumes date from the medieval era and were lent by Mrs Mason of Bury Farm. Hilda's dress was gold brocade and purple velvet with a padded bust, the crown was purple and trimmed with pearls as was the front panel and belt.*

down the walls for the purpose of rebuilding and enlarging the church, the greater part were too much mutilated to be accurately defined.

The church is a mixture of styles – all the windows were inserted into the old walls long after their original construction, the three windows on the south side Decorated or Transitional, while the single east window is Perpendicular. On the north side of the chancel, however, a long, narrow lancet window with plain chamfered jambs was in perfect condition. This window was inserted in the new wall in place of the more modern square window there before. The three-storied tower was left alone, except where a firmer buttress was constructed abutting the wall of the nave at its north-east angle.

Only the tower of the altered and enlarged church remained almost as it was. The upper part of the gable of the chancel and its side walls was taken down and rebuilt with better materials. A new aisle had been added to the south side of the nave, extending to the south-east angle of the tower. The new porch retained the style and character of the old, with identical materials used, and had been brought forward to the centre of the new aisle, flanked with buttresses to correspond with those at the east and west ends of the church.

In the 1660 Parish Register a charity by the gift of Mrs Mary Wort, set up in approximately 1706, paid out of certain tenements in the village, was worth 12s. per annum to the poor. There was still a

meagre amount of money in the Worts Charity, administered by the Parish Council, in the 1970s – eventually it was merged with the Nursing Comforts Fund which provided walking-sticks, bedpans and commodes among other aids to the sick and convalescent. Codford and Stockton, then as in the beginning of the twenty-first century, had an equal right to nominate tenants for the Stockton Almshouses, founded by the benevolence of John Topp, the possible builder of Stockton House, who died in 1635.

Milestones and Mile-posts

The A36 through Codford boasts several listed cast-iron mile-posts and boundary posts from c.1840, a silent reminder of the early Victorian age. An article by the then Deputy County Architect, R. Haynes, in the 1968 Wiltshire County Council publication *Leisure in Wiltshire* entitled 'Wiltshire Milestones', outlined their history. The following is taken from a section on iron mile-posts:

Although there were many ironfounders in the Westbury and Warminster area, and also over in the boundary in East Somerset, who were using local iron ore and coal imported from the west during the nineteenth century, few cast iron mileposts are to be found in the county. The most splendid of these are on roads radiating from Warminster. Large and of a 'classical' design (bearing in fact an appearance much more akin

Codford St Mary Men's Choir, 1894. The picture includes: *Reg Ford, Revd Ashton, J. Flemming, Albert Simper, Reg Ford, Syd Doughty, Fred Kill, John Sparey.*

Codford High Street, early 1900s. (Photo Hibberd Bros, Heytesbury)

to memorial tablets of the same period) they show the miles to Salisbury, to Bath or more specifically to 'Warminster Town Hall'. They bear the initials of 'C & M' or 'C & M.W. 1840' and were probably cast by Carson & Miller, Scottish ironfounders who worked in Warminster from 1820 onwards. This firm cast milestone plates and a number of their parish boundary signs are also found by the roadside dated 1840. This date may have had some significance as it coincides with a Turnpike Act (3—4 Vic. C21) consolidating all Acts in force for the Warminster roads.

The Nineteenth-Century Population

The population tables from 1801–1901, as published in Colt-Hoare's *History of Wiltshire*, offer an insight into the two Codfords through the century. In 1801 George III had been on the throne for 41 years, in a Britain of 10.4 million people; the Act of Union of Great Britain and Northern Ireland came into force and Thomas Jefferson became president of the United States. Codford St Mary had a population of 187 and Codford St Peter, including Ashton Giffard, 393.

In 1811 the Prince of Wales was made Prince Regent when George III was judged to be insane. During the Peninsula War, Arthur Wellesley, the Duke of Wellington fought off Messena at Fuentes de Onoro with 34,000 men on the 5 May. On 11 May, under General Beresford, the combined Allied British, Portuguese and Spanish soldiers won a great victory fighting the French under Marshall Soult at La Albuera. The Codford St Mary population had dropped by 12 to 175, and in Codford St Peter there were 73 people less – the population was listed as 320.

By 1821, the coronation year of George IV, there had been a significant increase in the population of Codford St Mary, with 258 people, while Codford St Peter and Ashton Giffard between them showed a population of 347. Great Britain's population had doubled in two decades to 20.8 million.

By the next census, in 1831, the House of Hanover were still on throne. A year earlier at the age of 64 William IV had become king. Codford St Mary's population increased to 287, Codford St Peter's to 387, and Great Britain's decreased to 13.9 million – perhaps because the indigenous population were colonising and fighting around the world.

The Victorian age that was to last for the next 60 years into the twentieth century, was four years old in 1841. Great Britain's population was now 18.5 million, Codford St Mary's 338, Codford St Peter's 253, and, on this single occasion, Ashton Giffard was listed separately, as having a population of 141 – the combined total of the two latter villages equalled 394. With this breakdown we can see that Codford St Mary (Codford Magna – Great Codford) remained the largest of the three settlements, as had been recorded in the Domesday Survey of 1086.

By 1851 Great Britain had once more reached the 1821 population of 20.8 million. In the year that saw the introduction of the first double-decker bus, an Australian gold strike in Victoria, New South Wales and alcohol prohibition enforced in the American States of Maine and Illinois, Codford St Mary's population was 390, Codford St Peter's, once again including Ashton Giffard, was 401, an increase of seven. There were 395 males and 397 females living in 156 inhabited and one uninhabited homes. A total of 190 people were listed as agricultural labourers, there were 101 scholars, 40 people were in domestic service, there were 16 paupers, 12 laundresses, eight woolstaplers, seven seamstresses, four school mistresses, three farmers, two landed property owners, two straw-bonnet makers and one gentleman.

At Ashton Gifford John Ravenhill Esq. was the 53-year-old magnate living with his wife, three daughters aged 28, 25 and 13, an 11-year-old son, his sister-in-law (recorded as a gentlewoman), and two teenage nieces. The eldest four girls were seamstresses. It appears there were a cook, housemaid, kitchen maid, ladies maid, footman and coachman employed at the house.

In Codford St Mary, at what is known as East Farm, Anthony Notley (aged 64) farmed 1,000 acres and employed 32 men. On the day of the census an agricultural labourer, 37-year-old James House and pauper Mary Woods (74) were apparently residing in his field barn. In Codford St Peter John Chisman farmed 950 acres and employed 31 labourers. He had a young family, an eight-month-old daughter Elizabeth, while eight-year-old William and four-year-old Louisa were being educated at home by a 25-year-old governess, Loveday Saunders. There were three female servants aged between 15 and 19.

Saddler John Bendel had a son of 16 who was a harnessmaker, his 14-year-old daughter was a letter carrier, the three younger children were scholars and he employed James Monpris (17) as an apprentice. One of the local masons was James Doughty (39) – he and his wife Mary had four sons (aged 11, nine, six and two) and a daughter (aged four). Another Doughty, this time a gamekeeper, had eight children, Isaac (20), Sarah (15) and Elizabeth (10) were all agricultural labourers, Mary (eight) and Joab (six) were scholars, the little ones were Thomas (four), Maria (three) and William (one month).

Isaac Flower was the surgeon, living with his wife Margaretta, his five-year-old son and two daughters aged three and two, three general servants and a groom. Widower James Raxworthy was a woolstapler who employed 12 men, possibly including his two teenage sons – he had an unwed daughter of 26 and two servants. Thomas Feltham was the butcher – he had seven daughters and one son, Henry. Maria Shore was one of the schoolmistresses – at 29 she lived with her parents who were in their late fifties. Her three brothers, all in their twenties and her

17-year-old sister were all agricultural labourers.

In 1851 Revd Henry Wightwick of Codford St Peter was 41, and his wife Sarah was 12 years his junior. Their children Mary (eight), Lucy (seven) and Henry King (six) were scholars at home, Walter (four), Alice (three) and Austes (?) (one) were in the nursery. Revd Wightwick's 60-year-old mother-in-law, Lady Elizabeth King, was also living in the rectory together with a lady seamstress, a governess, a housemaid and two nursemaids.

Will Collins recalls that many years later, so the story goes, the reverend was having a card party with three friends in his large drawing-room with French windows. Two of the players are thought to have been the squire, T.K. Harding, and Charles Notley (in 1851 he had been 22, living with his parents Anthony and Mary). The men gambled and drank copiously through the night. In the morning the sweep arrived to clean the chimneys. Unable to make anyone hear at the door, he wandered through the garden and into the drawing-room through the French windows. 'Be you ready for I' the blackened apparition demanded. The men were horrified – they believed the Devil had arrived to carry them off! Somehow the story was related to the *Bath Chronicle* who published the story – incorrectly implying that it had happened over a Saturday night and into the Sabbath. Revd Wightwick had no objection to being portrayed as drinking and gambling, but he took great exception to it being thought that he did so on a Sunday and threatened to sue. The paper retracted and all was well. In the 1970s his granddaughter, Miss Joan Wightwick, was still living in The Cottage in Codford St Mary. She had lived through her life in Codford with her bachelor brother Henry, who predeceased her, moving into Warminster to a nursing home in old age, dying at the great age of 99.

The year 1861 saw the outbreak of the American Civil War, the emancipation of Russian Serfs, the first horse-drawn trams in London and the death of Prince Albert, the Prince Consort. Great Britain now had a population of 23 million, Codford St Mary 404, Codford St Peter 359. This was the first time the records show that St Mary's population was greater than the combined Codford St Peter and Ashton Giffard. According the *Victorian County History* a large wool-stapling business in Codford St Mary was closed, as was a racing stables, resulting in the loss of local jobs.

Great Britain had 26 million people by 1871, when Codford St Mary's population was 349 and Codford St Peter's 326. This was the year Stanley met Livingstone at Ujiji, that the FA Cup was established, William I, King of Prussia, was proclaimed German Emperor and Grigori Rasputin was born in Russia.

The first Boer War ended in 1881, Disraeli died, flogging was abolished in the British Army and Navy, and the population of London was 3.3 million. Codford St Mary was now a village of 340 people, while Codford St Peter housed 319. Ten years later, in 1891, Codford St Mary had 18 less people at 322, and Codford St Peter had a population of 260. Queen Victoria still had ten years on the throne, Russia was beset by widespread famine, in Japan an earthquake claimed 10,000 lives, and American W.L. Judson invented the clothing zipper.

The first census of the twentieth century was set against the backdrop of the death of the Victorian age and the succession of Edward VII. This was a time of conflict – the second Boer War (1899–1902) was being fought, the Boxer uprising ended, American President McKinley was assassinated and the first British submarine was launched. Codford St Mary 's population was at its lowest in 80 years, with 277, and Codford St Peter's was at its lowest in at least 100 years, with a population of 242 – 60 years earlier, when Codford St Peter and Ashton Giffard were counted separately, there were 253 residents in the single village of St Peter's.

The nineteenth century had begun in the late-Georgian era, which included the Regency period, concluding in the final days of the Victorian age. The British Empire's influence had spread across the globe – British exploration, conquest and invention had flourished, and while Britannia certainly ruled the waves, in Britain there was unprecedented peace and prosperity. In the Wylye Valley life followed its gentle course, like the river after which it was named. In the first few years of the century a congregational chapel was built at Codford St Mary – over the years the gentry were the churchgoers and the businessmen and farmers attended chapel.

The three rural settlements that make up the present village of Codford were mainly agricultural and relatively self-sufficient. In the middle of the nineteenth century the coming of the railway offered the opportunity to trade and travel further afield. In September 1851, the Wilts, Somerset and Weymouth broad-gauge railway reached Warminster. They were taken over by the Great Western Railway that same year. The line was extended and by 1856 it had reached Salisbury, with stations at Wilton, Wishford, Wylye, Codford and Heytesbury.

Notes:

Revd Henry Wightwick was the rector of St Peter's from 1841 until his death at the age of 74 in 1884. He was known as one of the most hospitable men in the valley and was a great friend of the Duke of Albany. He is buried close to the eastern boundary at the front of the church, across the wall from the house he lived in for so many years; at his funeral in June 1884 there were 40 wreaths.

Others mentioned in the 1851 census lay in the churchyard; many of Revd Wightwick's family, surgeon Isaac Flower, farmer John Chisham, John Ravenhill with his wife, daughters and his son John Richard are all buried close to St Peter's Church.

The Valley of Death at Balaclava, from Raglan's viewpoint.   *Balaclava monument, October 2004.*

A Hero of the Crimea

On 25 October 1854 the British faced 25,000 Russians; the 93rd Highlanders of 'The Thin Red Line' checked the Russian advance; the Heavy Brigade mounted a successful charge on the Russian Calvary; the Light Brigade responded to a misunderstood order to attack the guns. The commanders were on the high ground, with a clear view of the battlefield – the officers in the valley had a more restricted view and Lord Raglan's order was vaguely worded and open to misinterpretation. Lord Cardigan led his men in a valiant but ultimately suicidal charge against the wrong guns, at the end of a narrow valley strongly defended by riflemen and calvary. The Light Brigade took the battery but was unable to hold it. It was possibly because the French Chasseurs d'Afrique covered the retreat that there were as many survivors as there were.

Colonel Hunt once lived at Little Ashton in Codford St Peter. He was one of the 195 survivors of the Charge of the Light Brigade (according to the late Miss Joan Wightwick) into the mouths of the Russian guns at Balaclava; to the end of his life the screaming of a hare reminded him of the wounded and dying horses at Balaclava. He was an excellent shot and if someone didn't kill an animal cleanly on a hunt he would 'go mad' (according to the late Paul Cole).

Looking across Second World War battle remains to the valley of the charge of the Light Brigade.

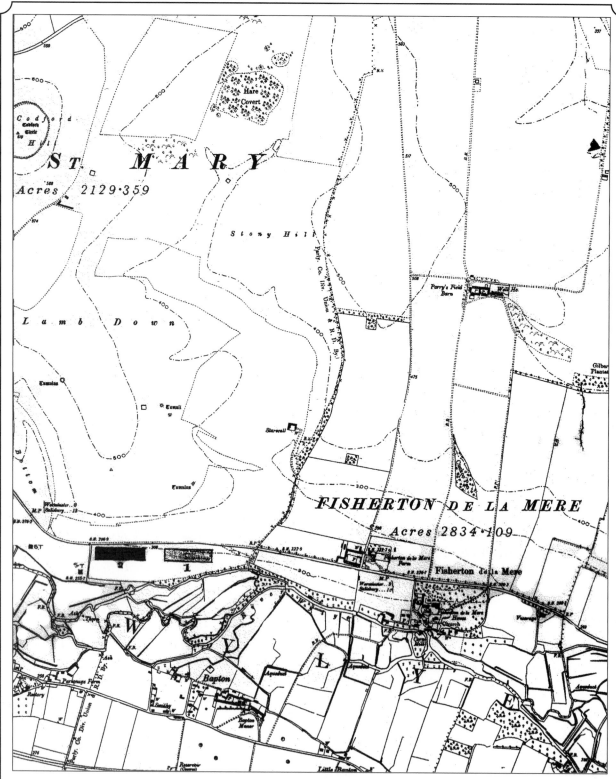

A 1915 map of Codford St Mary, with Codford Circle on Lamb Down and Fisherton-de-la-Mere.

Chapter 5

The First World War

The twin villages of Codford St Mary and Codford St Peter were ideally situated for military use, with their proximity to the railway and to the training areas of Salisbury Plain. At the outbreak of hostilities no less than 24,000 troops arrived in the vicinity in September 1914. Codford had 15 camps while the surrounding satellite villages had a further 12. Reminiscent of the gold-rush towns of Australia or America, almost at once temporary shops sprung up as villages utilised available space to accommodate the facilities needed by the influx of military personnel.

The men were under canvas while the huts were being constructed. In October the weather turned wet and cold – roads and fields turned into a morass of sticky mud from which there was no escape. The camps were on Manor Farm, along the Chitterne Road, around St Mary's Church, in Cherry Orchard close to the Woolstore, at Hillside, by the railway station and south of the main road towards Salisbury. There was a Red Cross Hospital near St Mary's Church and Codford Military Hospital was established at The Punchbowl – in 1916 this became No. 3 New Zealand General Hospital after the New Zealand Command Depot was established in Codford.

British Army Units in Wiltshire, 1914–18
Terry Crawford

This list is based on *British Regiments, 1914–1918* (Samson 1978) by Brigadier E.A. James, whose record of infantry and cavalry unit locations during the First World War is arranged by unit rather than place. James compiled his work from regimental histories, which often gave imprecise locations: 'Ludgershall'

could well mean 'Perham Down' or 'Windmill Hill', for example. Codford and Larkhill Camps each had satellites that were sometimes referred to by their own names and sometimes by that of the major camp. The list is titled 'Codford', but may include Boyton, Corton and Sherrington.

10th Black Watch: October 1914
8th Border Regiment: autumn 1914 [to billets in Boscombe in November]
11th Cameronians [Scottish Rifles]: *autumn 1914*
8th Cheshire Regiment: Oct 1914–Feb 1915
10th Cheshire Regiment: end August–early winter 1914
11th Cheshire Regiment: autumn 1914
13th Cheshire Regiment: autumn 1914
8th Duke of Cornwall's Light Infantry: autumn 1914
8th East Lancashire Regiment: Sept–Nov 1914
10th Essex Regiment: May–late July 1915
8th East Surrey Regiment: May–late July 1914
9th Gloucestershire Regiment: Sept–Nov 1914
12th Hampshire Regiment: 30 Sept–late Nov? 1914 [billets in Basingstoke]
16th Highland Light Infantry [1st Glasgow] *Aug–Nov 1915*
3/6th, 3/7th, 3/8th Lancashire Fusiliers: 1915–April 1916
11th Lancashire Fusiliers: formed at Codford Sept–31 Dec 1914
15th Lancashire Fusiliers: Aug 13–Nov 1915
19th Lancashire Fusiliers [3rd Salford] [Pioneers]: *Aug 25–mid Nov 1915*
12th Middlesex Regiment [Duke of Cambridge's Own]: *May–late July 1915*
16th Northumberland Fusiliers: Aug 21–mid Nov 1915
17th Northumberland Fusiliers [Pioneers]: *Aug 21–mid Nov 1915*

High Street with temporary shops, during the First World War.

Street scene at Codford St Peter during the First World War, with Woolstore Camp behind the wall. The cottages askew next to the telegraph pole are at French Horn.

Above: *One of the Codford camps with horses in the foreground during the First World War.*

Below: *A general view of some of Codford's First World War camps.*

Above: *Codford St Mary with a cyclist coming from Church Lane, some time during the First World War.*

Below: *An 1886 map, reproduced in 12 October 1914, showing temporary buildings (darker shading) which were beginnings of the military camp.*

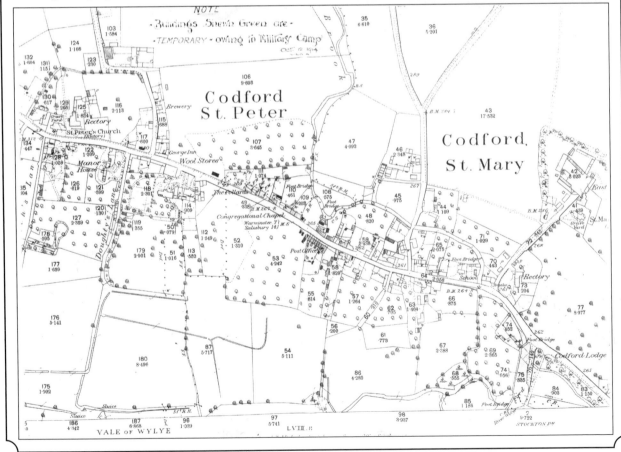

8th Oxfordshire and Buckinghamshire Light Infantry [Pioneers]: *Oct 1915*

7th Queen's Own [Royal West Kents]: *May–late July 1915*

7th Royal Berkshire Regiment [Princess Charlotte of Wales's]: *Oct–Nov 1914* [to billets in Reading: Nov 1914]

8th Royal Berkshire Regiment [Princess Charlotte of Wales's]: *Oct–Nov 1914*

8th Royal Lancashire Regiment [King's Own]: *Oct–Nov 1914*

11th Royal Fusiliers [City of London Regiment]: *May–July 1915*

7th King's Shropshire Light Infantry: Oct–Nov 1914

8th Suffolk Regiment: May–late July 1915

14th Royal Warwickshire Regiment [1st, 2nd and 3rd Birmingham]: *Aug–mid Dec 1915*

15th and 16th Royal Warwickshire Regiment: Aug–mid Dec 1915

10th Royal Welsh Fusiliers: Sept–Nov 1914

10th Welsh Regiment: Oct 1914

14th Worcestershire Regiment [Severn Valley Pioneers]: *March–June 1916*

Headquarters 18th Division May–July 1915

Additionally, on 1 October 1914 the *Wiltshire Gazette* reported the 8th and 9th Loyal North Lancashire's and the 11th Cheshire's to be at Codford. It also put the 9th Gloucestershire's, 7th Royal Berkshire's, 8th Duke of Cornwall's, 8th Royal Scots, 10th Black Watch, 7th Oxfordshire and Buckinghamshire's and the 7th Wiltshire's, all said by James to have been at Codford, in nearby camps at Sherrington, Boyton and Corton.

Alleged Fraud At Codford Camp
From an extract taken from the
Warminster Journal, 12 March 1915

At Warminster Town Hall, on Saturday, before the Marquis of Bath (in the chair), Mr G.N. Temple, Mr K.J. Bradfield, and Revd G.H.S. Atwood, Henry William Hawkins of Salisbury, a timekeeper at the Army Service Corps Camp at Codford, was again charged with making false entries in the pay book during the months of January and February, whilst in the employ of the Secretary of State for War; there was a further charge of conspiring with a man named Ernest Thomas to get diverse sums of money from the Secretary of State for War with the intent to defraud.

The Magistrates Clerk said Thomas was charged with a different offence altogether, that of endeavouring to obtain the sum of £1.3s.11d. from Henry Mason with intent to cheat and defraud. Ernest Thomas, a ganger at Codford Camp was then charged as already stated and with conspiracy with Hawkins.

Mr Jackson said they were in no doubt aware, the War Department was carrying out extensive works

that side of Salisbury Plain, and that defendants were in the employ of Sir John Jackson. Hawkins was a timekeeper, and Thomas was a ganger. It would have been comparatively easy to put the accounts in such a way as to obtain public money through Sir John Jackson when such money had not been earned. In this case it was Hawkins's duty as timekeeper to go several times a day to see that men were on the job, and to make certain entries in a book which was in the possession of Sir John Jackson. For the fortnight ending the 20 January and 7 February the entries were all in Hawkins's handwriting, and also up to the 15 February, when he was discharged, and the book had to be made up by someone else in the office. Mr Jackson went on to state that the evidence showed that there was collusion between the two defendants and that they had attempted to derive benefit by conspiring together. The Bench would commit both for trial if they considered the depositions justified it, or they could commit either of them.

Richard Banner Lumby, a cashier on the works at Codford, produced two time books, the entries of which were in Hawkins's handwriting. On the books were the names of Tubb and Ford, and for the fortnight ending 22 January it showed these men had worked 143 hours each, having earned £3.17s.3d. Tubb had 'subbed' £3.12s. and Ford £3.10s., and at the end of the fortnight, after deducting insurance and unemployment money, Tubb was paid 4s.2d. and Ford 6s.2d. For the fortnight ending 3 February there appeared for the first time a man named Bright, and all the entries in that book were in the handwriting of Hawkins. In that fortnight it was shown that Bright worked 143 hours, that he earned £3.17s.5d. and that he 'subbed' £3.10s., leaving after deduction 6s.4d. to come to him, which was paid.

When questioned, a witness, who handed out the wages to the workmen, stated that it was possible for one man to collect wages for other men, as he did not know the workers by name. The timekeepers were always in the office when payments were being made out through the window to the workers. It was the responsibility of the timekeepers to check the men and see the payments were made correctly.

Henry Herbert Mason, cashier in the same employ, said he took over paying at Codford after the last witness became ill. He produced his book showing entries for the fortnight ending 17 February and giving the name of Bright in the handwriting of Hawkins. It showed that Bright worked 80 hours and earned £2.14s.3d., that he 'subbed' £2.10s., and had 2s.9d. left over to him at the end of the fortnight.

There were no other entries in that book, because Bright apparently left the job. Hawkins left the job on Monday, 15 February. Calculated from the remaining entries Bright was owed 2s.9d., but he did not collect it. The witness further stated that there had been entries in the name of Tubb and Ford in the handwriting of Hawkins, and showing that they had been 'subbed' sums of money, leaving 10s.7d. each to be paid to them at the end of the week, but the money had not been paid. Bright, Tubb or Ford had not applied for these sums.

On Saturday, 20 February Thomas came to the pay office to make applications for money. He said 'I have some men away ill I want to draw their money.' He did not give the cashier their names and numbers, and was told to make a written application to the head cashier. Thomas said that the men did not make applications themselves because they were isolated through fever at their lodgings.

There were other cases of men who knocked off Saturday and did not come again. It was suggested that Thomas drew the three unpaid sums, as well as his own.

Edwin Alfred Cook, timekeeper for Sir John Jackson, said there were only two timekeepers there now. He remembered Thomas coming to him on Saturday, 20 February, after paying out was over. That day the wages were paid in one of the huts, and Thomas came to the time office and said he had three men out of his gang that were ill, and asked how they were to get their wages.

Edwin told Thomas to write to Mr Beck the head cashier. He then went away. The witness did not ask him anything about the men, their names, or their numbers. On Saturday afternoon he asked permission to leave, and left. The witness saw him on the following Monday afternoon, 22 February, when he said 'I have seen the three men in Salisbury, and they have orders from the doctor not to write to anyone, as there is a case of spotted fever in the house where they are lodging.' The witness replied that they would have to wait.

Edwin sent for Thomas to come to the office and asked him to provide the addresses of the three men in his gang, which he did – a house occupied by Mrs Burch at Rampart Road, Salisbury, but Thomas did not say she was any relation to him.

Mrs Annie Burch, of 41 Rampart Road, Salisbury, said Thomas was her brother. She denied there had ever been a case of spotted fever in her house, and also that she had a lodger there. She did not see her brother on Sunday, 21 February, but she did see him on the previous Thursday week, 25 February, when he came to her house. He had said 'If a letter comes for me, care of myself, take it in.' He did not say what she was to do with it and went away again. He said perhaps it might come up from Sir John Jackson's office or it might come by post. She did not know any men named Bright, Tubb or Ford.

PC Hillier said he executed a warrant on Thomas on 27 February. He cautioned him and read the warrant over, and the prisoner replied 'What's your opinion of my job? How do you think it will work out? I suppose it will mean a lock up for it. I was drawn into it by doing a kindness.'

PS Zebedee proved executing a warrant on Hawkins on 27 February at 3.30p.m., when he saw him at Salisbury Police Station, where he had been detained. Thomas was questioned and read the warrant, and in reply he said 'I know nothing about it. If... be proved.' He then brought him to Warminster.

Mr Trethowen, in addressing the Bench on behalf of Hawkins, asked them to say there was no case. The charge now against this unfortunate man was conspiracy. When he was first charged with making false entries he said 'That remains to be proved'. Now the charge was conspiracy it gave them the chance to say just what they liked about Thomas. But they did not give any evidence of it. One would have thought that the prosecution would have shown that he did make a false entry in this book, but there was not the slightest evidence. Here they had names down in a book, three names, and whether the prosecution had been attempting to prove they were there or not on three days he did not know. He supposed that these men 'subbed' at the weekends and were actually paid in the middle of the week. He thought that the magistrates must either find that there was no case or it must go for trial, and he contended that on the evidence the prosecution had brought there was no possibility of a jury convicting Hawkins. What had he done? Although it was alleged these men were not there at the time they were put down for, there was no evidence of it. Even supposing these men were not there on these two or three days on which he said they were, even then they had to be satisfied that Hawkins put them down for some fraudulent purpose of conspiracy with Thomas. How could he do so? If he made a false entry in the book and it put something into his pocket they may say there was something in it, but it had been stated he certainly could not take the money himself, and if he did not take it who could have taken it? The obvious inference was that someone took it. They had not the slightest evidence to show that these men were not there on the days when Hawkins entered them into his book.

Mr Marshall said that, following up the remarks his friend had made as to whether the three men did actually exist, or whether they were dead men or never existed, he pointed out that if they did exist it was obvious the money must have been drawn out by someone. It would be suggested that Thomas had drawn out the money, but he ventured to say that if Thomas had appeared four times at the pay office in one morning it would have been noticed. He thought that they had depended too much on coincidence, and suggested that there must be evidence of consort to do the illegal act. There appeared to be no actual evidence that the two men now charged had anything to do with each other.

After the Bench had retired for some time, and the defendants had stated they reserved their defence, the chairman said they stood committed for trial at the next Quarter Sessions to be held in Salisbury on the charge of conspiracy, and also they would be indicted for obtaining money under false pretences and for false entries.

Hawkins's solicitor applied for bail, as he was a married man, and his father was well known in Salisbury. Mr Marshall applied for bail for Thomas, and both men were allowed out on bail on substantial sureties.

The Lost Soldier
Private 212 Granville Horrocks

Granville Horrocks had served with the 1/10 Manchester Regiment but was finally stationed at Codford Camp with 3/10 Manchester Regiment, a Reserve Battalion which never saw any active service. He was 46 when he took his life on 5 April 1916 – he was buried at St Mary the Virgin, Wylye, but is not commemorated on the memorial in the churchyard. The fact that Granville Horrocks committed suicide, together with the fact he was not a local man, may have been the reason why his name was not included at the time it was commissioned; according to its inscription it was 'erected by the parishioners of Wylye'.

When Nigel Lampard began research into the local casualties of the First World War he discovered that Granville Horrocks was a forgotten soldier – he is not listed on any of the three memorials in Oldham, Lancashire where he was born in 1870. He discovered that Granville had married Mary Jane Whittaker at St Mary's Church, Oldham on 30 September 1900 and that the 1901 census had him as living with his widowed mother Jane, who was recorded as the head of the household and with his new wife Mary Jane. Granville's occupation was an ironworks labourer and his wife was a cotton reeler. No children were recorded in the household.

His medal card at Kew under the Manchester Regiment lists him as being entitled to the 1915 Star, British War Medal and Victory Medal. His entitlement to the 1915 Star and his four-figure service number, 2121, suggests that he was on active service before Gallipoli. Sadly, the Manchester Regiment's Museum has no surviving records as to when their regimental numbers were issued.

The inquest was reported on 29 April 1916 by the *Salisbury Journal*.

Soldier's Suicide at Wylye
Extraordinary letter to a Commanding Officer

The Coroner for South Wilts (Mr F.H. Trethowen) conducted an inquiry at the Wyvern Hall, Wylye, on Wednesday into the circumstances attending the death of Granville Horrocks, a private in the Manchester Regiment, whose body was recovered from the river Wylye on the previous Sunday.

Private Granville Horrocks's grave at Wylye. (PHOTO NIGEL LAMPARD)

Lieutenant-Colonel P. Bamford, commanding the 10th Reserve Manchesters, said the deceased was a Private attached to the 3/10 Manchester Regiment. He was about 40 years of age and he believed his home address to be 50 Bloom Street, Oldham. He was an old soldier. He went to Egypt with the 1/10 Manchesters in 1914, and had sunstroke then, and went to hospital. He was afterwards at Gallipoli, where he was wounded. After then he was attached to the 3/10th and sent to Codford. While witness was at Codford deceased wrote him a letter, and in consequence witness saw him, as the letter was unintelligible to him. He said he did not want to be kept in England. He wished to go out and fight in order that the young men might be left behind. Witness told him he wanted to keep him there until he was quite fit. Deceased was so very strange in his manner that witness saw the medical officer about him. He seemed to think that blame was being thrown upon him in connection with an engagement that took place at Gallipoli. Witness had made inquiries and could not find that anyone ever suggested that he had done wrong then. Witness produced a letter which was handed to him of April 15th. He reported the matter to the Police. He saw the deceased the day before on parade, and then noticed no difference in his appearance.

In answer to the Foreman, Colonel Bamford said the deceased seemed quite pleased when he spoke to him after he received the first letter. The letter referred to by the witness in his evidence was read by the Coroner as follows:

The Hospital Camp at The Punchbowl during the First World War.

SIR.- I have put myself on the draft A class, but the division has been hunting me down so much while I have been here that they do not want me, but intend to do murder; but I will stop them. I am only too willing to go out, for I am not afraid, otherwise I would not have gone out if I was afraid, for I had the chance of coming home, and would not leave my regiment. I had a serious illness. I collapsed on the desert through vaccination and fell asleep, and was exposed by the sun, which drove me out of my mind. If I had only been left bleeding away on the open nothing would have been said. I had a bullet hit me, but lost it when I swooned over from loss of blood. I went under an operation. A lot had been done there, and I know all about it. You must have me buried here, as my wife will not have the means. I have sacrificed my life for the honour of my regiment, but I will tell you must tell your officers in command to

put men in the right position, and give them a fighting chance, also the N.C.O's. I never had the chance. I died for the blunders of others. God Save the King. Don't make any bother; they will think I'm not right.

Private Thomas Weston, of the 1/10 Manchester Regiment, stationed at Wilton, said he knew the deceased well, and had worked with him in civil life. He saw him about 9.20pm on April 4th and again on the morning of the 5th at about 6.30. Witness spoke to him, but he did not answer. He had complained that men who had been in England a twelvemonth had not gone out and that those who had done their 'bit' would have to go again. He was well enough when witness saw him on April 4th, and nothing he said to witness made him think he was likely to take his life. From what he said to him he thought he wanted to go out to the front again.

Ernest Moore (aged 14 years), son of Herbert Moore, journeyman gardener, Fisherton-de-la-Mere, said that at 7.45am on 5th inst. he was at the Mill Hatches at Fisherton-de-la-Mere, when he noticed a cap on the bank by the hatches. He picked it up, and found the letter which had been read. He took the badge of the cap and the letter to Mrs. Bamford, the wife of Colonel Bamford.

P.C. E.J. Scarvin, Wylye, said that the letter referred to by the last witness was handed to him by Colonel Bamford. Witness went to Fisherton-de-la-Mere on April 5th, and since that time had been keeping observations on the river. On 23rd inst. about 7.15pm he found the body of the deceased lying face downwards in the river Wylye about 800 yards up-stream from Wylye Mill. With assistance he got the body out, and took it to the Bell Inn. He searched the body and found 5s.4d., and the deceased's identification disc.

An ANZAC hut from the First World War.

St Mary's Church and St Mary's Cottage from the Commonwealth War Graves (known locally as the ANZAC Cemetery) in 2003. (PHOTO BRIAN MARSHALL)

The ANZAC Cemetery, the ANZAC hut, used by the Codford Scouts, and listed cottages in 2003. (PHOTO BRIAN MARSHALL)

The ANZAC cemetery, off Church Lane.

The ANZAC service in 2004.

Lieutenant Allan Lindsey Saunders R.A.M.C., stationed at Codford Military Hospital, stated he saw the body of the deceased at about 7.30pm on April 24th. Deceased had been dead some time. He noticed no signs of any injury. From what he saw and what he had heard, death was probably due to drowning. Sunstroke did have an effect on the brain, and the letters read at the inquiry seemed to show that deceased was not of sound mind.

A verdict of 'Suicide during temporary insanity' was returned.

New Zealander Command Depot

The following passage is taken from *Hornchurch During the Great War: an illustrated account of local activities and experiences*, by Charles Thomas Perfect (published 1920):

Soon after the advent of the New Zealand Division in France at the end of April or the beginning of May, 1916, and after their first entry into action on the western front, a large number of wounded, and the usual toll of sick, began to filter through to England.

It was then realised that Hornchurch was far too small for the purpose of a Command Depot, and that,

Revd Ian Duff and Australian officers on 25 April 2002 at the ANZAC Day ceremony, 6.30a.m.

moreover, it was necessary to establish a Convalescent Hospital there. Such 'details,' therefore, as had been at Hornchurch were now moved en bloc to Codford.

The Codford Quilt

On the other side of the world, in East Taieri, New Zealand, the wives and mothers of the Kiwi soldiers who were in Codford while serving in the Army during the First World War, knitted socks, balaclavas and gloves to be sent to their boys. They also lovingly sewed colourful squares for a very special cot cover, with some of the following sentiments:

New Zealand Brave Boys; Wishing you a speedy recovery; Anzacs answered the call; July 25th 1916. Success to our Arms. Maggie Craig, East Taieri; East Taieri Briton loves her soldiers Brave Jane Irwin...

These words surround a centrepiece with a kangaroo and an emu flanking a flag in the centre, a kiwi at the top and a uniformed soldier beneath the flag, with native leaves on either side of him and 'Done by women of East Taieri 1916' stitched below.

When it was completed the patchwork 'quilt', as it became known, was sent across the oceans to England. The thin pink-coloured cot cover was used in No. 3 New Zealand Military Hospital until it closed in 1919, when it was passed into the keeping of the local baker, George Conduit, whose shop (rebuilt after a fire in the 1970s as The Stores House, at 116 High Street) was at the top of the hill across from St Peter's Church. George House Conduit was born on 28 October 1876, he was 40 when the ANZAC troops arrived in Codford – he frequently visited the hospital and often played cards with the New Zealanders. George died during the Second World War in 1941, on 24 May; he was married to Marietta Jane Young (20 December 1877–30 December 1958).

Eventually the quilt passed to George's daughter, Lillian Maude, whose grandson Stephen Pope married a New Zealand girl. Lillian attached the

The Codford quilt, made in New Zealand during the First World War.

The Australian Badge, cut into the chalk hillside, 2005.

following note to the cot cover and gave it to Stephen when he left England for New Zealand:

This cot cover once belonged to the New Zealand Military Hospital Codford St Mary Wiltshire during the First World War. When the hospital closed it was given to my father the late George Conduit of Codford who frequently visited there. It was greatly treasured by our family as we have known so many of the staff. It came into my possession on the death of my mother in 1959. I have often wondered about the good ladies who embroidered it. What a lovely thought for the boys in the hospital so far from home.

It gives me great pleasure to give this now to my grandson Stephen and his wife Janet to take back with them to New Zealand and hope they will treasure this little bit of NZ history.

Signed L.M. Pope.

At the time of writing George's great-grandson has a dairy farm at Mokotua, south-east of Invercargill in South Island, where the quilt is a treasured possession. So the story turned a full circle, the Codford quilt was taken back whence it came to 'the Land of the Long White Cloud'.

The Australian Rising Sun

This badge was known locally as 'The Codford Badge', 'The Australian Badge' or 'The Rising Sun' – never the 'Lamb Down Badge', until someone used the name on an internet site. Locally, during the early- to mid-twentieth century, the hill was also known as 'The Pimple.'

The seven-pointed badge had been hurriedly adopted, according to tradition, by the newly appointed Commander-in-Chief of the Australian Forces, a British officer, Major General Sir Edward Hutton, KCB, KCMG in 1902 for the Australian contingents at the time of the second Boer War. It represented a 'Trophy of Arms', comprised of mounted cut and thrust swords and triangular Martini Henry bayonets arranged in a semi-circle around a brass crown. It was slightly modified in 1904 and the Australian Imperial Forces wore the badge with pride throughout both world wars.

The Codford Badge was cut into the south-facing hillside over the Wylye Valley by Australian forces stationed in Codford in 1916. Initial work was started by the 13th Training Battalion, Australian Imperial Force. The badge was then embedded with green, brown and clear beer bottles to make it shine.

The badge cutting was at least in part worked on as punishment. The Down was used for physical exercises, men with full packs toiling to the summit of the steep hillside, stripping off to their vests in the icy winds and waiting until the PT officers were ready. Not surprisingly in the winter months men succumbed to sickness and the hill was known to the troops as 'Misery Hill'.

In the Second World War the badge was covered over to prevent it being used as a navigational aid. When it was uncovered after the war ended the glass had either washed away or sunk into the chalk landscape. In 2005 it measures approximately 175 feet in length and 150 feet in height, and the design has been considerably simplified.

The first working party of ANZAC liaison officers in Europe on 'Operation Long Look' was in the mid-1990s. Under five successive Australian liaison officers based in Warminster – Dave Killcullen, Tony Egan, Craig Shortt, Cameron Richardson and David Bishop – the work parties of ANZAC officers and villagers have gathered in the summer to re-cut, re-chalk and maintain the badge.

In 1916 Codford was a New Zealand Command Depot. The New Zealand No. 3 General Hospital was in the village on The Punchbowl, a valley surrounded on three sides by the tree-covered curve of the Down. Soldiers were sent to the depot for rehabilitation after being wounded or taken ill, and it was also a training area, 3 miles from the edge of Salisbury Plain.

After the First World War a small area was dedicated as a Commonwealth War Grave Cemetery for the ANZAC troops who died between 1916 and 1919: 66 New Zealanders and 31 Australians. Most of the deaths were in 1917 and 1918. The details of their deaths are likely to have been filled in by relatives after hostilities had ceased, so we are reliant on their accuracy for the information. A total of 14 men are listed as dying of pneumonia, while in 42 cases the cause of death is given as 'sickness'. Only two of the soldiers are recorded as having died from influenza, but it is likely that many of the deaths listed under the general heading of 'sickness' were caused by influenza. Three men succumbed to meningitis and bronchitis, one of a kidney inflammation and two of pulmonary consumption. One died of machine-gun wounds, another in an aeroplane accident. We have no cause of death for 26 of the men, although we know that at least one died after being injured by a grenade in a training accident.

Every year since 1999 an ANZAC service has been held at 6.30a.m. on ANZAC Day.

Notes:
Taken from the 'The Royal Australian Regiment – History of the Australian Army Rising Sun Badge' website.

The Australian Badge has evolved since its inception just over 100 years ago. The original design of 1904 has been slightly modified as to the wording on the scroll and the style of the crown. After the Second World War, in 1949 the scroll was altered from 'Australian Imperial Forces' to 'Australian Military Forces.' Some 20 years later the wording was changed to 'Australia' and the Federation Star and Torse (heraldic) Wreath added. On the 75th anniversary of the ANZAC landings on Gallipoli there was strong feeling that there should be a return to the traditional accoutrements worn by Australian soldiers during two world wars. Co-inciding with the 90th anniversary of the Army commemorated on 1 March 1991 the scroll now clearly identifies 'The Australian Army.'

The Origins of ANZAC

At the outbreak of the First World War Australia and New Zealand were both quick to offer support to England. Thousands of volunteers from all over Australia and New Zealand eagerly enlisted. The offer of help was readily accepted by England and in early 1915 a force of five infantry divisions and one light division were provided by Australia, and one infantry division was provided by New Zealand. They sailed for the Greek Island of Lemnos to be made ready for the Gallipoli campaign.

At 0400 hours on 25 April 1915, the ANZAC Corps were put into long boats so they could be landed at dawn. The intention of the commanders was to land the ANZACs at the lowlands below Suvla Bay, but a strong tide and current forced the initial landing to be misplaced and the force landed facing steep cliffs and well defended Turkish positions. Despite this the Turks were forced back – due only to the grim determination, aggressive fighting spirit and outstanding courage displayed by previously 'unblooded' troops.

The ANZACs fought continuously and improved their position until the campaign was abandoned nine months later. Of the original force landed, 66 per cent were killed or wounded. The morale of these fine men was never broken and they strongly resented being withdrawn. Since those times, 25 April has been set aside as a national holiday, when Australians remember those men and women of all three services who fell in all wars.

ANZAC Requiem

On this day above all others we recall those who served in war and did not return to receive the grateful thanks of the nation. We remember those who are still where they were left; amid the scrub in the valleys and the ridges of Gallipoli; on the rocky and terraced hills of Palestine and in the cemeteries of France.

We remember those that lie in ground beneath the shimmering haze of the Libyan Desert. At Bardia, Derna and Tobruk, and amid the mountain passes and olive groves of Greece and Crete, and the rugged hills of Syria and Lebanon.

We remember those who lie buried in the jungles of Malaysia, Singapore and Burma. In New Guinea and in the islands of the Pacific.

We remember those who lie buried amid loving friends in Great Britain and in unknown resting places in almost every land and those gallant men whose grave is the unending sea.

We remember those who died as prisoners of war, remote from their homeland.

We think of those members of the woman's services who gave their lives for ours in foreign lands and at sea.

We recall too, the staunch friends who fought beside us on the first ANZAC Day and ever since – men of

Codford High Street during the First World War, with the High Houses, YMCA and temporary building on the right-hand side of the road. The cottage jutting out on the left is the old bakery.

The First World War camp along Beanis Path. Also in the picture are the two listed cottages, with washing on the line, and the ox barn (far left).

New Zealand – who helped create the name of ANZAC.

We think of every man and woman who in the crucial hours of World War Two died so that the light of freedom and humanity might continue to shine.

We think of those gallant men who died in Korea, in Malaya and in Vietnam and in the pursuit of peace since then.

May they rest in the knowledge of their achievement and may we – and our successors in that heritage – prove worthy of their sacrifice.

Lest we forget.

Messages From 'The Drain'

There exist many postcards from the First World War, sometimes dog-eared, with indecipherable scrawls written in faded ink and blurred postmarks from Codford, describing the village from an outsider's point of view. Given the dreadful weather conditions during the First World War, with men under canvas in the early months, rain pouring from a dark grey sky, it was not surprising the troops nicknamed the village 'Mudford', 'Codford on the Mud', otherwise known as 'The Drain'. The unmade roads turned into rivers of mud, the rain soaking into the chalk landscape of the Wylye Valley and the open expanse of Salisbury Plain.

There follow several extracts from the postcards:

The Corporation Dust Cart
Sure a corporation dust cart
Overturned itself one day,
And all its filthy effluent
In a Wiltshire village lay.

And when Headquarters saw it,
It smelt so good and damp,
They said it's just the place
To build a Field Artillery Camp.

They thought they'd call it Codford
With the accent on the Cod,
And they put the blankety-blanks there
And commended them to God.

And then they built some rat traps
Which down here they call huts,
And we only wish they'd shove them
Where the monkeys shove their nuts!

On a photograph of St Mary's Church, with its gates across the road to the south, it is written:

The old church in a corner or practically in the middle of the camp the iron gates are taken down to make room for a roadway. I'm quite comfy, except for the mud which is awful.
Marshall.

I am here
Somewhere in Wiltshire
Its very queer.
I cannot tell you where
Codford's our mark
Stonehenge is over there
Just send that letter you cannot do better
Its sure to land
Somewhere
I am here

Temperance Tea tonight – I am not gone. Ned will tell you what a pickle we've been in today.

Well I have had another weeks leave and I went to Scotland and had a good time. When I came back they put me on a job working for an old farmer – I was driving the threshing mill for him. The weather is very cold here just now, very hard frosts in the mornings and very cold winds in the day time. I will be going back to France shortly now.

The Lodge is opposite number 5 Camp and is the lodge to Stockton House which stands in the centre of the park. This is the Salisbury road via Wylye.

You can take it from me we have a jolly time. The lights are on all night so it does not make any difference what time [it is]. Ours is getting an expert at finding his bed in the dark. They have been officer's quarters [?] and we three are the only privates in them so you see it is just like a bat and we make life as best we can. I might say it is not bad either.

One picture postcard shows the Congregational Institute and staff, dated June 1916. Written on the reverse is:

This is the place where our church parades are to be held. There is a fine library here. It has been pelting with rain today, so instead of weeding we have been sleeping in huts. 'Great need of men!' 'Your King and Country need you!' – to come and weed the garden! carry on. What of Lord Kitchener!

The Church Army Institute was behind St Mary's Church – the huge First World War building was still on the site at the beginning of the Second World War, when amongst other uses it was a venue for boxing matches. During the Second World War it was known as Institute Camp or Rectory Field Camp, with the camp entrance opposite the old ford. The 6th Guards Armoured Brigade Officer's Mess and 2nd Battalion Welsh Guards camp was located on this site. The Institute shed burnt down early in the second global conflict. Gordon Norris, the baker's son who was a child during the Second World War has provided the following letter from an unknown publication. Mrs K.R. of Martock wrote:

Talbot's Stores at the bottom of Chitterne Road on the High Street, during the First World War.

Floods around Talbot's Stores in the High Street, 1915.

The Chitterne Brook, looking towards St Mary's First World War camp.

Men, mules and horses at No. 8 Camp during the First World War.

Would Mother Run Off With A Fisherman?
'I'll be driven down to Codford,' my mother would say, usually when she had her oldest pinny on to clean the range. It was a chore she hated, but when she was in a really bad temper she took her revenge by scrubbing and polishing until her back ached.

'Be careful and watch what you say,' I'd whisper to my brother Ron, 'She's in a really dreadful mood.'

The only cod I knew about was the fresh fish that came on the wagon every Wednesday morning. The fishmonger generously gave the head to our cat.

Codford could also be connected with that horrible looking lump of dried stuff hanging from the hook in our pantry. I'm sure that was cod.

Surely Mr Giles the fishman wouldn't drive her away on that smelly old horse and cart? Mum did say she'd be driven.

Years later she explained why she had said it. Codford St Mary is a small town where there was an institution for mentally disturbed people!

This anecdote is interesting – it is likely that the Institute shed was the source of confusion – no evidence has been found to suggest that there was ever an institution for 'mentally-disturbed people' in the village. Of such misunderstandings are myths and legends made!

Sources:

The Corporation Dustcart – first three verses courtesy of Will Collins as he remembers them. Will believes he first heard the poem from John Stratton. The messages and the fourth verse were on postcards in David Falcke's collection – the wording was slightly different but the essential meaning was unchanged.

Right: *Lover's Walk, commonly known as Crouch's Lane, during the First World War.*

Below: *The Wesleyan Soldiers' Institute, during the First World War.*

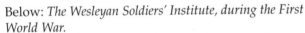

Chapter 6

Between the Wars

The Codford Cabby

The following poem comes from a faded newspaper cutting, possibly from the *Warminster Journal*, provided by Gordon Norris. On the back of the poem, under the heading of 'Warminster' there are several advertisements:

St John's Parish Room – Whist Drive and Dance, Wednesday, January 31st, 1923, at 7pm. Admission 1/6.

County Court – The next sitting of the Warminster County Court will be held on Monday, February 19th. Plaints should be entered at once.

Handpicked Blue Boiling Peas with special soaking tablet. 1lb., 3¹/₂d.; 2lbs., 6¹/₂ d.; 3lbs., 9d. – Marshman and Son, Warminster and Frome.

Special Monthly Meeting at Congregational Church on Sunday evening next at 6 o'clock: Rev. G. Manning. Subject: 'The True Light'. All are welcome.

A Codford Cabby

In the village of Codford many sensations occur, and the latest experience of the new 'cabby' has been translated in verse by someone on the scene:

Have I been a cabman long, sir?
Only half an hour or so,
I was only once upon the Railway,
But that's some time ago.

So you'd like to hear the story,
How I drove the fiery steed;
With a gent inside the ceb, sir.
Ah. That was a drive indeed.

I was waiting at the Station,
And the day was clear and bright,
When in came a brand new brougham,
And she was a dainty sight.

They had just hitched in the hoss, sir.
When a gentleman came along.
'Can you drive me to Charing Cross, lad.
Through the Strand you can't go wrong.'

I was up on the box in a jiffy –
And I shook up the fiery steed,
'Right O,' said the fare inside, sir,
And away we went at some speed.

We tore by the Station Yard, sir,
And over the railway track,
When the gent inside, he got nervous,
And thought he'd like to go back.

But that hoss went like the wind, sir;
And cared naught for dales or hills,
For wagons or milkmen's carts, sir;
But his was the pace that kills.

My hat blew off in the wind, sir;
But never a wit did he stop,
Till Heytesbury hove in sight, sir;
And there by the pub did he drop.

And that's how I drove the ceb, sir;
Thanks; yes; I don't mind if I do,
For whenever I tells the story,
I gets 'usky and dry; so would you.

Country Folk and Commerce

Looking back more than 70 years to 1927, the Codford entry in *Kelly's Directory* opens a window to the way things were in another age. The two villages of Codford St Mary and Codford St Peter were in the Hundred of Heytesbury, the Rural Deanery of Wylye, the Archdeanery of Sarum and the Diocese of Salisbury.

Codford St Mary had its own railway station 7 miles south-east of Warminster and 14 miles north-west of Salisbury. It was on the Salisbury to Westbury branch line of the Great Western Railway.

The area of 2,122 acres of land was described as having light chalk soil with chalk and flint subsoil, with a rateable value of £1,928. The chief crops were wheat, barley and oats. The principle landowners were J.M. Stratton and C.W. Edwards, and the lord of the manor was William H. Yeatman-Biggs of Stockton.

The church had been restored in 1879 at a cost of £1,200. The living was a rectory with a net income of £442 including a residence and four and a half acres of glebe land. It had been held since 1924 by Revd Cyril Henry Meyrick MA. There was also a congregational chapel which had been founded in 1778.

Codford St Mary had an elementary school (mixed) which had been built in 1875 and enlarged in 1889, with a striking clock added in 1899. It had room for 124 children but the attendance was usually

St Mary's Church with the ford bridge in the foreground, during the early-twentieth century.

Codford St Mary School in 1926. Left to right, back row: Miss Bartlett, Hazel Rogers, Ron Mould, Jean Ford, Stella Rogers, Jack Fry, Ben Sheppard, Miss Scull; middle row: Dorothy Davis, Alice Bevis, Gladys Sparey, Brenda Doughty, Percy Conduit, Reg Bell, Eric Bell; front row: Ken Poole (?), Willie Earney, Eddie Earney, Maurice Spiller, Raymond Spiller, Joan Simper, Earnest Davis. Ben Sheppard and Percy Conduit both died during the Second World War and are remembered on the Victory Bell in St Peter's Church.

around 50. Miss Bertha Scull was the schoolmistress.

The 1921 census recorded the population as 314. The private residents were listed as Mrs Chisman, Charles Edwards, Houghton-Brown of Manor Farm, Ernest Winbolt Lewis in the Poplars, Revd Meyrick in the Rectory, Revd Henry Steer (Congregational) and Mrs Wightwick in The Cottage. The sexton was James Fleming, and the sub-postmaster Ralph Stanley Parker. There was a carrier, Harold Couchman, who went to Salisbury on Tuesdays and Warminster on Wednesdays and Saturdays.

The commercial listing had only one farm of 150 acres or more – Codford Farms Ltd owned by J.A. Lush. There were two banks, both agencies. The Midland Bank was open on Fridays from 10.30a.m. to 2.30p.m. and Lloyds Bank, managed by Mr Lockyear, was open on Fridays from 10.30a.m. to 2p.m.

The range of commerce was impressive and the list is reproduced below:

Harold Couchman – motor proprietor
William F. Dewey – ironmonger
George William Goodsall – draper
Mills & Son – boot dealers
Chas. Mines – hairdresser
David Norris – baker
Ralph Stanley Parker – stationer and Post Office
Albert Simper – bicycle director
Bert Smith – saddler
John Martin Sparey – dairyman
Thos. Stacey (retired) – stationer
David George Stone – farm bailiff to Stratton
Robert Stokes – grocer
Edward Wightwick – estate agent
Chas Wood – poultry farmer

The doctor Ernest Winbolt Lewis MD Ch.B. Edin. physician and surgeon was the medical officer and public vaccinator for No. 2 District, the Warminster Union surgeon to the Great Western Railway and the Post Office, the medical officer for the Board of Education and to the Stapleford district Wilton Union.

Codford St Peter was noted to be 92 miles from London by road and 112 by rail. It had a railway station with a stationmaster, William Pope. The village also boasted a police station with Sergeant William Reakes in charge. In 1921 the village had a population of 318. The closest adjoining hamlet was Ashton Gifford, three quarters of a mile to the west, while the closest money order and telegraph office was at Codford St Mary.

The living at St Peter's was again a rectory with a net income of £483. It had been held since 1915 by Revd Edward Denny MA. The elementary school (mixed) had been built in 1841 and had room for 80 pupils, although the attendance was usually around 50. Miss K. Gasson was the schoolmistress.

In an area of 1,668 acres with a rateable value of £2,920, the chief landowners were J.S. Collins and Stuart Carey Houston. The private residents were listed as:

Little Ashton – Major P. Brian Allott
Ashton Gifford House – Mrs Hawley Broughton
Manor Farm – Arthur Collins
The Rectory – Revd Denny
Manor House – Major Stuart Carey Houston
Overton House – Miss Hulbert
Bradwell Grange – Colonel Ralph Sneyd
Misses Wightwick

Listed under Codford St Peter were:

James William Axtell – butcher and poulterer
Ernest Belbin – farmer [Bury Farm]
Harold Frank Bell – shop keeper
William Clark – farmer [Lower Farm – more than 150 acres]
Arthur Collins – farmer [Manor Farm]
William Dewey – petrol service station
Dyer & Son – coal dealers and hauliers
Walter Ford – builder
Frank Stanley – George Hotel
Mrs Mabel Gregory – grocer and beer retailer
George Hinton – bee farmer
Vosper Veale – haulier
William White – smith
Wiltshire Working Mens Conservative Society – secretary W. Ford.

In the 1921 census the population for Wiltshire was 292,208, consisting of 144,917 men and 147,291 women. The joint population of the two Codfords was 632.

In 1927 the Wiltshire Constabulary consisted of a Chief Constable – Lt Col H. Llewellyn DSO, a deputy, seven superintendents, 12 inspectors, 40 sergeants and 232 constables. Codford was a sergeants' station with the telephone number 12.

Ron Sutton's Brook Tale

Before the war the gangs used to meet, Codford and Stockton, along the Brook, on the bridge just going out of Codford. One Sunday we was [sic] there, Maurice Spiller, me and Walt Conduit. Maurice said to Walt 'I'll throw you into the river if you ain't careful.' He picked Walt up and held him over the bridge – because of the weight they fell over, and as they fell they turned over. Maurice went down first and Walt Conduit went on top of him. Walt got out clean and Maurice was mud all over. The Spillers were always noted for being clean, not a speck on 'em and he had to walk up the village, back home, covered in stinking, slimy mud all over.

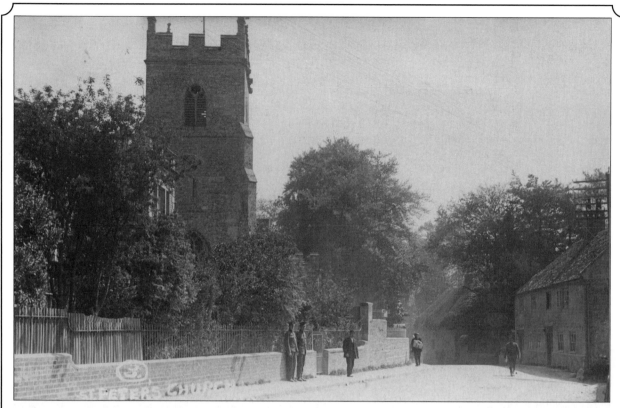

St Peter's Church during the First World War. Stable Cottage can be seen on the opposite side of the road.

Codford GFS in 1932 at Heavens Gate. Left to right, standing: Miss Scull, Margaret Weston, Bunny Withers, Hazel Cooper, Mrs Meyrick (the wife of the rector of St Peter's); front row: Jean Ford, Marion Bosworth, Alice Bevis, Joan Simper, Doreen Bosworth, Eileen Simper, Brenda Doughty. Marion and Doreen Bosworth's father was killed in the Second World War and is remembered on the Victory Bell.

St Peter's School in 1924. Included in the picture are: *Paul Cole* (back row, second right), *Doreen Cole* (middle row, first left) *and Malcolm Davis* (front row, second left).

Codford St Mary Church outing, 1928 or 1929. The picture includes: *Mrs H. Simper, Kitty Bevis, Grace Daisch, May Conduit, Clare Simper, Fred Doughty, Reg Ford, Revd Meyrick, Louis Hampton, James Fleming, Mr Chick, Mr Cooper, William Cooper.*

The Simper girls – Clare, Joan and Eileen on the gate by St Mary's Church, c.1928.

Left: *Mrs Norris, the baker's first wife, with Barbara on the bike and Dulcie in the pram, on the footbridge by the ford, in the early 1920s.*

Below: *Shepherd Mr Portingale and his flock, 1930s.*

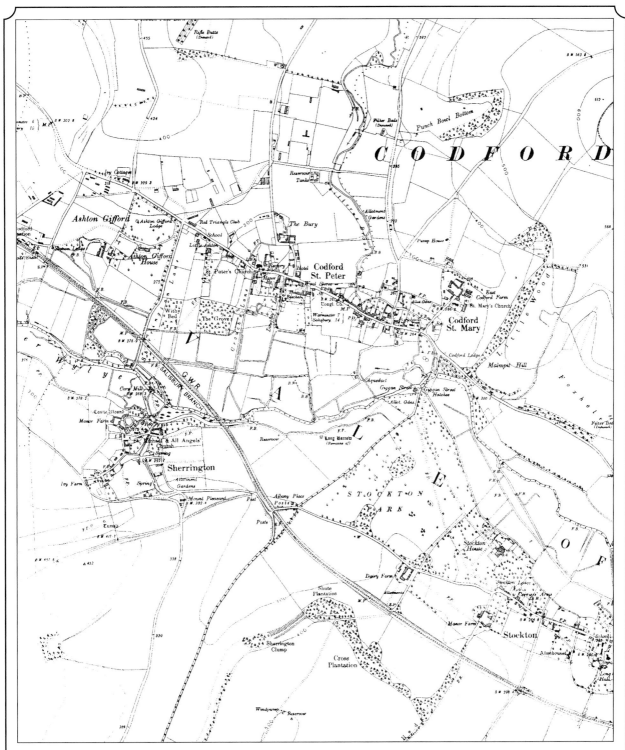

An Ordnance Survey map of the Codford area, 1926.

Possibly a shooting party, sometime in the 1920s or '30s.

Left: *Ron Sutton in the 1930s.*

Below: *Codford St Mary High Street during the First World War, with white railings and the Chitterne Brook, opposite the thatched cottage at the end of Church Lane, and St Mary's School.*

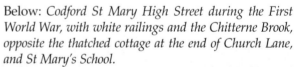

Codford St Peter's School, 1936. Left to right, back row: *Miss Whittle, ?, Betty Goodsall, Judy Thomas, Joan Belbin, ?, ?, Grace Morgan, ?, ?, Miss Gasson (later Mrs Cluff);* third row: *?, Peter Plowman, Ken Harvey, Ken Axtell, Maurice Phelps, Sid Andrews, Sonny Gage, ?, Ken Stokes, ?, George Goodenough;* second row: *Pam Case, Doreen Morgan, Jill Parkins, Hilda Marden, ?, ?, Jean Phelps, ?, Stella Fry;* front row: *?, Ken Marden, ?, Derek Stone, Tony Thorn, John Plowman, Gordon Norris, Les Barnard, ?, Les Whatley.*

Right: *The modern bridge is located where the foot-bridge across the ford used to be, by the white railings in Codford St Mary.* (PHOTO DAVID MASON)

The bridge across the Wylye, c.1994, looking towards Stockton. (PHOTO DAVID MASON)

Codford St Peter's School, 1937. Left to right, back row: Miss Gasson (later Mrs Cluff), Hilda Marden, ?, Betty Goodsall, Joan Belbin, ?, ?, Doris Morgan, teacher Miss Doreen Cole; third row: John Plowman, George (Tojo) Goodenough, Maurice Phelps, Sonny Gage, Les Smith, Ken Axtell, Ken Harvey, Gordon Carter, Les Barnard, Cyril Bailey; second row: ?, ?, ?, ?, Stella Fry, Pam Case, ?, Jean Phelps, Les Whatley; front row: Derek Stone, Ken Stokes, Donald Morgan, ?, Gordon (Tich) Norris, Dennis Blake, ?, Bill (Skinner) Meaden, ?, ?.

Left: *Village children paddling in the 1940s.*

Below: *A Vickers tank crossing the ford, 1938.*

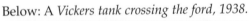

Chapter 7

The Second World War

It was with an inevitable feeling of familiarity that, 20 years after the last troops had departed from the village, the 260th Field Company Royal Engineers arrived to build the camps of the Second World War. Once again Manor Farm bore the brunt of the occupation, with land used around St Mary's Church, in Cherry Orchard, on glebe land behind St Peter's Church, and at Hillside huts sprang up with remarkable rapidity. The Pioneer Corps had a camp near Ivy Cottages; in the later stages of the war this was where the Polish troops were based.

Malmpit Hill was used as a 'dump', while at The Punchbowl there was a rifle range used by British and American troops. When the tank men arrived the Chitterne road was lined from Codford to New Zealand Cottages with tanks, half-tracks and Bren-gun carriers. There was water-proofing pool and three petrol stations guarded by sentries along Chitterne Road; the hard cobbles can still be seen in 2005. These were laid at road junctions because the heavy tanks turning on unmade roads churned up the surface.

In the autumn of 1941 the 6th Guards Armoured Brigade moved to Codford – when they left the 1st Northamptonshire Yeomanry were in Codford briefly, followed by about 1,000 men of the American 3rd Armored Battalion. When the troops moved out to participate in the invasion of Europe the villagers awoke one morning to an eerie silence, as the huts and the pup tents stood abandoned and forlorn – the Americans had disappeared overnight.

6th Guards Armoured Brigade

In September 2004 Codford Parish Council organised a dedication ceremony with a plaque to commemorate the presence of the elite Guards Regiments and their tanks in the Second World War. A total of 63 years earlier, in September of 1941, with national expectation of an imminent invasion from across the Channel, the 1st Battalion Welsh Guards arrived in the village; they camped close to the main area of settlement, some were in 'Woolstore' or 'Cherry Orchard' Camp and others in St Mary's Camp, also known as Institute Camp, around St Mary's Church close to the ford. The 3rd Battalion Scots Guards moved to Codford 'B' Camp and, in mid to late November, the 4th Battalion Grenadier Guards moved to Codford 'A' Camp, both situated on Manor Farm. On 27 November 1942 the Welsh Guards were replaced by the 4th Battalion Coldstream Guards,

who had been changed from a Motor Battalion into an Armoured Battalion in the 6th Brigade. The Battalion's heavy tanks moved from Heytesbury to Codford to join the remainder of the Brigade in a camp with tank standings.[1]

Initially, during training on Salisbury Plain, the Guards were in Covenanter tanks, but in the early months of 1943 the first Churchill tanks arrived as part of the re-equipping process.[2] It was in the Churchill tanks that the Guards Armoured Division proved their valour and determination as they fought across Europe.

General Ronald Buckland was one of those who returned and clearly remembered the village as it was when he was a young officer in the Coldstream Guards. He recalled:

We arrived in Codford on 22nd November 1942 relieving the Welsh Guards. Over 200 Officers, NCOs and men then went on a course at the Armoured Warfare School in Mongton [?] and Lulworth in Dorset. We moved to Yorkshire 26–29 April in seven troop trains, anyone in the village who is old enough will remember all the palaver of the loading of tanks onto trains as we had to be such... in order not to hit bridges. By the time that we had moved to Codford St Mary the Brigade had become 6th Guards Tank Brigade and had left the Guards Armoured Division and joined 15th Southern Division but the other Battalions were all there as part of Guards Armoured Division.

It is not known who wrote the following extracts, which have been taken from the *London Times*, published 9 October 1944. Both extracts were reprinted in the official divisional newspaper, *The News Guardian*, in May 1945:

The Guards Armoured Division 1944–1945

THE GUARDS ARMOURED DIVISION has proved itself one of the most formidable fighting formations ever to leave England. Goebbels has labelled the Division 'MONTGOMERY'S MURDERERS' and 'CHURCHILL'S BUTCHER'S', but the Guards consider that such abuse from such a source is high tribute to their fighting capacity. I SAW A GOOD DEAL of the Guards Armoured Division in the months when the Allies were preparing to break out from the Normandy bridgehead. Those were particularly difficult months for Armoured formations. The country was unfriendly to tanks, and the infantry had to bear

Above: *The private road on East Farm goes through the site of a camp in both world wars. It was also known as St Mary's Camp or Institute Camp (in the Second World War).*

Top right: *Remains of Second World War military buildings at New Road.*

Above right: *Site of military buildings during the Second World War at New Road.*

Right: *The Second World War surface at Punchbowl Farm.*

Below: *Karen Johnstone, furthest from camera, behind the Woolstore with veterans and wives of the 1st Northamptonshire Yeomanry who trained in Codford as part of the 42nd Armoured Brigade between May and September 1943. The photo was taken in the late 1990s.*

The cooking stove in the Woolstore, which was used during the Second World War.

the chief brunt of Operations. But the Guards were unhappy about it. They know the Guards traditions of infantry and old-fashioned cavalry were superb, but they felt that they still had their spurs to win as armoured fighters. More than one Guards Armoured Division officer or man asked me in those trying days when they were itching for a chance to really test their quality; 'What are the other people saying about us?' They need not ask those questions now. Their record in the bridgehead was good; since the closing of the Falaise Gap and the beginning of the Second Army's northward thrust across the Seine through Belgium into Holland it has been magnificent.

THE GUARDS WERE ORDERED on 27 Aug to move forward from the Falaise region across the Seine and push on as fast as possible. They met with some stiff fighting and minor skirmishing on the way, but by 20 Sept they were in the Nijmegen area – 490 miles in 25 days. On the night 30/31 Aug they advanced 89 miles from the Seine to the Somme, it was the longest advance that any division of any nation has ever made in military history. Four days later the Guards broke their own records. They advanced 93 miles from Douai to Brussels on 3 September – and though enemy opposition on that day was not resolute anywhere, the advance was certainly opposed. They had to halt at several points to clean up determined enemy pockets which tried to hinder them.

IT WAS A GREAT moment for the Commander, Major General Allan Adair, when the Guards reached Arras. It was at Arras in the last war that he won the Military Cross while serving as a junior officer with the Grenadiers; and it was a great moment for the Irish Guards when they were chosen to capture Douai. There the Germans in 1940 cut up the Irish Guards in a furious engagement. Now the tables were turned.

THE GUARDS WERE ecstatically welcomed when they entered Brussels on the night of 3 Sept. In fact the fervour of the welcome actually delayed the troops in completing their occupation of the city. General Adair called up his men by wireless 'Hello, have you reached your objective yet?' 'No' came back the reply. 'What is the trouble?' the General asked, 'Are you meeting opposition?' 'Yes, the population' answered the unit commander. A little later he came through to the General by wireless: 'Hello' he said 'Thank God it's raining, we are moving towards our objective now.'

THE GUARDS' COURAGEOUS part in the capture of the vital Nijmegen bridge in co-operation with the American Airbourne troops is a matter of history. A curious story about one of their armoured-car squadrons from the Household Cavalry at about the same time is less widely known. The armoured-cars were patrolling when they saw a small ship with four barges in tow. The armoured-cars manoeuvred into position, opened fire and sank three barges and damaged the ship. They signalled the news to Divisional Headquarters, which replied, 'Congratulations. Brilliant naval action. Splice the mainbrace.'

NEXT COMES THE Daily Mail's description of how the Division's armour smashed open the road to the plains of North Germany.

IT WAS MIDNIGHT, pitch black: and forward elements of the Guards Armoured Division halted for orders. The orders came – short, curt and definite – 'Get going and go fast', they said.

THE GUARDS GOT GOING: Their lightning advance against every kind of opposition opened up the road for streams of British armour to pour onto the plains of Germany. In the van were a battle group of Scots Guards riding on Welsh Guards tanks. Battle was joined at Nordhom, where the Guards group fought their way to the bridges in the town which was blazing fiercely. Then came the long, thrilling 15-miles dash to LINGEN.

IN THIS ADVANCE the Guards are breaking no records. They are up against the desperate remnants of the famous German 8th Parachute Army who have blown bridges and cratered roads every few miles along their path. The Guards crossed the Rhine on Good Friday. They broke out of the bridgehead the same day and re-entered Holland to liberate Aalton, Groenio, Enschode and Oldenzall. Over the frontier again and

Heating stove in the Woolstore, used during the Second World War.

The men's room in the Woolstore during the Second World War.

they captured Bentheim, strongly held by parachute troops. In four nights the Division's sappers were ordered to build 11 bridges. Each one was ready on time.

THIS TIME THE going is tough. But the Guards are tough men.

OLD WINE IN NEW BATTLES

THE SUPERB FIGHTING traditions of the Brigade of Guards have been the source and mainstay of the spirit that has carried the Guards Battalions, the Gunners, the sappers and the Services of this Division from victory to victory in its long journey from the ORNE to the ELBE.

THERE WERE THOSE who shook their heads when the Division was formed. 'Why turn' they said 'the most famous infantry in the world into mechanics and gunners? A Guardsman in a tank is rather like a pig in a poke.' The critics are answered now, when the fame of the G.A.D. stands equal with that of any armoured division on either side in these six years of great armoured battles. The tanks that rushed NIJMEGEN BRIDGE in daylight and raced blind through the night to cross the EMS at LINGEN were manned by men who knew every risk of armoured battle and added the élan of the dragoon to the skill and cunning of the driver.

AND, IF THE armoured brigade created new precedents and examples of valour, the infantry emulated and equalled the old. The men who held the line at TILLY, cleared the WAL banks at NIJMEGEN and broke the German paratroops could not have upheld more worthily the unequalled Guards infantry tradition. The writer was one asked in Brussels by an American Colonel what the 'Eye' flash stood for. When told the American said 'I reckon you are lucky to be with that crowd – I was in North Africa and I saw the Guards take LONGSTOP HILL, by God, no other troops could

have faced such fire. But the Guards went up the hill as if on parade and down the other side with their bayonets in the backsides of the Krauts!' And they did the same in Europe.

THERE ARE MANY CROSSES, crowned with black and brown berets, in cornfields of CAGNY, by the roadside in the deep valleys of the Normandy Bocage, by the banks of many a Belgian Canal, Dutch Dyke and German River. But those of us who are left may well be proud to have played a part [some a big one, some a small one] in the great deeds of the Guards Armoured Division when it marched – more often than not in the forefront of battle – with the British Liberation Army through France, Belgium and Holland to Germany to complete its task on the shores of HELIGOLAND BAY. Some of us may live long enough to be able to say that we played a part, too, in the Liberation of Germany from its own worst enemy, its baser self.

Among these soldiers were the young guardsmen who were the most popular troops to arrive in Codford in either war. They had practised their war games on Salisbury Plain and driven their tanks along the roads and lanes of the Wylye Valley; they had lived in the hutted camps in the fields and on the hillsides; drunk and danced and dallied with the villagers; and then they had fought and died in their tanks from the Normandy beaches into the heart of the Third Reich.

The close ties between the Guards and the village have been commemorated by an exchange of plaques on the wall of the Woolstore Theatre, organised by the Parish Council liaising with the regiments. Codford's connection with 6th Guards Armoured Brigade, consisting of the 4th Battalion Grenadier Guards, 4th Battalion Coldstream Guards, 3rd Battalion Scots Guards and 2nd Battalion Welsh Guards was celebrated in September 2004, when veterans and representatives of the four regiments gathered for an intimate ceremony of dedication. This was followed by a buffet lunch in the Manor House at the invitation of John Torrie. Among those attending were some who had arrived in Codford as unblooded young soldiers in 1941, who had fought across the battlefields of Europe and who had survived the conflict.

Notes:
1 The War Diary of the 2nd Bn Welsh Guards.
2 '6th Guard's Tank Brigade – The Story of Guardsmen in Churchill Tanks' by Patrick Forbes.

The Drummer Boy

Drummer John Tilbury joined the Grenadier Guards in 1937 when he was just 15. He enlisted in the Boy's Service and was sent to join the Corps of Drums. When the Second World War started he was stationed at Windsor, and before he saw active service he came to Codford with 4th Battalion

Grenadier Guards when they joined the 6th Guards Armoured Brigade and sampled the joys of life in the Wylye Valley. While in Codford he wrote the following ditty sung to the tune of 'I'm a rambler, I'm a gambler, and I'm a long way from home':

I'm one of the lads that they call Inter-Com,
If you can't find my scout car,
You know where I've gone,
I know all the 'wad' shops from Codford to Frome!
But I'd rather be having a good scoff as HOOME!

In a scout car, in a scout car,
I ramble along,
I'm one of the lads that just beating the gong,
I know all the 'wad' shops from Codford to Frome!
But I'd rather be having a good scoff as HOOME!

John Tilbury was a scout car driver with the battalion during the invasion of Europe. He saw action in France, Holland and Germany; in February 1945 he was with the Grenadier's during the massive attack on the Siegfried Line. Towards the end of 1945 the following articles were published:

Life In Codford Barracks

The 4th Bn Grenadier Guards has at long last gathered all its Companies for the first time since it left Kent in the summer of 1944.

A very changed Battalion it is too, for of the forty or so officers who sailed across the Channel on 19 July 1944, only ten are left, and Guardsmen seem to come and go with alarming rapidity.

The large Barrack Square is perhaps an all too adequate reminder of the joys of serving in Wellington Barracks, Windsor and Pirbright, but the eyes of the hopeful are already turned to the snow-laden clouds which are reputed top cover everything to a depth of several inches with that type of snow that prohibits Drill, PT, or any form of military activity.

The barracks at Euskirchen, which so lately housed some 5,000 Russian DP's have been turned into a very comfortable, if somewhat grim looking home from home. Theatres, Canteens, Gymnasiums are being constructed out of derelict blocks and already the sound of revelry by night in the Sergeants Mess indicates the creation of a new gang of Cardinals, captained by Sgt. Major Spralley; one of the remaining foundation members of the Mess.

Shades of Codford

After months of segregation in far-flung Mechernich, Vodelsang, Satzvey and Wachendorf the 4th Grenadiers are united once more in the big camp at Euskirchen, formerly occupied by Russians. They have christened their new abode 'Codford Barracks', after the ramshackle collection of Nissen huts on the edge of

Drummer boy John Tilbury, c.1937.

wind-swept Salisbury Plain in which they spent two grim winters while preparing for their important role in the invasion of the Continent.

Nobody who was there will forget Codford easily. Gunners, drivers and wireless operators sat shivering in bare, cheerless classrooms, endeavouring to master the theory of their trades, while slightly more fortunate tank crews ploughed through the mud in their Covenanters towards Tilshead.

Covenanters were eventually replaced by Churchills – the very earliest types of Churchills, with a thing called flexible drive, which was sure to break when the tank was far from home, so that some luckless person in the turret had to jump the primer continuously to enable the driver to limp back in bottom gear.

With the camp really in the grip of winter, the nightly visit to the NAAFI, although only a short distance from the rest of the huts, became as much of an ordeal as a trip to the North Pole, and it was customary to draw lots or to consult a roster to decide who was to go for tea.

John Tilbury was a member of the Regiment's Guard of Honour at Westminster Abbey for the royal wedding when Princess Elizabeth married

Above left: Surface for turning area for Second World War tanks near Long Hedge.

Above right: Fuel depot area from the Second World War.

Left: Major Richard Carr-Gomm of 4th Battalion Coldstream Guards.

Below: The Woolstore stage was used during the Second World War when troops bussed in local girls for dances.

6th Guards Armoured Commemoration, in September 2004. The picture includes: Major Barrow (Coldstream), David Greenacre (Welsh Guards), Brian Marshall (Grenadier), Sir William Marlow (Irish Guards), General Buckland (Coldstream), Major Carr-Gomm (Coldstream), Sir John Johnston (Grenadier).

Prince Phillip. The present Queen was made Colonel of the Regiment in the Second World War and her first official engagement alone was to inspect the Grenadier Guards at Codford in 1941 – during her visit she drove a tank, had tea at Stockton House and lunched in the Mess at Codford.

Memories of A Coldstream Guardsman, c.1942
Major Richard Carr-Gomm

Major Richard Carr-Gomm OBE was a distinguished soldier who was responsible for setting up the Abbeyfield Society to help people aged over 65, and the Carr-Gomm Housing Society to help the lonely, regardless of their age. He was not just involved at the organisational level but at the practical level, helping physically with the work, even to the extent of scrubbing doorsteps in Bermondsey!

His great-great-uncle Colonel Gomm was the longest-serving soldier in the British Army; his father bought him a commission in the Coldstream Guards at the age of ten. Colonel Gomm became a Field Marshall and, as Field Marshalls stay on the strength of the Army until death, he had been in the Guards for 81 years when he died in 1875 at the age of 91. He served in the Peninsula War (1808–14) and was on Wellington's staff at Waterloo, the final battle of the Napoleonic Wars.

Richard Carr-Gomm was a tank commander, wounded in action at the battle of Caumont outside Caen on 14 July 1944. A shell hit a high bank and exploded; as his head was exposed he received facial burns and shrapnel wounds to his face and ear. He was sent back to England and hospitalised in Cardiff, and thus he missed the inland fighting through France, Belgium and Holland. He returned to the European theatre of operations in time to take part in the Rhine crossing; and was again wounded when an exploding shell hit his tank, 'Elephant II'. This time his burns were less severe and were treated in a field hospital in Germany:

Codford and Marston Bigot near Frome were part of the second line of defence, reserve troops were held in readiness to be sent to the beaches in the event of the expected invasion from Europe. I served with the 4th Battalion of the Coldstream Guards during the earlier part of the '39–'45 war, it was at this stage, after the immediacy of the invasion was past, while we were at Marston Bigot, that the War Office decided that there were too many foot soldiers and they had better put the surplus to better use. They said they would go away now and then come back in a month and tell us whether they were going to put us into tanks or parachutes. So for four weeks we were left to walk about while they made up their minds.

It was, for me, a great relief when, on their return, they said we were too tall and heavy for parachutes and, therefore, they were going to send us some tanks and we

must learn to fight in them. Next week the tanks arrived and we were either sent on courses to learn how to drive and shoot guns from them or told to get in and practise round the camp.

We were very soon sent to Codford and it was there that we began to learn our new trade. A good way of training was to drive across the Plain chasing rabbits. Doing this would train the two gunners, who kept their unarmed guns on it, the commander in giving directions, the wireless operator in keeping everyone in the picture and the driver in speed and handling. Often the rabbits just gave themselves up and sat and waited in dejection; then we would let them go.

With Battalions of the Grenadier and Scots Guards we became part of a completely separate 6th Guards Tank Brigade. Now, with the heaviest possible tanks Churchills (my tank weighed 70 tons and needed nine gallons per mile in petrol), we were sent from Codford to practice on different terrains until we ended up in Kent before taking off for the invasion of France in early summer 1944.

I had eight troop of number 2 Squadron. Each troop's three tanks were named after different first letters of animals, and ours was E (elephant, eland, elk) of which my tank was called 'Elephant'. It was a tank later adopted by Brighton after a 'Salute the Soldier' week, and was, eventually, blown up (a few days after I had been wounded and left it) in Normandy 1944. I always looked on 'Elephant' with affection, and my friends even used to send me Christmas cards with elephants on them.

Codford was part of this odyssey and is a warm and happy memory. The Nissen huts were home and the village and its people were friends, long-suffering and kind. I am glad to have this chance to wind back history and remind myself of those times.

The American Invasion

The Americans wrote with relish and enthusiasm of their time in England. For many the land of their forefathers, the 'old country' – which they imagined peopled by the likes of Sherlock Holmes, with pea-souper fogs, ancient castles, helmeted policemen, double-decker buses, red postboxes, pubs with timber beams and warm beer – was as exotic as America was to the average English cinema goer. The silver screen offered matinée idols, cowboys and gangsters, wide-open spaces, guns and musicals; the English were fascinated by the Yanks, an emotion that was reciprocated with equal fervour.

Spearhead – The 3rd Armored Division

The 3rd Armored Division left New York Harbour on 5 September 1943, arriving in Liverpool ten days later. They entrained for the West Country, 16,000 men stationed within an area of less than 100 square miles, about 1,000 in the immediate vicinity of Codford. The Maintenance and Supply Battalions, Battalion HQ, the gun park, and the tank and repair

Above left: *The Second World War mural, painted by the Americans, in the Woolstore.*

Above: *US troops in Codford, 1943/44.*

Left: *American 3rd Armored Division mounted battalion 'at ease' in a camp with The Punchbowl behind, c.1943/44.*

American GIs waterproofing their jeep, 1 April 1944.

depot workshops were close to St Peter's Church; at the western extremity of Codford, at Hillside, were the 32nd Armored Regiment. A mile away, around Stockton House, were the 3rd Armored Division Combat Command HQ, the 45th Medical Battalion and the Trains HQ. The GIs had marched from Codford Station, never-ending columns of unblooded troops, entering the village which was to be their base for the next nine months.

The narrow, unmade roads of the Wylye Valley villages were unsuitable for the armoured vehicles of a heavy tank division and the winter of 1943/44 was unkind to the new arrivals. The lower areas of the village became a morass of sticky wet mud. The Americans, ever resourceful, were determined to provide hard standing for their tanks and sent lorries to the Mendips for stone. Off the New Road, in a field to the east of Mayflower Farm, the heavily loaded lorries arrived to deliver their cargo. There were not enough tipper lorries to accommodate the amount of stone required – an estimate was that 10,000 tons of Mendip stone found its way to the site. The Americans used mobile cranes to hoist up the front of the flatbed lorries and the stone then cascaded from the back. Due to this rough but effective method of unloading, the field was strewn with their front axles. The hard standing is just inches beneath the surface of what is a green-field site in 2005.

The 3rd Armored left Codford for Omaha Beach in Normandy between D-Day + 10 and D-Day + 13 (16–19 June 1944). They were later followed by other American troops such as those below.

Thunderbolt – the 11th Armored Division

'A' Company, 56th Engineers, landed during the morning of 9 October 1944, excited by their first glimpse of land, passing the Isle of Wight in the late afternoon to drop anchor in the port of Southampton. On 10 October at 1500 hours they disembarked, boarded a train and began their journey through the countryside to Melksham in Wiltshire, where for the next five weeks they attended classes and lectures, hiked and made their equipment combat ready.

(For further information on the 11th Armored Division visit www.11tharmoreddivision.com.)

Passes to London, Bristol and Salisbury were in the books so most of the men had their first view of 'Big Ben', 'The Tower of London', 'St James Cathedral', 'Westminster Abbey' and 'Piccadilly Circus'. The most interesting to us were our first sights of actual warfare, namely the many bombed out ruins in English cities.

'Any gum chum?' was a new phase we learned from the English children.

Moving our camp to Codford Camp No. 2, our final preparations were even more rushed as we made things

Early spring in 1944, outside the dispensary of B Company 45th Medical Battalion, 3rd Armored Division at Stockton House. Most GIs are in working uniforms. Sgt Don Mahr is on the far right with a box of medical supplies.

battle ready. Our last and most memorable relaxation was a battalion dance at which we had our first glimpse of real, clean fun. The vehicles shipped ahead of us to cross the Channel. Some of us sent home last minute letters through the NAAFI Club in the camp. John McHugh one of our original men now with 277th Combat Engineers dropped in for a last minute visit and wished us all luck. Our last night was spent in restless speculation on what the future held in store for us.

December 14th 1944
At 0430 we were hurriedly awakened and after hastily dressing we had our last meal in Codford Camp. Going back to our Nissen huts we rolled our bedrolls, packed up our equipment, trucked it all out on the road and then of course we policed and cleaned up the area and huts as much as we could. As it was still dark in a cold, grey dawn we didn't do too good a job.

They gave us a couple of sandwiches for our lunch and at 0730 we started for the Codford Railway Station. Our vehicles had all gone ahead the day before, occupied by our drivers and assistant drivers and they were scheduled to cross the Channel on L.S.T. [Landing Ship Transport] Boats. It was about one and a half miles to the Station and quite a hike with all our ammunition and other necessary junk in our packs and belts.

After an hour or so waiting, our train pulled into the Station at 0930. It took our battalion about ten minutes to load up and then we took off, heading south. Going through Salisbury we took a few pictures and Buch our photographer took some movies of the cathedral. This cathedral has the tallest spire in all of England, rising majestically a little over four hundred feet above the green lawn at its base.

By 1045 we were in Southampton Railroad Station, passing the dock from which we unloaded when first landing in England. After dismounting we lined up in

Above, left and right: Mr and Mrs Minty standing in front of their house at 65 High Street, after it was accidentally demolished by an American tank during the Second World War.

Left: GIs in front of their hut at Stockton House in 1944. B Company, 45th Medical Battalion, 3rd Armored Division. Left to right, back row, standing: Moore, Reynolds; middle row, kneeling: Mahr, Preston; front row, sitting: Kounlick, Anderson, Lawn and Korski.

Below: A GI with a jeep in 1943/44.

columns of twos and started out for the marshalling camp. We saw quite a lot of bomb damage but none of it as extensive as in London, Bath or Bristol. We walked for over an hour passing many civilian homes, which were occupied by British Tommies. It was in this city that we saw more British soldiers than in any other place at any time. It was a long hard, hot walk and the fellows were all cussing and raising hell. A baker's wagon stopped and he threw a couple of loaves of bread to the fellows of our Platoon, it was fresh and really tasted good.

Around 1230 we finally got into camp. It was in a park in the suburbs with houses on one side. The macadam roads were nice and hard of course, but to get to our six man pyramidal tents we had to wallow through a sea of mud. However, it was nice and dry in the tents and only ten of us in a tent in army cots. Very cozy!!?

For dinner we had C rations [meat and beans with hard biscuits] and ready-made coffee. We went back to our tents and managed to scrape up a little more food, which we were saving to satisfy our hunger. After dinner we fixed a fire because it was getting cold and foggy.

At 1745 some of the fellows in our Platoon decided to go to a movie. It was an extra long Nissen hut. Italian Prisoners of War and a few Quartermaster Negroes had already flocked in and by 1830 the place was packed. The projector was operated by a Navy lad as was the rest of the camp doings. We saw the 'Hairy Ape', which everyone enjoyed very much, it was really a good show. Even the Italians who couldn't understand a word of it, enjoyed the show. After the movie we returned to our tents and brewed a pot of coffee.

For lamps we used an evaporated milk can, filled it with gasoline and stuck a rope down into the can. It worked! We went to bed early with thoughts of Louisiana and the Desert manoeuvres. Not much speculation as to where we were going.

The 575th with the 11th Armored

The following story is told by Major Clyde Gregory:

First a word about how the 575th Anti-Aircraft Artillery Battalion came to be with the 11th Armored Division. After approximately 15 months training in the United States at Fort Bliss, Texas and Camp Carson, Colorado the Battalion pushed off from New York on 30th October 1944 to polish off the Luftwaffe in some section of the ETO [European Theatre of Operations]. Some felt that we should join the Timberwolf [104th] Division whom we had met and manoeuvred with at Camp Carson. From the G-2 from the 7th hole we knew they were in France. Our advance party, which was to inform us of what was happening, had been sent out about a month ahead of us. After 15 days of hard labor as the ship's crew we found our advance party in England. They had spent approximately a month arranging a mud hole for us in the vicinity of Omaha Beach, however, for some reason they were sent back to England and arrived there one day ahead of the Battalion.

We very quickly settled down for the winter near Nantwich, Cheshire, England. A few of the officers and men had the opportunity to visit London and hear and see some of the things the V bombs were doing to that city. Our schedule of events was interrupted, however, by orders from higher headquarters. On 26th November we were attached to the 11th Armored Division. We moved from Nantwich to Codford to join our new comrades on 1st December 1944.

Upon arrival at Camp Codford, Wiltshire, England, we were welcomed by Brig. Gen. Charles S Kilburn, the Divisional Commander. We were officially made a part of the Thunderbolt, 11th Armored Division, and given the privilege of wearing the Division shoulder patch which the G-4 would supply in plentiful quantities. However, it was later found that the shoulder patches had low priority for shipping space and there were none to be had. We were happy with our new assignment and felt that we were part of one of the roughest, toughest fighting teams ever thrown together.

On joining the 11th Armored Division we were informed that we would head shortly for combat with one of the Armies on the Continent. Speculation and rumour ran high, but the majority seemed to favor Patton and his 'Kraut Busting' Third army. We started the mill turning and for the next 15 days worked on a 24-hour schedule getting our equipment assembled, test-fired and ready for combat. Jeeps and half-tracks blossomed out with additional armor, wire cutters and 'Bustles.' On 16th December we left England for France where we were to complete any unfinished work prior to combat.

580th Battalion

John E. Sengstacken was with the 580th AAA stationed in Codford between 24 December 1944 and 7 March 1945. He recalled:

We were in a holding area in a camp run by the Brits and using Italian POWs for cooks and light labour. They were the happiest bunch of prisoners I have ever seen.

I was just a PFC at that time but my job was a jeep driver so I spent a lot of time in the camp office and available as a taxi mostly for officers going to Winchester or to be picked up from there. Still but one of the things I recall was a PA system and we had phonograph records that we could play on it when there was no announcement to be made. A recording of 'Frankie and Johnnie' by Guy Lombardo got a lot of use. Stupid thing to recall but I had very little use for the Guy Lombardo orchestra. Dorsey, Goodman and Shaw were more my kind of thing.

We had an AAA firing practice range at Bournemouth on the beach where one of our gunners did his best to shoot off the target that was being towed by an airplane [he aimed for] the cable or rope so that we would have a rest while they landed and fixed it for another go round. He did it once!

Above: *Annie Fry, Bill Fry (bus driver for Couchman's) and Joan Dredge (née Fry) holding her daughter Sheila, c.1949.*

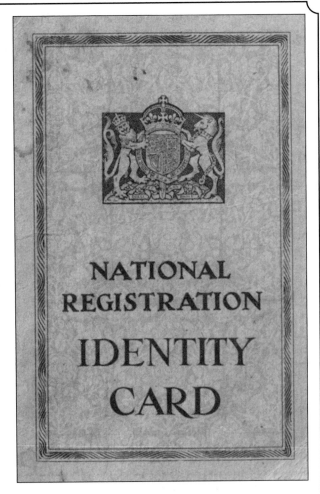

Above: *Joan Dredge's identity card.*

Sheila Dredge (now Poolman) aged three and a half.

Below: *Daphne and the late Maurice Handford with their son Nick. The Handfords lived in Manor House Cottage. Maurice was born in Salisbury and was a horn player. From 1949–61 he was the principle horn in Sir John Barbirolli's Halle Orchestra; in 1963 he was appointed joint associate conductor of the Halle, and from 1966 was the only associate conductor. From 1971–75 he was the principle conductor for the Calgary Youth Orchestra.*

Chapter 8

From the Second World War to 1980

Squatting At Bury Camp

Joan Dredge (née Fry) was born in Codford in 1924. She had two brothers, George and Jack, and three sisters, Annie, Olive, and the youngest Margaret who died at the age of 13. Her father Bill Fry worked as a bus driver for Couchman's and the family of six children lived at French Horn in the cottage furthest from the road. Mr Couchman used to do film shows in a hut that has long since been demolished – the youngsters paid three pence to see 'Mickey Mouse' films, which always seemed to break down halfway through the performance.

When she was four Joan was sent to live with an aunt at Southsea – it was a common practice to send one child to live with a relative when families were large and money was tight. She remembered a very happy existence until her aunt died of a stroke, and six-year-old Joan returned to Codford. Within a year her mother Alice had died. Her father later remarried and his second union resulted in four more children, two girls and two boys. Joan's early school years were at Codford St Mary School and she recalled that Miss Scull was very strict, and that she would take the boys into the porch to give them the cane.

Joan didn't get on with her stepmother and as soon as she left school at 14 she was put into service at Bartle (?) House at Sherrington. In 1942, aged 17, Joan volunteered for the ATS, serving throughout the war years with an anti-aircraft battery using the Vickers Predictor. In 2005 she still has her Instrument Drill book dated 30 October 1941 with its sequence instructions: 1) 'To Come Into Action'; 2) 'To Check Dials'; 3) 'To Line Up'; 4) 'To Go To A Stand By Bearing'. After the D-Day landings she joined the Ordnance Corps, leaving the Army after serving for four years to marry Bob Dredge of Fisherton in January 1947. Her new husband was half owner of a garage in the High Street; at the time of writing there is a bungalow on the site at 55a High Street.

The newly-weds moved into two rented rooms in Bury House. The house was up for sale and the tenants were under a month's notice. When Bury House was sold to the Forbes family, Bob and Joan moved across the road into a redundant Army hut at Bury Camp. For the next four years home was a tin hut with no lining – there were no facilities, no electricity, no bathroom. The Army had left a range and a wood burner in the hut. Bathing was in a tin bath in front of the fire, food was cooked on the range and an oil primus stove. Their very first winter in Bury Camp was bitterly cold,

but Joan had never been happier. She was working in Warminster at the creamery; it was piecework, making Fennings teething powder for babies. Joan recalls the awful winter of 1947 with snow 6 feet deep – the buses didn't run and she would walk to Codford Station to catch the train into work each day.

Eventually the council decided to take responsibility for the huts, and the squatters became tenants, paying 7s.6d. a week in rent. The council added facilities, the Dredges erected partition walls, and their first daughter and later twin boys were born while they were living at Bury Camp. In the 1940s mothers put their babies out in their prams into the gardens most days for the fresh air. Rain, shine or snow, any weather but fog, the Dredge children slept contentedly outside the hut in a field which, just a few years before, had been a scene of the hustle and bustle of military life.

It was due to the intervention of Mr Bee, a Parish Councillor who owned the Mace shop and off-licence at the top of the hill near St Peter's Church, that the Dredge family were allocated one of the brand-new council-houses at The Grove. Built on the withybeds, 20 The Grove was to be Joan's home for the next 39 years.

George V Postbox

Codford had a rare George V postbox at the local Post Office until the autumn of 2000. Wooden Ludlow boxes dating from 1910–35 are very unusual and there are no more than five remaining in the BA postal district. Because the boxes were made from wood they were easily damaged and subject to wear and tear – the Codford box was repaired on at least four occasions. When the High Street Post Office closed it was felt that relocating the box to New Road Service Station would be unwise. Despite misgivings about dismantling the box in one piece, the Royal Mail successfully retrieved and refurbished the original postbox and, accepting that it is a part of Codford's history, generously donated it into the keeping of the Parish Council. It is now on permanent display in the small room of the village hall.

The Codford Club Comes of Age – c.1970
Harry Cole

The Codford Club has now completed the first 25 years of its life and to understand how it began one has to go back a long way – more than fifty years in fact. For it was on Broadleaze that the YMCA had a large building for the troops who were stationed here in the First World War. At that time the frontage of Broadleaze was full of temporary shops of all kinds and the YMCA building, which was also of a temporary nature lay a bit off the road. It was used for some time after the end of the First World War in November 1918.

There was a concert given in this building on February 11th 1920 by the Codford Choral Society, Mr J.H. Perry who was the Congregational Minister here being the conductor. The programme was typical of the time, Glees by the Choral Society, Miss D. Billett [soprano], Mrs Erskine [cello] and Mrs Aylward [violin]. However after it had served its purpose it was demolished and the field returned to its former use with one exception, that was the building taken over by Mr H. Dewey and converted into a garage. Mr William Pond who was succeeded by Mr John A. Lush, his son in law, tenant of Middle Farm, Codford, used it for a time.

The owner of the property was Mr Charles Edwards who with his brother John was in business in London with matches, they were descended from a Tilshead family named, I believe, Savage. It was therefore not surprising that when the Second World War got going, the YMCA looked for a site for another YMCA, thought of Broadleaze and accordingly approached Mr Charles Edwards for permission to erect another there on the same ground. Not withstanding that Mr Charles Edwards was a very religious man – a fundamentalist I believe and a founder and treasurer of the All Nations Bible College, he dug his toes in and said NO! NO! which was exactly what we who knew him expected he would do. Whereupon the War Charities Commission who were financing the erection of the building clapped a compulsory order on him to acquire the land. He now shifted his ground and agreed to the erection of the

building if at the end of the war it was completely removed and the land reinstated. This was the situation and it is certain that if Mr Charles Edwards had lived there would never have been a Codford Club, at least, not there. But things did not happen that way, Mr Charles Edwards died in 1945 and was succeeded by his brother John, a partner in business – he was a religious but a more approachable man. Charles Edwards preached at you, always – John talked to you, but he had got old and his circle of friends and acquaintances became limited.

He lived in a double-fronted timber-framed house in Chitterne Road [Forde House in 2001], there were two monkey puzzle trees in the front garden and 'DAT DEUS INCREMENTUM' on the lintel over the door, it is where Mr P. Jensen now lives – it was here in its dark and grubby interior I used to go and talk to John Edwards. He did not get out a lot and he would talk of things in Codford of a bygone age, the reading-room where they used to play chess, this was the room over Mr Vine's shop where he played with his friends all long since dead. He was looked after by an old housekeeper named Edwards – a distant relative I believe and it was about this time the war having ended that the idea of setting up a Social Club became a need to be met if possible. Mr John Edwards approved of this idea and we discussed it a great many times but beyond saying he would give the village a piece of ground in Broadleaze it got no further. HE DID NOT and I could not get him to make a written bequest of anything.

In the meantime we used the Woolstore Theatre for social events and Colonel Sneyd who was the then owner offered to let us have the hall on a lease for seven years. This might have had to do except we could not regard it as a permanent home and the cost of upkeep would have been heavy. The war was over and the YMCA building on Broadleaze would soon have to be

Sunday school outing, early 1930s. The bus was owned by the Cornelius family. The picture includes: Revd Meyrick, Mrs Conduit (far left), Ron Sutton (far right, next to driver), the Ford sisters (the two girls with suitcases), Percy Conduit (centre, wearing cap), Walt Conduit (behind and to the right of Percy). Percy and Walt's sister is to the right of Walt, and Giles Conduit is the little boy with his back to the camera.

demolished. John Edwards was quite ready to let us have it if we could get it but he was the owner and we had no standing with the YMCA authorities.

John Edwards died in October 1946 and at the funeral I met Mr Walter Edwards the younger brother and the Solicitor who acted for the Edwards' estate. We talked over the situation, which was that the residue of the estate was left to the All Nations Bible College and the Trustees were Barclays Bank – there was nothing in the will which would enable us to have either the land or the building. Eventually Walter Edwards said he would write to the residuary legatees to know if they would carry out John Edwards' wishes in respect of the land and building, the Solicitor said he would do his best for us with the trustees of Barclays Bank, it was not a very encouraging situation but we hoped something might come of it.

A letter from Walter Edwards, written after the funeral, resulted in the residuary trustees agreeing to carry out John Edwards' wishes and give Broadleaze to the village, despite opposition from the Lush family who were taking over Middle Farm from John Edwards. The way was now open to call a village meeting, this was done and the first committee appointed to get the Club going, I was appointed Chairman and for the next ten years worked to get the Club established. The result is that today the village has a property worth in the region of £25,000 paid for and free from debt and the best social centre in the Valley.

The Conveyance document was made on 13 May 1949 between Barclays Bank Ltd and Codford Parish Council. It was signed by George William Goodsall and Henry Wightwick on behalf of Codford Parish Council. The first committee consisted of two Parish Councillors, and representatives of the Mothers Union, St Mary's and St Peter's Parochial Church Councils, the Trustees of the Congregational Chapel, the Choral Society, the WI, the British Legion, the Youth Organisation, the Tennis Club, the Codford Orchestra plus two village members elected at the Annual General Meeting.

Lights in the Sky

In the late 1960s and early '70s Warminster was the UFO capitol of Britain – the Warminster 'Thing', lights, flying saucers and cigar-shaped objects in the sky, mushrooms of smoke and crescents of fire, strange sounds and mysterious strangers. The *Warminster Journal* had the scoop of a lifetime; journalist Arthur Shuttlewood documented the unfolding events in 1967 with his book, *The Warminster Mystery*. The sightings began on Christmas Day 1964; many people reported eyewitness sightings, describing the objects as 'Things'.

One man who never really talked about what he saw one dark night in the skies above Codford was local police officer PC 388 George Russell. PC Russell had been in the Metropolitan Police before transferring to Wiltshire – a countryman with calm good sense and a no-nonsense approach, a man not given to imaginative speculation. He vividly remembers his one encounter with the 'Thing' while on night duty in Codford:

Me and John Trenholme were patrolling at night, from recollection about 1–2 in the morning. We were driving along the High Street past St Peter's Church towards Warminster for our grub break. Suddenly we became aware of something over to our right, it was very low in the sky. At first I thought it was a helicopter, it was about that size, and looked like the glass front of one. It was a huge great dome, the surface glowing orange, like a light in the cockpit. Then I realised if the inside was illuminated the pilot would be unable to see out into the darkness! I was also aware that there was no noise. After a moment the 'Thing', moving unbelievably quickly and totally silently, sped off towards Manor Farm then off to the north-east. We turned around to follow it but it disappeared from view in the direction of the Plain.

The bottom of Chitterne Road – on the left is the ox barn, and further over the bridge is Forde House.

A photograph taken c.1902. This is the site of Forde House in 2005, in Chitterne Road. The man in the shop doorway is Mr Savage, owner of the property, with his son. The lady on the left is Mrs Bennett, mother of C. Bennett; the lady on the right is the midwife, Mrs Kill, the sister of M. Ford.

PCs William Ponting and William Henry Hillier outside the New Inn, Corton, in 1917.

Left: WPC Maria Forey and PC John Wyeth, local beat officers, in 1987.

Below: The Old Police Station was built in 1951 and is pictured here as a private residence in the mid-1990s.

Chapter 9

Country Policing

Wiltshire Constabulary Warminster Division – 70 Years On

In 1903 the Codford beat included Boyton, Corton, Upton Lovell and Sherrington. In the photograph opposite the time is 'the Great War', the year is 1917; two local police officers stand outside the New Inn (now The Dove Inn) at Corton. The men pose in front of the thatched cob wall, hands behind their backs. They are PC113 William Ponting, stationed in the village and PC219 William Henry Hillier of Codford.

PC Ponting is the younger of the two, born in Malmsbury on 25 October 1894 – he was 19 when he joined the Wiltshire Constabulary as a 4th class constable. His records show he was 6 feet 1 inch tall, fresh complexioned, with brown hair and blue eyes. A gardener prior to joining the police force, William Ponting was unmarried and apparently healthy, as his only illness appears to have been appendicitis. After training he was posted to Trowbridge, on 10 October 1914, remaining there until 29 April 1916 when he was transferred to Corton. After just three years' service PC Ponting was discharged due to sickness on 31 August 1917; it therefore follows, looking at the trees, that this photo was taken in the early part of 1917.

PC Hillier was also a Wiltshireman, born on 4 October 1888 in Calne, joining as a 4th class constable on 27 March 1911 aged 22. PC Hillier was a married man with hazel eyes, dark brown hair, a fresh complexion and he stood 5 feet 10 inches tall. Both men were vaccinated immediately on entry into the Wiltshire Constabulary; neither man had any Army experience. PC Hillier had been a groom in civilian life, interestingly he appears to have been able to ride a bicycle but not a horse! His illnesses are listed as lumbago, febricula and influenza. He was stationed at Bradford on Avon from 14 May 1911, at Codford from 15 February 1912 and at North Tidworth on 5 November 1919.

Almost 70 years later, landlord of the Dove Inn Michael Rowse and his wife Jane were intrigued when the photograph reappeared. They showed it to their local policeman, John Wyeth. We have obtained a date of 1917 and, with the help of the Scenes of Crime Officers, it is possible to distinguish part of a number of one of the men's uniform.

At the time of writing it is exactly 70 years since the photo was taken, and everyone was enthusiastic to re-create the scene. In 1987 the Warminster East beat consisted of: Sutton Veny, Norton Bavant, Tytherington, Heytesbury, Chitterne, Upton Lovell, Stockton, Sherrington, Boyton, Bapton, Wylye,

Outside the Dove Inn (formerly the New Inn) at Corton 1987. WPC Maria Forey and PC John Wyeth pose in an updated version of the picture opposite. (Photo Wiltshire Constabulary Scenes of Crime)

Searching the crime scene are PC Ken Forey, Scenes of Crime Officer Barry Strange, the landlord of the Dove Inn, Michael Rowse, and PC John Wyeth.

PC Fred Read and Kate Stickley in the 1950s.

The Police Station (foreground) in Chitterne Road, as seen from the air. There are three farm cottages in Oxyard, and the thatched cottage beyond is Oxbarn, c.1987.

Codford, Fisherton-de-la-Mere, Knook and Corton. There were three beat officers, John Wyeth at Codford Police Station, Jim Ford at Heytesbury Police Station and WPC Maria Forey.

On 13 August 1987 off-duty police and Scenes of Crime Officers took a modern photograph. The trees were in full foliage and it was no longer possible to get far back enough include the attractive cottage next door in the shot. The Dove Inn looked much as it had seven decades earlier, except there was a beautiful creeper across the front of the building; the thatched cob wall showed its age with several obvious deep cracks.

John Neil Wyeth, PC421, joined the Wiltshire Constabulary as a cadet on 30 August 1966, the day after his 17th birthday. He served as a cadet in Swindon, Chippenham and Devizes, before joining the regular force on 29 August 1968. After training school he was posted as a probationer to Salisbury from 18 November 1968; to Alderbury from 10 May 1970; to Warminster from 8 September 1971 and to Codford from 20 October 1973.

Maria Louisa Forey WPC134 joined as a cadet on 5 August 1974, serving Devizes, Swindon, Trowbridge and Warminster. She joined the regular force on 30 October 1976, was stationed at Salisbury from 18 April 1977 and Warminster from 8 October 1978. She had been a beat officer on Warminster East from 1982.

So, slowly and inevitably the passage of time has crept on. If they were surviving in 1987 both William Ponting and William Hillier would have been in their nineties; in the early years of a new millennium they would certainly be dead. We may never discover what happened to them after they disappeared from the police records, but their images remain, young men captured for posterity in a pinprick of eternity.

A Country Policeman's Lot
Mr Read's Story

I moved from Castle Combe to Codford in 1951. Another police constable had been ordered to move from the Chippenham area but due to his impending retirement the move had been cancelled. On my arrival in Codford I found my family were to be the first occupants of a newly built police house complete with office. The house was just off the main A36 through the village on the Chitterne Road, on a plot of field, which had been used as a children's play area.

My new 'beat' included Codford St Mary and St Peter, Chitterne, Sherrington, and Upton Lovell. My duties consisted of cycle patrol, also covering Stockton, Fisherton-de-la-Mere, Boyton and Wylye when the policeman on that beat was off duty or on holiday.

In visits to shops, garages and public houses on the beat it was not long before I knew most people and after a stay of 12 years, nearly everyone. People were very

friendly. I had the assistance of a special sergeant and two constables at Codford and one constable at Sherrington and Chitterne.

I would visit farms in the area to be present when sheep dipping took place. There was a serious outbreak of foot-and-mouth disease in the area and part of our duties was to issue the movement of animal licenses and to perform duty at various entrances where outbreaks had occurred to stop unauthorised persons from entering the premises. We also had to see that the footwear of authorised persons and vehicles entering the farms were properly disinfected.

A check of unoccupied dwellings while their owners were on holiday was made, other duties permitting, also checks of the large houses where aliens were employed as servants to see if their visas were in order. All aliens coming to the area would have to register with the police.

Before leaving the Police Station I would contact Warminster by telephone for information, then while on patrol I would make static points outside telephone kiosks in case Warminster office needed to contact me.

The main trunk road, the A36, ran through Codford – it carried heavy traffic, from lorries transporting stone and gravel, as well as private vehicles at all times of the year. It was especially busy during holiday periods and the summer; it was necessary to spend a lot of time on the road due to accidents. A number occurred at the junctions of the A36 and the A303 at Deptford East and West. Holiday traffic from the provinces ignored traffic signs at these junctions, causing a large number of accidents at weekends and peak times, resulting in a large number of prosecutions. Dealing with a serious accident at Shrewton Hill in Chitterne I had to cycle the 3 miles between Codford and Chitterne, then obtain a lift from a passing motorist a further 2 miles to attend the injured driver. He had been attempting to overtake another vehicle in thick fog, collided with a car coming in the opposite direction and broken both his legs. The ambulance had to travel either from Salisbury or Warminster.

A welcome break from beat duty was serving a period of three months as an observer in a patrol car in different parts of the county. When on duty the driver would stop, and set down the observer to do a foot patrol through a village where there was no resident policeman. He would visit public houses during opening hours, making the acquaintance of the landlord and the customers. Other duties included visiting the church to check the offertory box was secure, speaking to the locals and going into shops and post offices. The idea was to show a presence to deter crime.

Whilst on motor patrol you would deal with accidents, report offences and offer advice as necessary to motorists and other road users. When on your beat you would stop and check any vagrants passing through. One I remember was John Henry Wheeler, his sole possessions on the carrier of his bicycle. He would stop and kneel down on the pavement outside St Peter's Church in

Codford, wet weather or fine, and say a prayer without going into the church. I had previously come across him when I was a policeman in Castle Combe.

On another occasion Mrs Daniels, who lived opposite St Peter's Church and was responsible for locking it at night, went to unlock the church door in the morning and saw, to her dismay, a tramp looking out of the window alongside the road. She telephoned the police station and I went to investigate. When she unlocked the door she found she had locked him in the night before. After checking that all was in order I took the tramp to the Police Station where I found he was not a 'wanted man' and that he had been checked a number of times in the county.

One time a lady tramp stayed in the church porch where she had shelter for the night, while on another occasion a tramp called William Shakespeare was arrested in Eastbourne, having stolen a bicycle from outside a house alongside the main road in Codford. I

had the unenviable task of going to Eastbourne to collect the prisoner and the bicycle by train.

Police Courts were held in Warminster every fortnight, and each month there would be a conference in Warminster, which was attended by all the town and country policemen in the area. Police matters were discussed; crime at national and local level was always on the agenda.

Owing to the position of St Peter's Church on a bad bend of the A36, whenever there were marriages or funerals, help would be requested for the parking of cars. This was due to the heavy traffic and the fact the junior school was situated on the main road. The duty was done as the children came out of school.

For some years I helped with the Codford Youth Club, which continued after I left in 1963. I was offered an office job at Police HQ in the Traffic Stats Department, and as I only had a short while before retirement I decided to accept the post.

An oral history day at Codford Primary School, c.2000. As part of a project exploring village life in the new millennium, PC John Wyeth (in old-style uniform) and PC Steve Price (in modern uniform) visited the school and are pictured here with pupils Dean Bolton, Katy Elliot, Lisa Stokes, Alex Wood, Michael Poolman, Richard Allerton and Adam Crossman. The children were shown police equipment from the 1970s and 2000 to explain how policing has changed in 30 years. The book that followed their research was called 'You Weren't There – So I'll Tell You', which told the story in their own words. (PHOTO PAUL MACDONALD, WARMINSTER JOURNAL)

Chapter 10

Agriculture

Bullet from the Boers

The following report appeared in the *Warminster and Westbury Journal* on Saturday 30 July 1904:

There is a story going about Codford of a farm labourer at work on a farm in the vicinity who came to the field the other morning with a large hole in his forehead.

On the bailiff asking him if he had been fighting, he replied 'No, that's where I was shot at Colenso, and the bullet came out yesterday.'

The bullet had been lodged in the labourer's head for four and a half years!

The Battle of Colenso was fought in South Africa during the second Boer War on 15 December 1899. While unsuccessfully attempting to relieve the siege of Ladysmith Sir Redvers Buller lost 1,055 men, 71 officers and 10 guns that day. He was eventually responsible, on 27 February 1900, for ending the siege which had lasted almost four months.

The Last Drowner
John Collins

The Collins family have owned Manor Farm since John's father came to Codford in 1913. He fought in the First World War, returning in 1918 to run the farm. John was an avid collector of rural artefacts and had a small museum that contained more than 700 items. He recalled:

The Water Meadows were dug about 150 years ago. Ditches were dug from the Chitterne Brook with a hatch by the riverside, and it goes out so far then the ground was in waves or layers. You had to keep the water flowing over, and then there was another ditch that took the water back to the river. You had to keep it flowing all the time, as the water mustn't get stagnant.

Our last drowner was William Whatley who worked on the farm for fifty years, he retired in the 1930s. The tool he used to cut the ditches is a prized exhibit in the farm museum. William was born over the farm boundary in Upton Lovell and one of the barns has his signature carved in a beam and a date 1879.

The Water Meadows were late being constructed in comparison to most people's – I think about 1840. Most of the water meadows were laid out in the late 1700s. They certainly weren't laid out in 1809 because I've got an old framed map in the office which shows the river before it was straightened. Above the road bridge it's

dead straight for a way to make it easier to lay out the ditches. They were kept up until the Second World War.

I can picture William Whatley scything round the corners at harvest time just before the war. In 1968 Mr Stratton who owns the meadow above Spots Pool wanted to do away with his ditches, level them off and plough them up. The Water Board would only give him a grant if the rest of the owners along the Chitterne Brook would do the same. We are by far the biggest owner of the Chitterne Brook, I think the rest, they were something and nothing, and it wasn't really laid out below us. So to oblige Mr Stratton we did the same.

The ditches were really becoming a bit of a nuisance; they would get filled in through lack of maintenance. It would be far too expensive these days to have a drowner on, all the manual work. All the handwork of having the little ditches chopped open. You flooded them, drowned them in the spring, then you got the first bite for the lambs and the sheep. Then in the summer they were out with the scythes for the hay. The chaps used to start about four in the morning, then in the heat of the day sit under a hedge for a couple of hours and drink cider.

Some places put cattle in the meadows in the autumn, but lots of people didn't like cattle going in the meadows at all, they used to tread in the ditches. The drowner would hate to see cattle going into his meadows! In the autumn they were wary of putting sheep in the meadows in case they got fluke.

My son-in-law Mark who is a London barrister likes to come down at weekends, getting out of his office and playing around in the meadows with his metal detector. I take all the things he finds to Salisbury Museum and they keep a record.

After the War when I saw how things were thrown away I decided to hang onto things that might be of interest. Among the artefacts found in the Manor Farm Water Meadows are: a latten brooch from 50BC; a rare fly brooch from AD50 (seven years after the Roman

The Chitterne Brook, looking north from the New Road bridge. (PHOTO DAVID MASON)

The Chitterne Brook, looking south from the New Road bridge.

occupation of Britain); Roman wavy edged horseshoes; a twelfth-century brooch; medieval packhorse bells; coins, including: an Emperor Gallienus, AD253–268; an Emperor Diocletian, AD284–305; silver sixpences from the reign of Elizabeth I, George II and George III, and a William IV 6d.; and badges and buttons from the First World War including those from Australian and New Zealand troops camped at Codford.

Manor Farm
Will Collins

Arthur Collins was studying law when he was diagnosed with TB; in the days before life-altering drugs a healthy, open-air lifestyle was necessary. Initially Arthur travelled to America and bought an orange grove in Santa Monica, California. However, with unprecedented frosts in a climate known to be temperate, the weather proved uncooperative to his new venture. On his return, just before the First World War, his father bought Manor Farm in 1913 from Mr Chisman for Arthur and his brother Edwin. When Edwin married Mr Collins senr set him up in a separate farm further down the Wylye Valley at Berwick St James.

By the start of the First World War Arthur's condition had improved enough, so that he was able to enlist, leaving Mr Chalker as farm manager. He was wounded in France on the Western Front and invalided out of the army. During the Second World War Arthur's health was bad, but he served on the Home Front, on the local Agricultural Committee, as an air-raid warden – he was also a special sergeant in the Wiltshire Constabulary. He had two sons; the eldest John was old enough to fight, while Will was still at school. John was eventually brought home in order to run the farm. Will remembered:

Manor Farm has just over 11,000 acres of land, to the north it goes over the Chitterne to Heytesbury Road, it has two fields of about 55 acres the other side of that road, all in Codford Parish. The western boundary is marked by a tree line, which is also the Parish boundary; the other side of the trees is in Upton Lovell Parish – it was the old Parish of Ashton Gifford. To the east a

couple of fields that go as far as the Chitterne Road until you come to Spots Pool, we go along the Chitterne Road as far as Lyons Seafood [Allied Lyons] then come back in. To the south Manor Farm land starts just beyond the veterinary surgery in Green Road; nearby Anzac Cottages also belong to the farm.

There are six barrows on Manor Farm – one of them was excavated in the 1950s by a group of people including the Revd Steel, who lived at Wishford or South Newton. They found one skeleton and some bits of pottery that are in Devizes Museum. That barrow is in the other field, and that has since been ploughed. All are round barrows [from the Bronze Age] and they are now scheduled ancient monuments and are protected. Some of the mounds have had rabbit damage over the years. There's a chap called Colt-Hoare who excavated them all in the early 1800s and he dug a hole straight down the middle, some archaeologists think he damaged them, they haven't been excavated since that time as far as I know.

On the hills looking eastwards into a lovely valley where there is a well, Will recalled:

One of our employees used to say an old witch used to bide about round there, and the trees down there which we planted some years ago, we've named that after it and we call it witches well.

A few years ago after a good year, we put in farm roads. I don't think these Downs had been ploughed since the Middle Ages, the cattle and sheep graze the landscape. The farm grows wheat and barley; we've got a herd of beef cattle, and a flock of sheep. We used to have sheep that were a cross breed called 'mules,' the rams we used were partly Suffolk and partly Charolais. Nowadays we no longer have our own flock but do take sheep in to 'keep' for other owners.

Looking down to the bottom field with the ribbon of the Chitterne Brook, its waters spreading across the fields after the February rainfall, into the field called Long Furlong which was last ploughed in 1879, Will commented that there was a lot of water coming from Imber at the moment:

The source of the Winterbourne is mostly from Chitterne, though in very wet years it begins at Imber. The only year in my lifetime that it didn't rise was 1975–76 because we had a very dry summer in '75 and an exceptionally dry winter, during the winter of '75/'76 it didn't flow at all. The only year that it never dried up was I think 1946, which was very, very wet.

This is the seventy-fifth year since records began – my father started to keep rainfall records in January 1930. 2000 was by far the wettest year in any of the previous 70 years, we had 46.61 inches of rain, the previous highest was 1960 with 42.68 of which 7.91 inches fell in October, so nearly four inches more than any previous year. Recent average annual rainfall has been just over 31 inches, however in 2002 the rainfall was 46.15 inches so it seems

At the bottom of Church Lane during the foot-and-mouth crisis, c.2001. Codford escaped infection.

East Farm yard looking north.

to be getting wetter. The water is collected through a funnel into a tube, and measured at 9am every morning from a receptacle in the kitchen garden. The tube must be completely level and as far from an object as its height.

Looking through the farm receipts from directly after the Second World War offered a glimpse of the way things were 57 years ago, when rationing was still in force, in a time before mechanisation, when the fields were planted with wheat, barley and oats and dotted with ricks made of hay, straw, and grain.

In June the Ministry of Food took 12 fat ewes for £44; one pig was sold for £12.14s.4d.; and in October the Ministry of Food took four fat heifers for £143.9s.6d. During both world wars Manor Farm land had been the site of hutted camps, for which rents were paid quarterly: December 1945 the Army Pay Office paid £17.19s. to rent about 40 acres for camps; in March 1946 rent for camps was £16.14s. and rent of the road a further £1.5s.; in June 1946 the military paid £18.14s.; and in October 1946 they paid £17.19s.

When the military decided they no longer required the camps they did not reinstate the land to its prewar state, preferring to pay the total value of the land, as this was less expensive.

From the farm outgoings it is possible to see that mechanisation began in 1947, with the purchase of diesel, a combine harvester, bailer, Land Rover, Rover car, and a Massay Harris Combine.

East Farm

J.M. Stratton and Co. is owned by the late Michael Stratton's four sons, Olly, Barney, Josh and Jake. In 2004 they employed seven people full time and two part time. The farm had originally been owned by the Biggs (now Yeatman-Biggs) family from Stockton. The present business was established when Jack Stratton bought the farm in 1921. Since then the land area has increased – Jack bought Chitterne Farm in 1930 for £3 an acre. Michael Stratton inherited from his uncle Jack and started farming in 1946 with 50 employees – it was a stock farm with very little arable land.

The Army used most of the farm for training troops, and it was not until the late 1940s and '50s that the land was ploughed for the first time.

Michael Stratton bought Manor Farm in Stockton in 1950, and part of Auckland Farm in 1962. The total area in 2005 encompasses 3,500 acres. The Strattons have made a massive investment in buildings, roads, a water system, fences and woodland, to transform what used to look like the present Army range into a productive working farm.

Punchbowl Farm

Greg Puddy was born at Cleeve House, home of the White Horse Trekking Centre. He was the seventh of Bill and Joan Puddy's nine children. Through his working life Greg managed Punchbowl Farm, which was bought by Captain George Davenport in 1963/4. Around 1998 Greg bought 150 acres, including the Punch Bowl, from Davenport, who retained 250 acres of the land, renaming it Sherrington Mill Farm.

A Farming Family
Ann Jessey's Story

Codford is my birthplace – I was born there on 4 October 1942. My birth name was Bridget Elizabeth Ann Lush and I was born at Bridlea Cottage (which was named for my mother's maiden name, 'Bridget Leach') across from Middle Farm House that was owned by my grandparents, John and Bessie Lush. My

Foot-and-mouth precautions in 2001, with St Mary's Church and East Farm House.

Greg Puddy leading the White Horse Trekking Centre cart; father Bill driving mother Joan with the whip.

father, Ron Lush, bought Auckland Farm in Chitterne Road about five years later, so we moved there and I lived there until my parents split up in 1958, when I moved to Salisbury with my mother and sister.

I attended St Peter's Primary School in Codford, where the principal at the time was Mrs Cuff; then St Monica's School in Warminster and then South Wilts Grammar School in Salisbury. My main reason for writing is to contribute a few titbits of information, the first being about my grandmother, Bessie Lush, who did a lot of work in the community during and immediately after the war. One of her tasks was to find homes for evacuees from London – a task in which she was very successful and in which she led by example, housing two Quaker families from Surrey in her own house for the duration of the war.

Bessie was also a dynamic force in the Congregational Chapel, organising charabanc outings to Bournemouth and Weymouth for the farm workers' children, who would otherwise not have been able to go. She also set up the Congregational Sunday School, as well as the youth brigade which met every Thursday night at the chapel. In addition she chaired the local branch of the Women's Institute several times and was the key organiser of the annual Codford Fête.

After she and my grandfather sold Middle Farm in around 1950, they moved to a house in Green Lane, where they invited the Longmans, a family of missionaries who retired from China, to live in part of their house, along with their daughter and two grandchildren. They became great friends of mine as I used to stay with my grandparents a great deal and used to go to St Peter's School along a route which passed by the 'squatters' camp', where the Polish refugees were housed. My sister was born at Auckland Farm in 1950 and had several Polish children as classmates,

including her best friend Rita Trojak, whose father had married and stayed in Codford after the war.

My parents were very involved with the Woolstore Theatre. Dad did all the lighting for the plays, helped build the sets and occasionally acted. He played the estate agent in the Codford Amateurs' production of 'Rebecca', which went to the National Drama Finals in London some time in the 1950s. My mother created the models of the sets for various plays, with my help of course! She and I also trod the boards now and then, once in some kind of Benjamin Britten operetta that was descended upon by sound crews from the BBC and broadcast on the radio!

I don't remember the Sneyds all that well, but I do remember Lionel and Phyllis Crawhall and I thought they were the ones who owned the Woolstore, because they lived right next door and she was a retired actress. They were the catalysts for most of the performances in my parents' day. I think they also founded the Theatre Club, which was the other troop besides the Codford Amateurs.

The American 3rd Armored Division was stationed in Codford during the Second World War. I had a brother (now deceased) who was born in 1944, and one of his godparents was an American soldier named Al Rafdal. Since 'Uncle Al' had given me a souvenir prayer book with his name signed in it, I always called him my 'American godfather', even though he was really my brother's godfather, and I have a photograph of him with me, my mother and father, my uncle Ken (Lush), two other American soldiers and Doreen Bosworth, a Codford girl who Al eventually married in 1951. In 2000 I managed to track down Al and Doreen in Des Moines, Iowa, where they were both well and had recently celebrated their golden wedding anniversary.

John Collins was a neighbour at Manor Farm and a frequent visitor to our house; I know he married very late in life. I do remember his brother, Will, but not as well as John, who at the time was the more gregarious of the two and used to get on very well with my father.

I remember 'Shep' Bundy especially well – my Dad was very fond of him because he was such an independent spirit and so smart. His oldest daughter Jean was a very beautiful girl – blonde in the same vein as Marilyn Monroe, but tragically she died from cancer very young. She married a young police constable who moved to Codford and they later moved to Devizes, where I think he became a Chief Inspector. Shep's youngest daughter Rosemary went to school with my sister Christine. When she married she lived in Auckland Farm, in the house built by my Dad.

Wally (Walt) Conduit used to live in one of those big tall houses in the High Street nearly opposite the Post Office. Not only did we go to school together, but he was one of the 'livewires' at the youth club organised by my grandmother. We both used to go on the coach trips to Bournemouth and Weymouth.

Chapter 11

Codford's Shops and Trades

From 1880 until 1980
(Not Including The Two World Wars)
Rosamund Willoughby

When we, the Willoughbys, moved into Overton House in 1954 there were 20 shops or useful trades – by 2004 there was only one shop combined with the Post Office, garage and petrol pumps. We have a purpose-built surgery with two doctors and various clinics, a large school with playing-fields and a regular bus service so we are fortunate.

The Station – Station Road

In 1844 Isambard Kingdom Brunel, the great Victorian engineer, submitted the first plans for a railway, and by 1846 the line between Westbury and Salisbury, passing through Codford, had been laid out. The GWR (Great Western Railway) opened a station for passengers in Codford on 11 June 1856. Almost 100 years later, in 1955, the station was closed to passengers. There was also a busy freight yard, which closed on 10 June 1963.

On the right-hand, Codford side of the level crossing was a large raised signal-box, which was finally made redundant in the summer of 1982, and later pulled down. Before the automatically controlled gates and flashing lights were installed on the crossing, a pair of large heavy gates were kept open to the road and had to be closed from the signal-box before the signals could be lowered for the trains to pass through.

On the left-hand, Boyton side of the crossing there was the stationmaster's house, the last occupants of which were the Wilsons (Sue Poolman's parents). Sue's father was a ganger and when he died in August 1968 her mother moved out. In the spring of 1969 the house was pulled down.

Codford stationmaster's house and level crossing.

Miss Ethel Simper, the schoolmistress at St Peter's School until 1922.

The nights were much quieter after June 1963 when the freight yard was closed and there was no longer the endless banging and clanging which echoed up through the valley, as the wagons were shunted in and out of the sidings.

In December 1914 a loop line from Codford at the Sherrington crossing was opened, which remained manned until 1923.

There was also a crossing-keeper's cottage on the left-hand, Codford, side where a railway pensioner named Pickford lived. His son Percy worked for Harry Cole in the piggeries, while his daughter Violet was the first woman porter at Codford Station in 1940. If you look over the fence by the small gate onto the crossing, on the left-hand side, you will see a very pretty rambling rose – all that remains of the cottage garden!

For further information about the railway, provided by Anthony Notley, see *Sherrington – A Wiltshire Village*, by Rosamund Willoughby.

Beavens (later Guinness) Barley Research Station – Station Road

Up the track to the right of the Codford side of the railway crossing, past the signal-box there was the Barley Research Station. During the First World War there were hutted camps in these fields and later in 1941–42 the site was bought by Beavens for use for their barley research – previously their barley had been grown on their farm in Boreham Road in Warminster.

In 1962 Guinness bought the site, intending to build a new malting there, but nothing came of it. In 2005 it is owned by West Crop Ltd for agricultural research. Guinness kept detailed weather reports – perhaps West Crop still do but do not publish them locally. Beavens, however, continue with their maltings in Pound Street, Warminster; these are the oldest traditional maltings in Great Britain, continuing directly from Dr Beaven in 1880. At the time of writing they are being restored and will shortly be open to the public. Dr Beaven introduced and grew the first pure variety of barley for British farmers in 1905 [according to Chris Garrett, head maltster at Warminster Maltings].

Hillside Café

The original café was a wooden hut, another redundant building from the wartime camp; the café was opened by someone called Hesketh who came from 'away' in 1925–26.

In the early 1930s George Writer came down from London and built the two bungalows, behind what in 2005 is the Little Chef, and installed petrol pumps, a workshop and garage for repairs, employing a mechanic called John Parker. This workshop was much used by Doughty's, the builders. The removal of the petrol pumps and the building of the café, The Happy Eater, later to become The Little Chef, all took place in the 1980s.

The changes to Hillside Café involved the replacement of the hut by a purpose-built brick building, slightly to the right of the original site in the 1980s.

According to Maurice Cole, during the Second World War Mrs Harris, the owner of Hillside Café, who was very left wing, was the local convener for Lady Churchill's 'Aid To Russia Fund'. Local volunteers would collect donations of 1d. a week. Just before the Labour landslide election at the end of the war there was a political meeting at St Mary's School, at which the local Labour candidate spoke. During his discourse he said that all the millionaires should be put on a boat and sent to a desert island as they were no use to anyone. A local farmer took exception to the remarks and interjected – ' Don't talk like a fool man', whereupon Mrs Harris clocked him from behind around the head with her handbag, to the amusement of a portion of the audience.

New Road Service Station

Major Houston of Codford St Peter Manor owned a number of the redundant wartime wooden huts and rented them out. There was quite a complex of these where the Smith's have their shop and workshops at the time of writing. Firstly, Mr Reeves had a small sweet shop and bar selling soft drinks; he installed the first petrol pumps.

Behind where the Post Office and shop are in 2005 was another building that ran parallel with New Road in the Cole family's field. This was used for whist drives, dances, concerts and drama groups before the Woolstore became available for village use.

Major and Mrs Houston (of the manor) gave the children of Codford and Sherrington an annual party which was held in this building. The Sherrington children were collected and brought up on a farm wagon drawn by a team of horses – an added excitement!

The Phelps family moved into the building in 1938 and remained there until 1959 (Margaret Ashman née Phelps was born there). Maurice Cole thinks they were the last occupants and that it was demolished in 1968.

Later, Mr Dean bought the garage site and continued with the shop, adding groceries as well as sweets and the petrol pumps, but there was no garage for repairs. He had a large greenhouse where the first workshop is in 2005, and grew excellent tomatoes for sale until he retired in 1970.

Major Houston sold to Mr Reeves in March 1950, and in July that same year the garage plot was sold on to Mr Walker, who kept it until 1954 when it was bought by Archie Dean. Some 13 years later the site was sold to Jim Hunter who had a house built, 'Denarus', behind it. When Jim Hunter sold to the Smiths he retained the house, remaining there until his death.

In 1971 Mr and Mrs Smith bought the site and business and moved in with their family; they enlarged the shop and built the garage and workshop. In 2005 there is a much enlarged shop, newsagent and Post

The New Road Service Station, c.1995/96. Mayflower Farm's old piggery, now the site of the Sound Post, can be seen in the background, on the hill.

John Smith driving the school bus in 1995 on the 50th anniversary of VE Day.

Office, together with the garage and workshops, the school bus service and coach line, all run by Brendan Smith, the grandson of the original Smiths, aided by his father John.

Mayflower Farm – New Road

A short distance along New Road, on the left-hand side, is Mayflower Farm. This was another of the redundant wartime huts – it was originally the Guard Room for the camps, which has been replaced by a modern bungalow. This was where Harry Cole, the father of Paul, Godfrey and Maurice, lived and farmed. In the large room at the New Road end Harry ran a small club for the village lads, where there was a full-sized snooker table, dart and ring boards, and they played cards with a charge of sixpence. There were also whist drives and dances – no village hall in those days!

Dyer & Son Coal Merchant

On the right-hand side of Codford St Peter's end of the High Street there was the coal merchant and haulier, Dyer & Son, with a large board on the roadside wall stating 'Dyer & Son Coal Merchant'. First came Henry Dyer. He was listed in the 1920 *Kelly's Directory*, followed by his son Jim Dyer. The Dyers also delivered in wagons all around the area – their coal came in railway wagons to the Codford Station freight yard and it was quite common to see two coal wagons standing in the goods yard.

The Dyers also had a smallholding and part of their land stretched from their High Street yard right down to the railway line [there was no bypass to divide it up in those days]. Helen, Jim's daughter, did a large part of the farm work including the expert laying of the hedges down Sherrington Lane, traces of which are still visible in 2005.

Kelly's of 1899 lists two names, one Charles Newman in Codford St Peter as 'Coal Dealer' and Job Oliver as 'Haulier and Coal Merchant'; Job probably followed Newman and both may well have been on the same site as Dyer.

The School

Still on the right side, beyond Dyers, there was Codford St Peter School. Latterly this was the junior school with the seniors at St Mary's. The building opened directly onto the road with a small covered porch, which evidently became too dangerous with the increase in traffic and children dashing out across the road to their parents. One small girl was knocked down by a car and the school was closed.

As Codford was still without a village hall both schools were used for meetings and other events, and as a polling station where villagers went to cast votes during elections. At the time of writing the building is a private dwelling (called Moonraker's) and, rather sadly, the little porch has been removed – the entrance is now at the east end.

Bee Farmer

George Hinton is listed in 1920 as a 'Bee Farmer' (bee keeper) living in 117 High Street with a 'small shop'. Number 118, Godfrey Cole's house, was the farmhouse for Grove Farm, and at some time numbers 117 and 118 were connected by doors upstairs and down, making it a much larger house.

Maurice and Godfrey Cole recalled Mr Hinton lived in a thatched cottage on the site of the bungalow built by Joe Trojak, occupied in 2005 by Maurice.

The Stores

Still on the right-hand side of the corner by The Grove entrance, where there is a red-brick house called 'The Stores' in 2005, there used to be an attractive small cob-built building which contained an inglenook fireplace. This was a grocer's shop and 'off license' owned by George Conduit from 1914 into the 1920s. He also had a small bakery.

Conduit was followed by Mrs Mabel Gregory who is listed in 1920 as 'grocer and beer retailer' – the premises were still listed as an off licence. The Gregorys closed the bakery, but installed a petrol pump on the roadside in 1924–25. They were followed by Mr Bee who was there for a great many

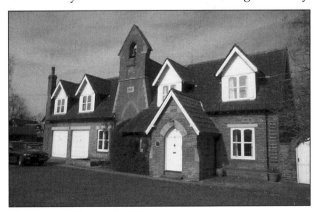

St Mary's old school, 2004.

Soldiers in the street outside the old school and cottages by the brook, in the winter sometime during the First World War.

St Peter's School in 1915/16. The teacher on the left is Miss Ethel Simper. Fourth from the left in the front row is Ron Davis.

The top class at Codford St Mary, c.1934. Pictured with Mrs Veale are, left to right, back row: *?, Mavis Couchman, ?, ?, Audrey Goodsall, Miss Scull;* middle row: *?, Pete Jenkins, Ron Sutton, Phil Thomas, ?, ?, ?;* front row: *Barbara Norris, ?, ?, Joan Conduit, Joan Fry, Dulcie Day.*

The lower class, left to right, back row: *Miss Bartlett (later Mrs Few), M. Carter, ? Cull, D. Barnard, ? Couchman or ? Barnard, Arthur Spiller, D. Sutton, ? Conduit;* middle row: *Dulcie Norris, ? Cull, D. Day, J. Day, E. Carpenter, ? Fry, ?, ? Andrews, Miss Scull;* front row: *J. Conduit, G. Conduit, J. Mills, B. Spiller, ? Jud, ? Tulk.*

A picture taken from St Peter's Church tower before The Grove estate was built in 1951. Mr Bee's store can be seen in the foreground.

Overton House, St Peter's Church and St Peter's Old Rectory with the new Rectory behind and Bury Mead on the far right, late-twentieth century.

years and was known as 'old Mr Bee' by 1954. Those were still the days when most of us had a 'book' into which your purchases were entered and an account rendered either weekly or monthly.

Mr and Mrs Wheeler bought the business when Mr Bee retired in 1955. They kept a prosperous small shop selling sweets, fruit and vegetables, bread and groceries. They kept the petrol pump and also sold paraffin from a large tank in their garage. Paraffin was still much used for lamps, heating and cooking.

The off licence remained with a large board on the east end wall of the building with the light over it. The off licence was useful on Sundays, when the shop would be open in the mornings – in those days there was no Sunday trading.

When the Wheelers retired in the 1970s Mrs Gale bought the business, but it gradually ran down and was closed for good. Mrs Gale then converted the building into a private dwelling. Sadly, one Christmas some curtains drying on a radiator caught fire and the whole building was gutted, Mrs Gale and her dog 'Tiger' both dying of smoke inhalation. The burned-out shell remained for a long time until the site was bought by a developer from 'away' and a much larger, and not very attractive, red-brick house was built in 1989–90.

Overton House – The Doctor

On the left-hand side of the High Street next to St Peter's Church is Overton House. This was the home of Dr Isaac Flower from the early 1840s until his death in 1889. Dr Flower, whose father was a doctor in Warminster, was the village doctor and had his surgery in what today is the dining-room, the entrance being the door in from the back yard where there is still a bell with a pulley, which rings out loudly on a good pull. Dr Flower was also the registrar for births and deaths for Heytesbury district; we were told he kept pigs in the field and drove about in a pony and trap.

St Peter's Bell-ringers

Bert Doughty's father, Albert Doughty, was a bell-ringer for 50 years from 1920 until he retired in 1970. The ringers with him were: Vic Pothecary, Walter Daniels, Albert Sheppard, Jack Whatley, Frank Samways (who lived next door to Doughty's Yard), and Albert Doughty.

Walter Daniels's wife was a Pothecary and she was born in the thatched cottage opposite the Rectory whose door opened directly down a steep stone step onto the road at the front, at the back of the Manor garden. This was the head gardener's cottage and Walter was the head gardener; probably Mrs Daniels's father Pothecary had also been head gardener.

When Walter died his bachelor brother, Harwood

Daniels, also a gardener, continued to live there until he retired and went to live at St Johns in Heytesbury. In 1962 the cottage was pulled down and no trace of it remains, except the large stone front doorstep.

On New Year's Eve every year Major Houston of the Manor gave the bell-ringers a dinner that was held in the Daniels's cottage. At about half an hour before midnight they would come up the road to climb the tower, in very good form. Villagers could hear them singing and laughing as they came. The bells were muffled before midnight to ring out the old year and unmuffled to ring in the new year.

The Thatches

Below the Manor on the right-hand side, the corner of Doughty's Lane (known locally as Frog Alley) and the High Street, is The Thatches. The Thatches is a comparatively recent name – in 1880 there was a butcher listed as George Leaver, most probably in this same building. In 1889 there was another butcher named William Lever – a different spelling but this does not mean anything; William Lever is probably George Leaver's son. There are no Leaver's or Lever's, or even a butcher listed in the census returns of 1871 or 1901.

Rustic Lane was also known as Doughty's Lane and Frog Alley.

Flag bearers for the Royal British Legion, Bill Axtell the butcher with his daughter Beryl. Behind them are the Congregational Chapel, the Sunday school and the Manse.

In 1919 or 1920 William Axtell (always known as Bill) bought the cottage, the business and the shop and continued as a butcher until he retired in 1956. Otterwell the butcher took over for a short time until he moved down the High Street. The cottage was sold and the shop turned into a restaurant called 'The Thatches' – when the restaurant closed the whole building became a private dwelling but kept the name.

The Timber Merchant

B. Davis, 'Timber Merchant', who also ran a green-grocery business, lived in what today is called Manor Cottage, next to the Woolstore. Davis had a large timber yard in Green Lane on the left-hand side, the site of what is today'Old Manor Cottage, 102 Green Lane, the first house on the corner of Bury Mead. When Davis retired the yard site was sold for building. The old or original Manor House is the small thatched cottage running parallel with the High Street opposite today's Manor.

Jim Davis driving his tractor, bringing wood from Stockton to the wood yard, 1958–59. Bob Dredge is on the trailer and Wilf Pearce on the road.

The George Hotel with Australian and New Zealand troops – Woolstore Camp was on the site of the present Cherry Orchard.

The George Inn

In 1899 Walter Cottle was listed, he was also farm bailiff to Mr Charles Notley (who farmed Church Farm, now East Farm, next to St Mary's Church in Church Lane), and in 1920 a Frederick St Germier is listed as of the George Inn. There have been a great many others over the years since 1920 – the George continues in 2005 as the only pub in the village.

The Wool Store

The Wool Store is opposite the George pub and is probably the most interesting building connected with the life and history of the village. Wool and sheep were the most important industries in Wiltshire – most of the wool was poor quality and coarse and was used mainly for felt and carpets. Hence it seems logical that there were carpet and felt factories in Wilton using local wool.

Apart from farming, sheep provided most of the work in and around the villages; Bert Doughty's grandfather was the last of the 'wool sorters', Giles Conduit was foreman wool sorter. Emily Conduit married Albert Doughty in 1914 – they were Bert and Fred's parents. In its heyday there were about 30 sorters and when it finally closed in about 1928 there were only five.

In 1880 there was listed George Dear, a woolstapler in Codford St Peter. In 1889 he was still here but there was also a William Dear, 'foreman of the Woolworks', and by 1920 there was an Alex J. Dear, a woolstapler. He was living in 'The Beeches' and was listed among 'private residents' as well as under commercial, so the Dears had gone up in the world!

The Beeches is the big house behind the Wool Store, later called Bradwell Grange then Flying Goose Furlong, which is the name of the field. It was later known as Grey's Mead and in 2005 is The Wool House.

Giles and Sarah Conduit, parents of Kit, George, Nan, May, Fred and William.

The History of The Flying Goose

Kate Forbes recalled that:

Mrs Briggs, who lived in what is now Wool House, started keeping ducks, I don't know if they actually did the plucking in the old kitchen in the house, but there was also the downstairs, the brick end of the old Wool Store. Anywhere they were plucking and dressing ducks the flies were terrific, after a while she bought a piece of land up the road and they moved their business, more especially the plucking and packing, up there.

The house was 'The Beeches' when my father knew it first when the Dears lived there, then Colonel Sneyd came and he called it 'Bradwell Grange', after he died in about 1948 and it was sold to the Briggs, she called it 'the Flying Goose'. Then it was sold it to the Simpsons, he was a London businessman and used to go up to London three times a week.

Per Jenson, who lived in 'Wool Cottage', met Major Briggs and went into the business. After their son was killed in a road accident they gave up and moved away. Jensen went into prawns rather than ducks and built up quite a big business, he then sold to Lyons; when Lyons decided to give up the management staff bought it.

The Wool Store and French Horn Cottages, c.1963.

We were told that the then open space behind the Manor vegetable garden, which opened onto green Lane and Bury Farm under the chestnut trees, was where the local sheep were brought for shearing. This area became hardcore standing for tanks during the Second World War. Until the old YMCA club huts were given to the village, the Wool Store became the village hall and was much used for all the local meetings, the WI, dances, concerts and drama – it was very much the hub of the village.

From 1948/49 until 1959 the Wool Store was home to two theatre groups – the Codford Amateurs and the Woolstore Theatre Club. In 1957 Harry Cole bought the theatre and things continued as usual until 1962, when he sold the theatre to the Wool Store Theatre Club. In 1964 the Codford Amateurs were disbanded as it was considered unnecessary to have two societies doing the same thing. The theatre has continued to flourish and is, we are told, the only village theatre in the country (see *The History of a Country Theatre* by Karen Johnstone for more information).

The Blacksmith

Opposite the entrance to Cherry Orchard there was a blacksmith called Trim, whose forge was in yet another of the wartime huts. Trim travelled around the farms carrying a large bellows and anvil in his pony and trap. There was another blacksmith's forge in Doughty's yard after the war.

A whist drive during the Second World War. The lady in the front is Mrs Hill who lived in the lane by the George, and next to her is the blacksmith, Mr Trim.

113

Outside The Poplars, High Street, with the Lloyds Bank sign on the right.

Codford St Mary from the air, c.1992.

The Poplars

On the left-hand side, below the entrance to Cherry Orchard, was the home and surgery of a succession of village doctors – it was quite usual for a doctor to have his surgery and dispensary in his own house. In 1899 there was a Dr Albam Ward, physician and medical officer for Codford St Peter and district, and also registrar for births and deaths for Heytesbury sub-district. A resident in St Mary's, he may have been the first doctor to live in The Poplars at 86 High Street.

Dr Ward was followed by Dr Ernest Lewis who we know did live in The Poplars – he was not only a keen cricketer (!) but a busy man. He was a physician and surgeon and medical officer and public vaccinator for No. 2 District Warminster Union, and surgeon to the GWR and Post Office, as well as medical officer to the Board of Education – all listed in 1920s *Kelly's Directories*. When Dr Lewis retired (or died – it is unclear) he was followed by Dr Christopher Houghton-Brown in 1947, who stayed until he retired in 1970.

The surgery's consulting room was in an annexe to the right of the front door, with a small dispensary between the surgery and the kitchen. Patients entered via the annexe door and waited on hard upright chairs in the passageway. When the Houghton-Browns came there was no window so it was rather dark and dismal until they installed one.

When Dr Houghton-Brown retired the Elcombs bought the house in 1970 – for a short time his successor, Dr Logan Taylor, used the surgery but lived in Sherrington, while Flat 37, on the ground floor in Cherry Orchard, was converted into a surgery with a waiting-room and dispensary. This continued as a surgery through a succession of doctors until Dr John Fishwick arrived in 1989. He continued in 37 until the new larger, purpose-built complex was built and opened in 1992.

The Ironmongers

Below The Poplars was 81 High Street, which in 2005 is called Mill Cottage. There was Dewey's the ironmongers shop, an excellent shop that sold almost everything – from hammers and nails, paints and paraffin to saucepans and china, garden tools and seeds. Dewey's is listed in the 1920 *Kelly's*. He also owned the garage opposite and when he retired Paul Cole took over both the garage and shop and installed petrol pumps. When Paul Cole retired the garage was taken over by Smith's of New Road Service Station and South Newton and later by Webb's Caravans.

The Village Hall

Opposite The Poplars, parallel with the High Street and backing onto the playing-field, was the village hall, always known as The Club because it had been

Outside Mrs Dewey's Hardware Store in High Street, early 1930s. Pictured are: Audrey Goodsall, Norman Dewey, Veronica (Vera) Chapman, Dulcie and Barbara Norris.

a YMCA club building and reading-room for the Forces during the war. It was then given to the village for use as a hall.

The building, another wood and corrugated-iron hut, consisted of a caretaker's quarters at one end with a kitchen shared with the main hall – not very convenient for the caretaker! There was a large hall with a stage plus an upright piano at one end (useful for accompanying *Jerusalem* for the WI and hymns for the Mother's Union). At the kitchen end was a wide wooden counter for teas, a portion of which was divided off with a security grille when Lloyds Bank opened for business once or twice a week. There was also a small lending library – this was before the mobile library started!

At the back was a Small Hall with a door out onto the playing-field. A monthly baby clinic was held in this hall where bottles of orange juice and cod-liver oil were handed out by Mrs Forbes (Kate's mother) and myself, and the District Nurse weighed babies and dispensed advice. For many years Miss Oxford came every month to make cups of tea and biscuits.

The windows of both halls had wooden shutters for the blackout, and over the war years each regiment which was stationed in the village painted their badge on to a pair of shutters – one special pair was painted by Rex Whistler but these were taken away very soon after the Second World War. The shutters have now been rehung on the walls of the new village hall.

The Drapers

83 High Street was Goodsall's, 'Drapers and Outfitters' – in 1920 Hibberd's Brothers is listed, but Goodsall's took it over in the early 1920s. This was a

lovely little shop, so clean and tidy selling every kind of haberdashery, reels of silk and cotton, elastic, ribbons, knitting wools and patterns, ladies and children's underwear, socks and stockings, and materials by the yard. In a smaller adjacent shop there were children's clothes and ladies dresses, skirts and blouses and coats. They were a great loss when they finally retired and closed.

[When I (*the author*) arrived in the village in the autumn of 1973 I can't recall who had the shop – I do know that very shortly after, certainly by 1976, John and Madge Bingham had arrived. My very clear memory is that they had a great many cats and dogs as pets and were selling rabbits, hamsters and guinea pigs as well as haberdashery, clothing and some fresh fruit and vegetables. On entering the shop during this period there was an all-pervading odour of animal – I certainly bought three gorgeous Peruvian guinea pigs, Chuckletummy, Clothears and Cuddlypuff, but could never have faced buying anything edible or to wear!]

The Wheelers bought the house and shop and sold fruit and vegetables and a few groceries and pet foods. Eventually it became just a pet shop until it too was closed for good, and yet another shop became a dwelling.

The Butcher

Mr Bell had a small butcher's shop between 118 High Street and what is the entrance to The Grove in 2005. In the early 1920s he moved down to one of the huts in what is now known as Tina's Yard; in the early 1930s he bought 82 High Street and built a shop front.

On the right-hand side of the High Street at the end of the playing-fields and tennis-courts there was a butcher's shop in one of the wartime huts. Howard Frank Bell had moved down from 117 High Street next to the old telephone exchange. He was followed by Laurie Pike. The building was later pulled down and the Otterwells took over the butchers with a shop on the opposite side of the High Street next to The Manse.

Later, after they closed, the small building became Wilkie's Fish and Chips and very popular they were – if a bit smelly! Wilkie's closed and the building is now a dwelling-house known as Whitcleave.

The Telephone Exchange

The first exchange was in the front room of 81 High Street, managed by Bell the butcher until just before the Second World War, when Herbert Smith took over until the automatic exchange was built. The small building remains as Wren Cottage.

The Grocers

In what today is called Tina's car park or Yard there was another of the wartime huts in which Robert

Ravenhill Cottage, the site of Lloyds Bank during the Second World War. (PHOTO BRIAN MARSHALL)

Stokes had his grocer's shop. Robert Stokes did well and expanded to open a much larger shop in Salisbury – the shop ran from Silver Street to the Canal (Boots the Chemist in 2005). It became the biggest and best grocer, baker and off licence in the area. When Stoke's opened a Salisbury shop the Doughtys helped them move from Tina's Yard to the Milk Bar.

The Banks

There used to be small branches of two banks in the village – the Midland Bank was in a room in 'The Manse' and Lloyds was in Paul Cole's old house (16 High Street). Bert Doughty remembers as a boy, in about 1926, being given two bags of money by his mother to take down to Lloyds Bank – one was the takings from Doughty's the builders and the other from the Langford Bakery van which delivered around the area.

The Baker

Norris the baker had his shop in the now empty premises on the corner of Tina's Yard and the High Street, with his bakery to the rear. His was the first steam bakery in the district. Norris closed in the late 1940s, after which villagers relied on Bryant's of Bapton, who also baked their own bread and delivered around the district.

[In 1973 the small shop on the corner of the High Street was a grocery store owned by Norman Green – his daughter Tina Alder had a hardware store behind. Later Mr Green moved his store to larger premises and when he retired Dan and Jill Fishlock took over – *author*.]

Sometime after Norris closed the shop became 'Tina's Antiques', while the present showroom was the Fishlock's grocery shop. They moved their shop down the High Street to what had been Chick's then Smith's Stores, until they too retired and the building reverted to a dwelling-house.

Mr Spiller on the steps to Norris's bakery, c.1930s or early '40s. The delivery van can be seen in the garage.

The Post Office

The Post Office was housed in what is today the garage of Home Close, previously called Shirley House, using one room in the main house, from early 1880 until just after the First World War in the early 1920s.

In 1880 Joseph Ford was listed as 'receiver at the post of money orders and savings bank.' Letters arrived from Warminster by mailcart at 6a.m. and from Bath at 4.50p.m., and were despatched by 1.30p.m. and 7.13p.m., on Sundays at 6.23p.m. In St Peter's 'here is a wall letter box cleared at 6pm weekdays and 9am Sundays.' This letterbox was in the wall of the vegetable garden opposite Overton House. When the traffic increased it became too dangerous to cross the road to post and collect letters as there was no pavement, and the box was moved across the road on to the wall of Overton House at the bottom of Rockworth path in 1970.

In 1889 Joseph Ford was still there and was listed as sub-postmaster. By then it was recorded that 'letters will arrive from Bath and Warminster by mail cart at 5.55am and be despatched to Bath and Warminster at 7.25pm, and on Sundays at 6.23pm.' Next came Stanley Parker who was followed by a succession of postmasters.

Home Close, the site of old the Post Office. (PHOTO BRIAN MARSHALL)

Mary Goodenough, Barbara and Dulcie Norris with an unidentified boy at the eel house by the ford, c.1930s.

Soon after the First World War the Post Office was moved across the road to 73–74, where it remained together with a very useful small shop selling sweets, soft drinks, writing paper, toys, cleaning materials and garden seeds. When the Post Office finally closed in 2000 it was turned into a dwelling-house, although the shop front remains, together with the name Old Post Office.

A new Post Office was opened in New Road Service Station behind the shop, and two pillar-boxes were erected, one outside the shop and another in Tina's Yard next to the village notice board, and the small letterbox was removed from Overton House wall.

Cobblers and Shoe Shop

There were a number of small businesses on the right-hand side of this end of the High Street. In 1880 in St Mary's there was listed William Davis, a bootmaker, but Joseph Sims was succeeded by Albert Sims, probably his son. In 1920 there was only Mills & Son 'boot dealers'; they were succeeded by the Snelgrove's who had an excellent small shop selling boots, shoes, Wellington boots, shoe laces and polishes. Snelgrove was a very good and useful cobbler who repaired boots and shoes, and gave them a beautiful polish at the same time, often delivering them back to the owner personally!

Mr Snelgrove died first and Mrs Snelgrove continued with the shop but there was no longer a cobbler in the village. When she died the business closed and the house was sold for a dwelling, although the shop front is still there in 2005.

The early-twentieth-century Post Office workers in Codford. Of the back two men, one is possibly Mr Griffiths. Left to right, in the front: Fred Sparey, Reg Cox, R. Ford, Mr Parker the postmaster, George Sparey, Harry Dawes, Bert Simper, William Conduit. There were several Sparey families in Codford at this time – George and Fred were not related as far as is known. George Sparey was killed in action during the First World War whilst fighting with the 1st Battalion Wiltshire Regiment, probably at Neuve Chapelle in October 1914. Fred Sparey died of malaria when with the 2/4th Wiltshire Regiment in India. His twin sister Alice began working as a temporary postwoman when he went to war, walking as far as Imber, 13 1/2 miles away, to deliver the post. She retired in 1959.

The Lodge, once the gatehouse to Stockton estate, prior to 1989, when the bypass construction began.

Soldiers and horses outside Simper's shop in 1917. The yard is now the site of 67a High Street and Westwood.

Simper's shop and the High Houses, which were possibly originally called Victoria Cottages.

Mr and Mrs Payne (he was the local colporteur – book-seller) next door to Simper's Store in the High Street, c.1912–18.

Middle Farm House. (PHOTO BRIAN MARSHALL)

Cycle Dealer

In 1899 George Simper was listed as a blacksmith and Francis Doughty as a builder. By 1920 they were listed as Doughty & Simper 'Cycle Dealers'. Simper continued as a cycle shop and repairer until well into the 1950s–60s, although he is not listed; Doughty was still the builder.

Clock Mender

Stan Simper was an excellent clock and watch mender, with his shop on the right-hand side beyond Garrett's yard. Eileen Simper married Jim Davis the timber merchant.

The Doughtys: Builders

In 1826 when Revd Thomas Davis was rector of Sherrington (see *Sherrington – a Wiltshire Village* by Rosamund Willoughby for more information) repairs and rebuilding took place at the Rectory and Samuel Doughty did the work, so they were already local builders. In 1880 Joseph Ford the postmaster was also listed as 'Carpenter'. In 1920 there was W.R. Ford – the Fords have their yard behind Shirley House in what today is Garrett's yard.

In 1928 the building business was taken over completely by Albert Doughty, Bert's father, who was always called Albert and never Bert! Shirley House was empty at the time and the Doughty family moved in – Bert was then 12 years old. Bert and his brother Fred took over the business in 1947–48 and their mother remained in the house until her death.

Their yard was behind the house and their hut-cum-workshop was where the Garretts' house is in 2005; the house was sold to Ken Garrett and they lived there until they built their present house at 67A High Street.

The Hairdressers

The first hairdresser was Mr Bell who lived in the Milk Bar and worked in an extension to Shirley House on the site of the present garage. Later the hairdresser was Charlie Mines, who had the word 'Hairdresser' painted in red letters across the end wall; a sign saying 'shaving' still exists over one of the garage windows at the time of writing. When Mines retired a young hairdresser came up from Ringwood until the business closed, while Mines continued to live at number 82.

The Dairy

At 70 High Street there was a dairy from which milk was delivered throughout the district. Mervyn Ashman was the milkman, delivering from his electric milk float for many years until he retired. In 1920 Morley Green and William James Mizen were listed individually as 'Dairyman'. In 1954 it was owned by John A. Lush of Middle Farm who was a dairy and arable farmer. Charlie and Gwen Thorne ran the Chestnut Dairy, certainly through the years of the Second World War.

Wylye Valley farmer Arthur Lush, not the same family as Lush of Middle Farm, who later moved to Butler's Combe in Crockerton, either took over Sparey's dairy or set up his own. He was followed by Green who came from 'away', possibly from London. Villagers were very glad to have a dairy in 1967 when the whole country was snowed in and they were cut off from the rest of the world!

A Mr Harris bought the dairy from Arthur Lush – he in turn sold it to Stanley and Audrey Grey who moved from Norfolk in 1963 with their daughter Rita. Mrs Grey taught at Codford School for many years. When the Greys retired their son-in-law, Charlie Woollard, took on the business for a time. In 1972 the dairy was bought by the Curries, originally Gordon and Marianne and his parents.

The Currie's four children – Sarah, Christopher, Laura and Charlotte – were all born before they moved out of the village, in around 1983–84. Gordon was active in local politics as a parish and a district councillor. They sold up when King Street Dairy of Warminster bought the business. The house was sold separately and the present large kitchen is on the site

Mr Chick (of Chick's Stores), Miss V. Evans, Mr Bosworth (remembered on the Victory Bell) and Miss May Conduit in 1937.

Middle Farm House, on the right. The man on the bike is outside Stacey's Newsagents and stationery shop.

of the covered yard and cold room. For many years until he retired Bob Carter continued to be the local milkman. In 2005 the milk round is much smaller – instead of doorstep deliveries most people buy from the shop at New Road Service Station.

Sydney Ingram – Saddler

In 60 High Street, below the Post Office, with his workshop in the garden behind his house, there was a 'saddler and harness maker' – listed in 1920 as 'Sydney Ingram Saddler of Codford St Mary'. Like Robert Stokes he prospered and moved to Salisbury where his shop remains at the time of writing – the long narrow shop on the corner of Catherine Street and the Old George Mall continues to sell high-quality leather goods, luggage, handbags, dog accessories, curry-combs and horse blankets. They are one of the few remaining private businesses left in the city.

Chick's Stores, Chicks Seed Warehouse, Seed Merchant

In the rather imposing building of 62 High Street, most recently Codford Stores, was Chick's Stores, owned by Ernest Edward Chick who was listed in 1920 as 'Shopkeeper and assistant overseer'. Later the shop became Smith's Stores when it was taken

over by Doughty's aunt May Smith and her husband. When Mrs Smith retired the house reverted to a private dwelling until the Fishlocks moved their business down from Tina's Yard.

Newsagent

In 1920 Charles H. Stacey was listed as 'shopkeeper'. He lived in 56 High Street, in what is called Wellin Cottage in 2005 and was a newsagent and stationer. He also sold soft drinks from a shop front built out from the house to the pavement.

The Milk Bar

The Stokes moved their small shop with Doughty's help from Tina's Yard to the corner of Chitterne Road and High Street. Eventually, Sparey's, the farmers who had a milk round, took it over and opened a Milk Bar with an Italian ex-prisoner of war named Carlo running it. The Spareys were then living next door in what today is Ravenhill Cottage.

The Milk Bar was very popular and prospered throughout the Second World War, and for some time afterwards; it was also named an official bus stop and listed in timetables. When the Milk Bar closed in about 1973 it was pulled down – Milk Bar Cottages were built on the site.

WI float in the parade to celebrate the 50th anniversary of VE Day, 1995. The ladies at the front of the float are, left to right: Kate Forbes, ?, Pat Meadows, Barbara Short, Caroline West, Sue Poolman. The driver is Alan Nash.

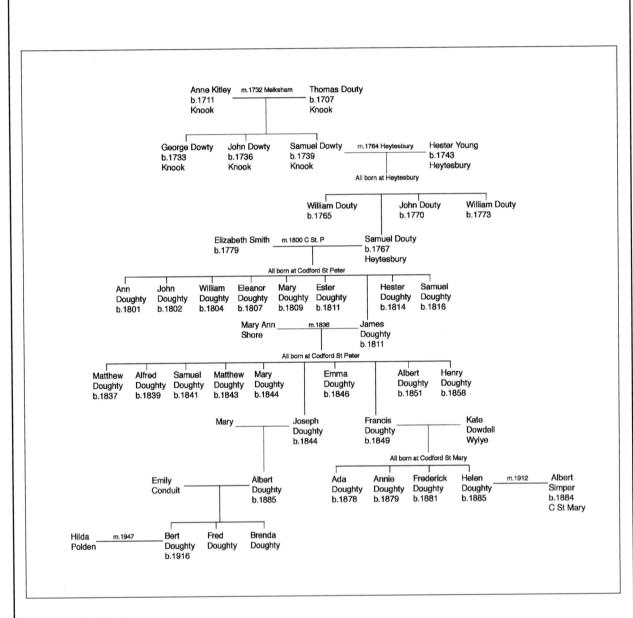

The Doughty family tree.

Chapter 12

The Twenty-First Century

The Village's Oldest Family

When Janet Hill (née Davis) took up her late mother's dream and began to trace her family history she little realised what an all-consuming passion it would become. It is thanks to her painstaking research and generosity in sharing her discoveries that so much information is now available on Codford's oldest family. A member of one of the remaining Davis families in the village, her brother Steve's children, Nicola and Christopher, are the seventh generation born in Codford. Related to other well-known local families, the Doughtys, Simpers and Spareys, the Davis pedigree can possibly be traced to Codford Everleys in the middle of the seventeenth century.

Francis Doughty (1849–1923) who married Kate Dowdell of Wylye, was born in Codford St Peter. He was the eighth of ten children of his father James Doughty, a 38-year-old mason also born in the village. Francis's grandfather, Samuel Douty, was a Heytesbury man whose parents and grandparents have been traced back to 1707 and the neighbouring communities of Knook and Heytesbury, situated less than 3 miles to the west of Codford.

In the 1881 census Francis was recorded as 'Master Mason employing 6 men'. His address at this time was Victoria Cottages, Codford St Peter – this entry was three properties away from the Post Office of the time. An educated guess, given the location and period of the houses known through most of the twentieth century as the High Houses, is that they were originally called Victoria Cottages.

Francis built the family home, Doughty House, now 66 and 67 High Street, in 1884, and moved in with his wife and three children, Ada, Annie and Frederick. The following year their youngest child Helen (Nell) was born.

Some of the other properties Francis built in the village were 67a, 67b, and the rank of red-brick houses and Post Office (prior to 2000) on the opposite side of the road. He is also believed to have built the clock tower on St Mary's School.

Kate Doughty died in 1928 and is buried with her husband in St Mary's churchyard.

Their daughter Helen (1885–1971) was born in Doughty House. She was a keen chorister and sang in local choirs including the Common Close Congregational Choir in Warminster. Helen was an apprentice seamstress in Warminster before her marriage in 1912 to Albert Simper of Riverside

Cottages, Codford St Mary; it was at this time that Doughty House was extended and divided into two properties, 66 and 67, to make a home for the newlyweds. Helen lived at number 67 for her whole life, from her birth until she died at the age of 86. Both she and Albert are buried in St Mary's churchyard.

George Simper (1851–1931) was born at Great Wishford, as was his father Edmund, who came from several generations of Simpers from Grovely Woods, situated between the Wylye and the Nadder Valleys on the Wilton estate. Edmund's great-great-great grandfather, William Simper, was born in Grovelly Woods in 1689. George was lodging in Salisbury at the time of the 1881 census and his occupation was recorded as a blacksmith. It was during this period that he met his future wife, a Winterslow girl, Eliza Shears. They were married in Salisbury in 1883 – he was 32 and Eliza was 21. The couple moved to Wylye for a short while before moving into Riverside Cottages, Codford St Mary, where they raised five children, spending the rest of their lives in the cottages close to the River Wylye and the Codford bridges. They too are buried in St Mary's churchyard.

Albert Simper (1884–1963) was the eldest of George and Eliza's five children. His brother Arthur was killed in Flanders in 1916 and his sister Ethel became a schoolmistress in Codford. Albert married Helen Doughty in 1912 and they had three daughters, Joan, Clare and Eileen. He worked with his father-in-law, Francis Doughty, in the building business and later had a cycle shop which was situated on the site where 67c The Cottage now stands.

Henry Savage and Sarah Anne Davis were both born into Codford families. Henry's mother was a Sparey and Sarah Anne's mother was Jane Everley, born in Codford St Peter in 1809. The couple married at Codford St Peter Church in 1856, with their first child John Savage Davis being born a few months earlier that year. The family moved to Stockton in the mid-1860s. Henry's brother William Savage was a baker and general shopkeeper at the bottom of Chitterne Road in Codford St Mary. The shop stood on the site of what today is Forde House behind the Milk Bar – it was destroyed by fire in the early 1900s.

John Savage-Davis (1856–1943) was listed as a 'bootmaker journeyman' in the 1881 census. He was living with his grandmother Jane Davis and his uncle William Davis. In June 1881 he married Keturah Cowdry of Heytesbury in the Independent Chapel at Codford. John bought The Bury at Codford and farmed there, also running wagonettes for the local

Above: *The Doughty family, with Francis, Kate, Ada and Annie behind, and Helen (Nell) and Frederick in the front, 1894.*

Right: *Herbert, Malcolm, Alice, Jim, Ron and Jack Davis, 1932/33.*

Below: *Helen (Nell) Doughty outside Doughty House next door to the Post Office, with a baby carriage outside, 1890.*

Nell Doughty, in a white blouse, on the ford bridge in 1900. The cottage behind is where she lived at Riverside.

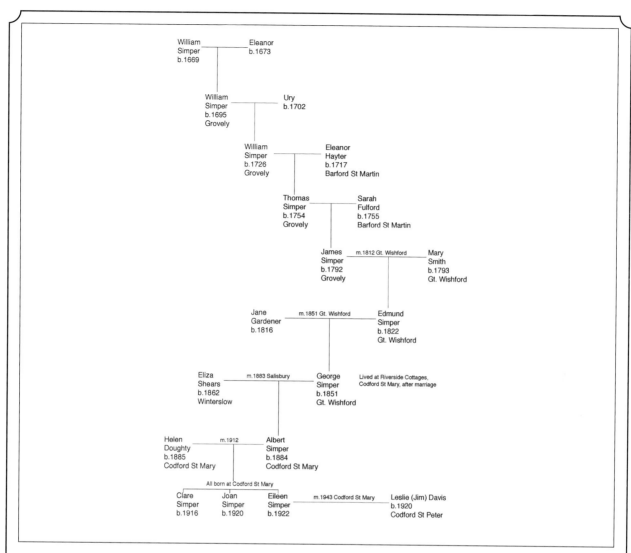

The Simper family tree.

George and Eliza Simper with their children Albert (in sailor's suit), Edward ('Ted') (sitting next to his father) and Stanley (on his mother's lap), c.1894.

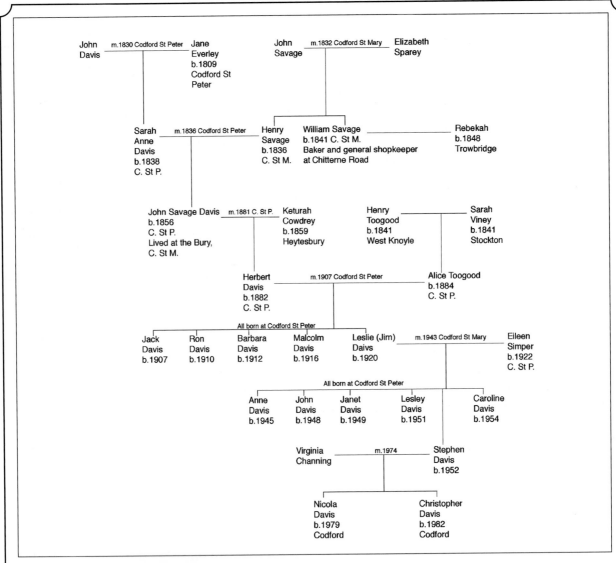

The Davis family tree.

Arthur Simper aged 18, just before he went to the Western Front where he was killed in 1914.

Malcolm Davis DFC in his RAF uniform during the Second World War.

The marriage of Jim Davis and Eileen Simper, with bridesmaid Joan Simper, 1943.

gentry. He sold up in around 1935 and moved to Croydon, London with his wife and youngest son Walter, returning to Codford after Keturah's death to live with his eldest son Herbert in Manor Cottage (next to the Woolstore). He lived there until his death during the Second World War. Both John and Keturah are buried in St Mary's churchyard.

Janet's grandparents, Herbert Davis (1882–1955) and Alice Toogood (1884–1951), were born and lived in Codford their whole lives; they were married in 1907 at Codford St Peter. Before moving to Manor Cottage they lived at Windwhistle Farm, which was behind the old council-houses in New Road. They had four sons, Jack, Ron, Malcolm (Malc) and Leslie (Jim), as well as a daughter Barbara, who died in infancy.

In 1917 Herbert was an Army driver in Russia for a Colonel Rollinson, and had to make a quick retreat because of the Russian Revolution. In 1918 and 1919 he worked in Canada for Gillards, a haulage company, before returning home to Codford to set up a wood business in Green Lane, Codford St Peter. Herbert and Alice, as well as her parents Henry and Sarah Toogood, are buried in St Peter's churchyard.

The Davis brothers were all born at Codford St Peter and all joined the RAF during the Second World War. Jack had joined the Metropolitan Police in 1934

and signed up with the RAF in 1942. He was a WO flight engineer, flying Liberators for up to 14 hours at a time over the North Atlantic on anti-submarine patrols. After the war he lived for a time in West Bromwich, returning to Wiltshire in about 1961. He was the landlord of the New Inn (now the Dove Inn) at Corton, moving to the Fox and Hounds in Warminster in 1966.

Ron was unable to fly because of a perforated eardrum, so he served as a flight mechanic based at Old Sarum and Larkhill. After the war he farmed at Ashton Gifford Farm for a time then moved to Bore Hill Farm, Crockerton, just outside Warminster.

Malc was awarded the DFC and various campaign medals – he was in 578 Squadron operating out of Burn near Selby in Yorkshire, flying Halifax bombers and completing 40 bombing missions. After his tour of ops he was posted to Old Sarum where he flew a De Haviland Rapide, transporting high-ranking officers and VIPs. He died from a brain haemorrhage in 1954 while staying in Codford at the George Inn. Malc is buried in Codford St Peter's churchyard.

Jim learned to fly with his brother Ron before the war at the Civil Air Guard at High Post near Salisbury. During the war he was stationed at locations around the country but mostly at Heaton Park near Manchester. He married Eileen Simper in 1943 and

The cast of The Mikado *at the Little Theatre in Codford (now the site of New Road Service Station), c.1927. Jim Davis is second from the left in the front row, and Kathleen Whatley (née Phelps) is first on the left in the back row.*

Dick Whittington at the Woolstore, with Angus Bramwell (Lazy Jack) and David North (King Rat). (PHOTO BRIAN MARSHALL)

Teechers youth production at the Woolstore Theatre in 2004. Left to right: Jess McCarthy, Harriet Green, Martha Fishwick, Michael Sides. (PHOTO BRIAN MARSHALL)

Wool sorting in the Woolstore during the late-eighteenth or early-nineteenth century. It is possible the bearded gentleman on the far left could be Giles Conduit.

Right: *Giles and Sarah Conduit outside 15 Codford.*

left the RAF in 1946, when he returned to Codford and went into the wood business with his father Herbert. In 2004 the wheel has turned full circle – Jim Davis remains living in the village with his son Steve, whose children are the latest Codford-born generation.

Few of us today are able to have this sense of continuity, to feel that our ancestral roots are deeply planted in the place where we live! To be able to trace ancestors in the same area back to 1669, and to know that the family link stretches back still further, means that it is possible that the lineage could go back to the time of the Saxons when the settlement was named – perhaps further still to the early farmers and the Bronze Age tribes.

The Woolstore

The only village theatre in the country owned by its own company, the Woolstore Theatre is at the heart of the Codford community; refurbished in recent years it is a centre for cultural excellence offering a wide variety of entertainment supported by people from the Wylye Valley and beyond. However, this is only part of the story of an industrial building that has been integral to Codford since its beginnings.

The importance of wool in the area stretched back through medieval, Norman and Saxon times to the Bronze Age tribes of the Plain. In 1379 Codford was the centre of an emerging specialised cloth-making area. Poll Tax Records show that in a 4-mile stretch of the Wylye Valley there appear to have been nine fullers and six weavers. According to *The Victorian County History,* Codford had two fullers, as did Boyton and Heytesbury, while Knook, Corton, and Upton each had one.

The Woolstore was built in around 1764, in the village of Codford St Peter at the bottom of the hill east of the church. It was originally used to store fleeces for holding and grading before they were sent to mills up and down the Wylye Valley to be washed, carded and eventually spun. Wool was a very important commodity; the fleeces were brought in by cart, remaining in the open courtyard until they could be dealt with; obviously if it was raining the fleeces became sodden and very heavy. In around 1834 the owner of the building decided to build an extension at the end of the building and cover it to enable the carts to unload in the dry. The Woolstore Theatre occupies this part of the building and the runners of the huge doors can still be seen in the theatre today.

The 1851 census recorded that Codford had three wool sorters, eight woolstaplers and one wool stapler's

129

Jon Nash played the lead in Teechers *in 2004. (PHOTO BRIAN MARSHALL)*

The back of Woolstore, 2004.

Left: *Production of* Dick Whittington *at the Woolstore Theatre in 2004. Left to right, front: ?, Mo Bell (Dick's cat), Matthew Mitchell (Dick), Jenny Begley (Alice), Derek Miles (Alderman FitzWarren), Robin Scard (the Dame). (PHOTO BRIAN MARSHALL)*

Below: *Wool sacks outside the Woolstore in the late-eighteenth or early-nineteenth century.*

Youth Dramatic Festival, 1 May 1946, One Morning Very Early. Left to right: *Dulcie Norris, Dianna Bartrum, Barbara Norris, Beryl Axtell and Sally Thergood.*

An interior door at the Woolstore.

The hoist window at the Woolstore.

wife. The woollen industry went into decline and the three-storied, seven-bayed building of Bath Stone and brick, with its hipped roof and arched ground-floor windows, began to be used for other purposes, including storage. During the First World War the extension was the Albany Ward's Empire Cinema, a picture palace with seating for 500. With thousands of troops in the vicinity – British, Australian and New Zealanders – the cinema was regularly packed to capacity. After the First World War this part of the Woolstore was used as a village hall, for entertainments such as dances, concerts and whist drives.

Bert Doughty was born in 1916. He lived at Riverside with his parents and remembers the Woolstore as a child. His maternal grandfather, Giles Conduit, was the foreman wool sorter. As a small boy he would be taken into the main building of the Woolstore and lifted into the tall wool baskets to tread the wool down. At one time, in the late 1920s, there were about two dozen workers in the building. When Giles eventually retired he worked as a gardener in the big house behind the Woolstore building.

In 1926 the theatre evolved from the main building with the arrival of Colonel Sneyd and his new young wife, more than 40 years his junior. They bought the large elegant house behind the Woolstore and renamed it Bradwell Grange; today this is the Wool House. Mrs Sneyd was an amateur actress and enamoured of all things theatrical, so her doting husband turned the annex into a theatre. Ron Lush of Middle Farm, and two Bradwell Grange employees, Jack Jeffries the chauffeur and gardener Bert Ford, built the stage. Mrs Sneyd and her friends performed all manner of plays for their own amusement, later giving performances for the wider community. The Sneyds eventually allowed the villagers, who had formed their own group, the Codford Amateurs, to use the theatre for their productions.

On 16 January 1931 an article in the *Warminster Journal* recorded 'The Woolstore's Debut':

Although bearing the name of the 'Wool Stores' the large building at Codford formerly used for the stapling of wool has been transformed by Colonel Sneyd into a very fine theatre.

Illuminated with electric light, and well heated, the residents of Codford are fortunate that there is such a commodious and well-equipped building.

Last evening the Codford Amateurs made their debut in the 'Wool Stores' theatre, and those responsible for promoting the production, which was in aid of Codford St Mary Church heating apparatus, had every reason to be gratified by the large attendance.

The programme opened with a sketch, 'The Strutham Amateurs,' and the scene was the Ladies dressing room, Strutham Town Hall. It was a delightful little sketch, which afforded the characters ample scope to entertain the audience. Mr J. Houghton Brown was a popular success, and Miss Parsons and Mrs Meyrick added the tinge of

humour necessary to make the sketch bright, while Mrs Sneyd, as the leading lady, proved a talented performer.

The audience was delighted by the ballet dances by Miss Gundred Charles, and she was encored.

Lieut. Col. and Mrs Lee gave a sketch, 'The Burglar and the Girl' in a manner that held the audience spellbound. It was a drawing room scene (2am) and the battle of wits in conjunction with revolver threats completely baffled the audience until the lady was conquered.

Mr Harry Cole was in great form as an entertainer. He combined funny stories, 'imitations with limitations' and concluded with the old favourite 'A Yard of Lace.' Mr Cole was recalled and again received applause for his efforts as a laughter maker.

The final item was a farce, 'The Bathroom Door,' and so well was it presented that the audience literally rocked with laughter. The scene was 'A Hotel Corridor,' and the characters: The Young Man, Mr F. Lewis; The Young Lady, Miss Houghton Brown; The Elderly Gentleman, Rev. C. H. Meyrick; The Elderly Lady, Mrs Bridson; The Prima Donna, Mrs Sneyd; The Boots, Mr. C. Houghton Brown.

The advent of the Second World War meant another change in the fortunes of the Woolstore. The 260th Field Company Royal Engineers (43rd Wessex Division) were the first troops to arrive in the village since the First World War. The theatre was used as a mess hall with the cookhouse behind in a corrugated-tin hut.

In 1943, when the 3rd Armored Division arrived in Codford, the main Woolstore building became a billet and a mess hall; there was a USO Club canteen and recreational area, and it also housed the American Red Cross. There are many features still in evidence early in 2004, including the huge cooking stoves (*see page 83*), a scenic mural painted on the wall (*see page 88*), the stage (*see page 86*) and sprung dance floor where the GIs be-bopped with girls bussed in for an evening's entertainment, one of the wood-burning heating stoves, the door of the men's room (*see page 84*) and a fire escape sign (apparently though a third story window without a fire escape) (*see page 135*).

In 1948, on 5 December, the Woolstore Country Theatre Club was formed. This was a separate entity from the Codford Amateurs, although some members of the latter joined both clubs. When Colonel Sneyd died at the end of 1949 Major Briggs became the new owner of the Woolstore building. He allowed the theatrical productions to continue until 1955. Major Briggs indicated his willingness to sell the Woolstore to the Amateurs, but unfortunately they were unable to raise the money. However, in 1957 the chairman of the Codford Amateurs, Harry Cole, bought the theatre for £325, and both local drama groups were able to continue using the facilities. The theatre could accommodate 110 people and at this time the price of a seat was 5s.

Above: *The new seating in the Woolstore Theatre, with lighting box at the back, c.2003.* (PHOTO ANTONY BARRINGTON-BROWN)

Right: *The fire exit in the Woolstore.*

Work to refurbish the auditorium of the Woolstore Theatre, c.2000. Pictured are: young Frank West, Michael Found and an unknown colleague. (PHOTO ANTONY BARRINGTON-BROWN)

Above: *The Woolstore production of* Mansfield Park. *The cast from the left are:* Kat Williams, Carl Fear, Cathy Byers, David North, Marilyn Latcham, Derek Miles (Squire Bertram), Sarah Williams (Fanny Price), Angus Bramwell, Maureen Marshall (Lady Bertram), Mike Walker *and* Mary Jones. (PHOTO ANTONY BARRINGTON-BROWN)

Left: *The bar and coffee bar area with the gallery leading to the store room above, c.2003.* (PHOTO ANTONY BARRINGTON-BROWN)

The core construction workers at the Woolstore Theatre, 2001–02. Left to right: Michael Found, 'the Gaffer' (project manager) Antony Barrington-Brown, young Frank West, Robin and Felicity Scard, Charlie Woollard. (PHOTO ANTONY BARRINGTON-BROWN)

Usher's Brewery was very keen to provide extra parking for the George Inn opposite and saw the footstep of the large Woolstore building as the perfect solution to their car-parking problem. The company wanted to buy it and tear it down! With this in mind, about seven years after Harry Cole bought the Woolstore, the brewery made an opening offer of more than £1,000 – no doubt being prepared to increase the price during negotiations. Harry Cole would have none of it and generously offered to sell the theatre to the Woolstore Theatre Club, who were eligible for grant funding, for just £100 more than he had paid for it – £425. In October 1964 the Codford Amateurs were disbanded, merging with the Woolstore Theatre Club, and the foundation for the successful local theatre was laid.

At the time of writing there are plans to renovate a building, which has become dilapidated over the years. The annex, owned by the Woolstore Theatre, has had a facelift, and there are plans to adapt the privately-owned main building into maisonettes.

So, in 240 years the Woolstore has evolved – it has provided work for the local people, sheltered and housed troops in two world wars, has been a centre of entertainment in one way or another for almost 90 years, and will provide accommodation and access to the arts in the early-twenty-first century.

Codford's Ghosts

According to local tradition it is widely reputed that the tangible spirit of one of the Australian soldiers who came to Codford between 1916–19 can be felt in the Woolstore Theatre to this day. While the ANZAC troops were in the village they certainly left their mark in the consciousness of the locals – one story is of a prostitute who gave some Australian soldiers the pox – it is said that she was murdered and thrown down one of the wells on Manor Farm. Another tale is that when the village cobbler upset one of the 'diggers' he returned in the evening with his mates to burn down the shop. The gang blocked the road so the fire appliance was unable to attend to the fire. A third orally reported incident is that a group took one of their own to nearby Stockton Park and hung him from a tree!

One evening three of the 'diggers', somewhat the worse for wear after a visit to one of the drinking establishments, decided to enter the Woolstore Theatre from the back. One apparently changed his mind and returned to barracks while the other two climbed a ladder and crept underneath the stage to listen to the film. One of the soldiers got bored and left the way he had come; the second, lulled to sleep by the darkness and no doubt the drink, woke to a deserted building after the film had finished and the audience had left. He felt his way through the pitch-black theatre until he reached the heavy sliding door and pushed it open – as he did so he slipped and fell.

The door was fitted with a counterweight, so it slid along the wall with a relentless inevitability. The soldier died as the door closed on his neck.

In 2005, to the right-hand side of the back of the stage, to the left of the pipe, it is always bitterly cold. In the 1930s it was necessary to turn the lights off using the master switch by the stage and cross the darkened auditorium – the last person out would usually ensure they were not alone, and some would carry heavy flashlights and talk loudly to keep their courage up. Various children have complained of the icy chill that sends shivers down the spine in this part of the theatre. In the 1970s an actress saw a man standing at the back of the stage in the shadows, yet there was no one to be found.

A less well-reported ghost can be found in the Woolstore building next to the theatre. Someone in the building reported having seen a man with a clay pipe wearing light leathery plus fours coming down the stairs from the upper floors. This figure is supposedly a man who may have either been drowned having fallen into a barrel of wet, greasy fleeces or been killed when the barrel overturned.

Across the road from the Woolstore is one of the village's oldest buildings, Old Manor Cottage. The building was derelict certainly through the twentieth century until after Second World War. It had a cellar with an underground passage that connected it to the next cottage up the lane by the George Inn. Maurice Cole recalls that there was a strong scent of violets in the cottage and that the village children called it the 'haunted house'.

Sometime in the 1950s the cottage was bought and restored using traditional building materials by Mauri Burford and her husband, who was the Diocesan architect. Mauri, who used to produce for the Codford Amateurs, was very psychic – she could feel a presence in the Woolstore and would never stay in the building on her own. Godfrey Cole, who was the last chairman of the Codford Amateurs, remembers that he would often go to the Old Manor Cottage to talk about the productions and that one day Mauri told him the following story. She was sitting in the downstairs front room writing at a table when she became aware that she was not alone. She looked up slowly and saw an old lady in period clothes sitting in a rocking chair beside the large inglenook fireplace. Mauri watched the old lady as she continued to rock backwards and forwards, her serene countenance never registering any recognition that Mauri was in the room. Mauri looked away for a few minutes and when she raised her head again the old lady and her rocking chair were nowhere to be seen.

The Cole family lived at Mayflower Farm, bought by Harry Cole after he sold a prize Wessex Saddleback gilt, Codford Mayflower, for a record 365 guineas after she won the Royal Bath and West Show in 1922. It was not until 1952 that this record price for gilt was bettered. The building was a First World War hut with a concrete veranda, and was used as a guard room for No. 15 camp. Harry and Lillian Cole were very friendly with the Gregorys who ran a taxi service and had the grocer's shop at the top of the hill by St Peter's Church. One winter's evening the Coles were playing cards with Mrs Gregory while her husband Harry was working when they heard footsteps on the veranda, walking up and down. They thought Harry had dropped his fare off and was coming to join them – however, he did not appear and there was no sign of anyone else. Harry and Lillian sometimes speculated that the footsteps could have been from a soldier of the First World War who died in the guard room.

The best-recorded ghost has been seen by various people in the area behind St Peter's Church along Green Lane. Christine Bailey had been told about the cowled monk-like figure by a woman she knew, who had seen the figure on the site of the present Bury Mead, but had never taken the sighting seriously. In 1957 Christine was returning from work on a dark, cold winter's evening, and as she reached the corner of Green Lane by the old piggery she saw an apparition. The figure wore a black cape and hood and she both saw and felt it touch her leg! In her own words she 'ran like hell'!

The second eyewitness to the ghostly monk was equally credible. Around 1984 Christine's son Scott was a 17-year-old on a youth training scheme. He left home at 7a.m. on a snowy winter's morning to meet Maggie Taylor, so they could travel in to town together. As he turned the corner at Rockworth, behind St Peter's vicarage, from about 20–30 yards away he saw a figure approaching. Scott moved to the left of Green Lane to allow the figure to pass. As he looked up in the dim light he saw that the figure was wearing a cloak, he did not note the colour, with a hood over the face. Scott said:

I stopped, and it stopped – I looked at it and saw there were no footprints in the snow; the figure was hovering above the ground and it had no feet! It glided towards me – I turned and ran down the lane by the George. I then walked up to The Grove and told Maggie, she didn't believe me. We went back to Rockworth together and there was only my footprints in the snow.

Neither Christine nor Scott is prone to exaggeration, nor do they make a habit of talking about their sightings, but if asked they are completely matter of fact and certain about what they saw. Maggie Taylor told me that she also saw the apparition in the same area some time later. She also believes there are others in the village who have seen the ghostly monk in the gloom as he glides across the glebe land around St Peter's Church.

By The Road Divided
The Codford Bypass

Until 1990 the main A36 trunk route from the south coast port of Southampton to Bristol and into Wales ran through the village along the route of the High Street. Codford was a village divided, with HGVs, local, military, agricultural and holiday traffic in a seemingly never-ending stream of vehicles. From the 1950s there had been talk of the need for a bypass – in December 1978 the scheme was entered into the roads programme.

Initial plans had been for the road to go to the north of the village, but by the time of the public consultation in June 1983 the proposed route was a single-carriageway road to the south of the village. In April 1985 the preferred route put forward by the Department of Transport had been modified to include a slight shift further south of the playing and recreation field, and the scheme had been extended at either end to include Malmpit Hill and the bend by the White Horse Trekking Centre, both notorious accident black spots.

In September 1986 the draft orders were published and in June 1987 there was a lively three-week public inquiry in the Codford Club. The decision to build the road was made public in February 1988, the River Wylye was realigned slightly, the stone bridge at Giggan Street was raised and construction began in April 1989.

The road was ahead of schedule when, in April 1990, the original contractors, Rush & Tomkins, went into receivership. In May 1990 a new contractor, HT Construction, was appointed to complete the outstanding work by August 1990, within the original contract period. In fact the 1.7-mile bypass, costing £2.1m excluding VAT, was opened by Parish Council chairman Major Euan Hutchings on 31 July 1990.

The environmental and social advantages of taking the main road from the village was felt immediately – children could walk alone on the pavement or ride their bicycles in the High Street, villagers were

The former gatehouse to the Stockton estate.

The first sod of the Codford bypass cut at Ashton Giffard, April 1989.

able to stop and pass the time of day without the fear of being drenched by a passing car or sucked towards the wheels of a juggernaut, and the ever-present noise and fumes were removed from the community. In the summer, to celebrate the freedom from traffic, there was a grand parade (including a tank!), followed by a street party for the whole village. It was the first time for decades that the High Street was deliberately closed to traffic.

It'll Be All Right On The Night –
Behind the Scenes at the
Community Play

It seemed like a good idea at the time – in 1996 Theatre In The Downs, a professional company from Chippenham, approached the village to ask if it would be the venue for one of six plays in the summer of 1997. I had been approached because I wrote village articles and liaised with the media, and Karen Johnstone was contacted because she was the chairman of the Woolstore Theatre; we were both parish councillors. It all sounded so simple – a small cast of professional actors with backing from the Woolstore Theatre Company and any other locals who would like to take part. The action of the play was to take place during a village walk in 1914 as war was declared, and real characters from the village would be written into the script.

Act One, Scene One: The Woolstore Theatre
in September

A village meeting was held and representatives from all the village organisations, as well as interested locals, came along to decide whether Codford should host a community play. The financial question was raised several times and representatives from Theatre In The Downs assured the meeting that this would not involve the village in any financial way, and the costumes were to be provided.

Act One, Scene Two: Inside the Woolstore
Theatre, nine months later.

The first run through of the play – prior to this there were preliminary meetings. Characters from the period were researched, the school was approached and venues agreed. In the intervening months Codford learned that it had to raise £2,500 towards the estimated £5,000 of the cost of the play, as well as provide most of its own costumes.

A village soup kitchen (a choice of soups, ploughman's and desserts) had been organised, projected ticket sales, grants from Rural Action For Wiltshire and the Small Grants Fund, plus a grant from the Walking Initiative to Theatre In The Downs on Codford's behalf had covered the costs. As we had been told the latter grant was expected to be £500 per village, Karen and I took it that this was part of the Codford contribution and not to go to the Theatre In The Downs.

The research was done; actors Mark Hyde and Tim Laycock (also Musical Director), worked with the children of Codford and Steeple Langford Schools, the Evergreen Club and the Women's Section of the Royal British Legion, teaching them songs and dances. There were several meetings with the Woolstore Theatre Company to walk the route and plan the dialogue.

The first general rehearsal – the weather was appalling and the forecast for the week of 26, 27 and 28 June was dire. The local store had sold two tickets for the first night on Thursday and ten for Saturday. Half the children at Codford School had a tummy bug, and had not been told what their costumes were for the 'Moonrakers' scene; the pony and trap booked months ago was unavailable at two days' notice, and several of the stewards were unable to make it. Only two scenes had been rehearsed, and there was no time for the final integral scene in the Manor Garden.

Act Two, Scene One: The First Night

By now Karen and I felt as if we were on the deck of the *Titanic*, playing with the band as she sinks! We were acting as cheerleaders and telling everyone how wonderful it was going to be. Behind the scenes we lost one of our banner carriers and, with one day's notice, had to find a lock-up garage for the vintage car. We were unable to find a vintage trap and were rescued by the White Horse Trekking Centre, who was planning to have a cart for any of the audience who might not be able to walk too far.

There were only about ten in the audience, well wrapped up against the damp, chilly evening, so the cart was able to deposit the lady of the manor outside the George Inn. During the course of the Promenade Play the beehive collapsed so that the small children from Codford School had to perform in the open. The Grim Reaper puppet, total height 12 feet, also collapsed – the puppet was on a rucksack on the shoulders of the Woolstore's Mike Walker, who was

Above: *The route of the Codford bypass, at the start of construction in 1989.*

Left: *Diverting the River Wylye before construction of the Codford bypass, 1988–89.*

View of the new and old A36 routes. At the top on the left is the village playing-field with the old Codford Club next to the garage site, c.1990.

Major Euan Hutchings, chairman of Codford Parish Council, opening the Codford bypass, 31 July 1990. (Photo Kitchenham Ltd, Bournemouth)

Above: *The western entrance under construction at the top of Sherrington Lane, July 1989.* (PHOTO DAVID WILTSHIRE)

Right: *Bypass Street Party, 1990.* From the left, those around the first table in the foreground are: *?, ?, ?, Ruby Holloway, ?;* second table: *Cath Lock, Joan Dredge opposite Ray and Pauline Herbert, ?;* third table, back: *Jim Holmes, Kath Holmes, Norman and Edie Bennett, Vi Bundy, ?, Gemma, Cynthia and Graham Carter;* fourth table, back: *Dark-haired girl possibly Mary Tipping, sitting opposite her father Revd John Tipping (in dark glasses).* Photographer on the pavement with tripod (left) is Jim Hunter. (PHOTO DAVID WILTSHIRE)

The bypass under construction, early 1990, with the River Wylye in flood.

Above: *Bypass route south of Codford, across the meadows, June 1989.*

Right: *Building the 'Bund', Codford bypass, June 1990.*

Below: *The road takes shape, 1989.* (*PHOTOS DAVID WILTSHIRE*)

The A36 at Malmpit Hill as the clearing begins for the new bypass, c.1988. (PHOTOS DAVID WILTSHIRE)

Looking to the bridge across the Wylye as clearing continues from Malmpit Hill.

The Codford end of Sherrington Lane, June 1989.

Above: *Work on the new road bridge, July 1989.*

Left: *Working on the new road bridge on Codford bypass, 1989.* (Photos David Wiltshire)

The new road bridge for Codford bypass under construction.

Chitterne Brook flowing towards the Wylye under the new road bridge, April 1990.

Above: *The bridge over the Wylye as clearing begins, 1988–89.*

Right: *Damming the Chitterne Brook by the bypass bridge, 1990.*

Below left: *Work to raise and strengthen the bridge during construction of the bypass.*

Below right: *Construction vehicles by the listed bridge over the Wylye.* (PHOTOS DAVID WILTSHIRE)

Above left: *The Wylye in full spate at Codford Bridge, March 1990.*

Above right: *The Wylye flowing beneath the bridge with the new pillars in place, April 1990.*

Left: *The bridge being raised after the river was diverted, June 1990.*

Below: *The Wylye has been dammed to accommodate work on the bridge, May 1990.* (PHOTOS DAVID WILTSHIRE)

Above: *The bypass at Malmpit Hill shortly before the road opened, April 1990.* (PHOTO DAVID WILTSHIRE)

Left: *New A36 bridge over the Chitterne Brook, c.1994.* (PHOTO DAVID MASON)

Below left: *In the distance the old A36 (now blocked up) can be seen, with the new bypass in the foreground.* (PHOTO DAVID WILTSHIRE)

Below right: *The junction at the top of Sherrington Lane almost complete, June 1990. This is the old A36 Warminster end of the village.* (PHOTO DAVID WILTSHIRE)

Construction of the new bypass at Hillside. Work is taking place on the White Horse Trekking Centre land to take out the corner.

Traffic lights at Hillside, July 1989.

Right: Bypass Party, 1990. Mary Barnard (left) and Iris Conduit are in the back seat with driver, Jack Beaman, and passenger Rita Hunter. Gwen Thorne is standing in the background. (PHOTO DAVID WILTSHIRE)

The White Horse Trekking Centre show-jumping area.

over 6 feet and had to cope with his own height again above him as he negotiated the route.

Act Two, Scene Two: Friday Evening

The *Warminster Journal* photographer turned up, thus increasing the non-participating audience by 25 per cent. One of the players, determined to remain in character, asked two ladies from Bratton if they had walked over or come in their pony and trap – the response was a bemused silence; however, one of them did agree to carry one of the beribboned staffs.

Act Two, Scene Three: The Last Night in the Manor Garden

Everything was all right on the final night! The wet day had calmed to a mild, dry evening – more than 60 people came along to watch and everyone had a wonderful evening, entering a time capsule back to the last days of innocence, surrounded by the sights and sounds of a community unknowingly at the brink of war! The audience enjoyed the show and it was far beyond their expectations.

The cast were on a high – it had been a fun experience, watching the children's eager faces as they performed, taking part in a communal project that re-entered the village's past and focussed on one moment in the history of Codford while making another.

The churches had provided a venue for the second scene, two organists, a choir, the bell-ringers, and Revd Brian Thomas of Wylye played Canon Maclean. The Woman's Section of the RBL and Evergreen members had served the teas as Mrs Ashton's Glee Club and two rural primary schools had performed, singing, dancing and acting with vigour!

The Woolstore Theatre served as the nerve centre of the play and the Company had its ranks swelled by the participation of the audiences and people from nearby villages, who also joined in with the fun. The George Inn had hosted the cast and been taken over during the production – filled to overflowing after rehearsals and performances; John Torrie had allowed his garden to be invaded and the White Horse Trekking Centre had donated a pony, cart and driver.

The Bratton Brass Band provided the music together with the strolling players Sharon Lindo, Georgina Brown and Tim Laycock, who conceived the play. The Theatre In The Downs Company had interacted with local people throughout the production, blending professional and amateur contributions seamlessly. The play itself proved a success story for those involved in the performance, either as participants or onlookers.

Off Stage: Behind The Scenes

During the period between conception and acceptance and rehearsal it had become apparent that, while the actors were brilliant, the organisational and communication skills left much to be desired. Karen had attended an Arts Conference in Devizes where Dot Macree, Artistic Director of the Theatre In The Downs was speaking – she learned of a Lottery initiative, Arts 4 Everyone, and, on hearing for the first time the 'One World Band', resolved to apply on behalf of the Woolstore in order to bring the band to Codford.

The following day she received a phone call from their Financial Director asking her to apply for 'Arts Express' funding for the community play. She refused, explaining that if funding was available it would be for the Woolstore Theatre – it was at this point that for the first time there was any mention of Codford contributing £2,500 towards the expense of putting on the play.

At the suggestion of the Financial Director a meeting between village and Theatre In The Downs representatives was arranged in January; Jacky Nicholas of the Community Council for Wiltshire attended this. It was agreed that once 50 per cent of the total cost had been raised, any profits would remain in the village to be shared between local charities. The intention was that any monies would be divided between the Woolstore Theatre towards a new floor and the village hall for refurbishment of the upper room.

At this time a breakdown of the financial commitment was requested as there were six communities involved and certain expenses would be joint while other costs were specific to locations. Karen divided the proposed budget into six in order to apply for a Rural Action Grant.

By the time Tim Laycock was due to rehearse with the schools there was a new administer, Michael Taylor. On 13 May everyone was told to provide their own costumes. They were given information packs and advised to go round charity shops.

The schools were very unhappy; due to an administrative error the actors arrived at Steeple Langford School a week late. The original plan appears to have been that the local school in Codford, where the action of the play was set, would only perform their bee dance one night, while the smaller non-local school at Steeple Langford was doing two evenings; in the run up to the performance the 'Bees' still didn't know what they had to wear and the 'Moonrakers' received their costume details on 24 June, the day before the dress rehearsal!

Meanwhile, at the Woolstore things were not much better! The actors arrived and had not been briefed about pre-play discussions, and Karen was handed two pages of handwritten script to go around to 11 people. She had to type and photocopy them, two days before general rehearsal.

The cost of tickets was set at £4, which was considered too high for the small rural communities, so the villagers lowered the price. The programmes were set at 70p – after debate the Theatre In The Downs agreed to sell them at 50p, but on the first two

The Community Play, 1997. The group on the right are, from left to right: *Louise McDonald* (front, in white blouse and hat) *with Corrie and Kelsey, Annelies Puddy, 'J' Claypoole, Derek Miles* (in top hat).

Community Players outside the George Inn, 1997. Left to right: *Greg Puddy, Len ?, John Wyeth, Romy Wyeth, Ken Axtell, Alan Kells and Maurice Cole.*

Community Play outside the Woolstore, 1997. Left to right: *Annelies Puddy, Kelsey, Louise and Corrie McDonald, Sandy Stokes immediately behind with the pole, Lee James behind, again with a pole.*

Community Play in Cherry Orchard, 1997. Pictured are: policeman Peter Leonard, mother Julie Barnard with Ruth and Faye, Sandy Stokes holding the pole and Mike Walker emerging from the Grim Reaper.

Community Play outside the Woolstore Theatre. Among those pictured are: *Derek Miles, Mary Jones, Maggie Piper, Doreen Axtell, unknown actor, policeman Peter Leonard.*

Community Play, 1997. The crowd gathers outside the Woolstore Theatre. Among those pictured are: *Karen Johnstone* (far right) *the then chairman of the Woolstore Theatre Company.*

The Bee Dance, June 1997.

Codford School perform their Bee Dance, June 1997. Holding the pole is Lee James, and with his back to the camera is the Theatre in the Downs actor Tim Laycock.

nights charged 70p and on Saturday they were sold at 75p. Although the audience had paid to attend the show Theatre In The Downs placed unlabelled collection buckets out as people left, and as most people wrongly assumed the donations were going to the Woolstore they made contributions.

The show was widely advertised locally, but when tickets were not selling as expected Karen asked if Dot Macree wanted her to put an advert in the Salisbury and Warminster papers to attract from wider afield. The village ended up footing the bill for £72.90 for advertisements, as well as the heating bill for the Woolstore Theatre and the bill for the emptying of the chemical toilets.

The whole process had been an enriching experience for those taking part and a valuable learning experience for those involved in making it happen. A few years later the Woolstore Theatre Company put on a community play without money from the public purse and it was a sell out every night!

The Village in 2005

There are six Grade-II listed buildings in the village – the old Woolstore, French Horn Cottages, 102 and 113 High Street, the Old Manor House and the Old Rectory at St Peter's. The bridge over the Chitterne Brook and 25 other properties are Grade-III listed buildings. The New Road ex-council-houses are the oldest social housing in Codford; the two former council estates at Cherry Orchard and The Grove were built after the Second World War. In 1972 Codford's first 12 executive houses were built on the site of the Second World War tank workshops at Bury Mead. For little over 20 years there was no further large-scale development. Wiltshire Rural Housing Association built six retirement bungalows in Cherry Orchard; in 1992/93 the Sutton Hastoe Housing Association built six local homes at Rickworth Place on land bought from the Church. It was agreed that later the other two thirds of the site would be developed commercially – originally six houses were proposed, but when Greenhill Place was eventually built there were 12 executive houses.

As the new village hall was built as part of a land swap deal the Shaftesbury Housing Association development is on the site of the old wartime building known locally as the Codford Club and the garages. Three large houses known as The Downlands were built opposite the old piggery in New Road when the Codford Bodyworks was demolished, and eight houses were built in the gardens of the Wool House, the four smaller dwellings were replacement buildings across the lane from where derelict old cottages had stood.

The four Granary Close houses off Chitterne Road were built where a wartime tin building stood. Until the 1980s this was occupied by an elderly Polish couple; Mr Kazinski had stayed when the Polish Army were demobbed in Codford at the end of the Second World War. His wife would toil in the huge garden, growing root crops and cabbages, digging and hoeing, pickling in salt-water brine in huge barrels. Mrs Kazinska moved after she was widowed and planning permission was granted.

In the period before Greenhill Place was developed the land had been used as an animal sanctuary – goats, sheep, dogs and cats were housed where Second World War huts had once been. Initially the huts were used after the conflict, to house families in need of accommodation, first as squatters and later as tenants of the local council until the housing estates were built and the huts were demolished.

Quinton's Place, the latest development, was the most controversial development in 30 years. It was the site of a fairly new bungalow, possibly 12 years old, surrounded on two sides by the old scrapyard. The yard had become more and more unsightly, with piles of rusting vehicles, so that when the owner asked the Parish Council to move the village policy limits to allow the scrapyard to be built on, it seemed a good idea. What the councillors were unaware of was that the bungalow was to be demolished and that the substantial plot of land that went with Quinton's was part of the package with the industrial site. Instead of six small homes there was an application for 15 houses – the Parish Council convinced the planners there should be no more than 13, two of which would be social housing. The proposal for 11 tall five-bedroomed town houses was universally opposed – villagers said they were an inappropriate development, they were out of place in their setting, too tall, too visual on the skyline in an Area of Outstanding Natural Beauty, and too expensive. There was concern about the drainage in a village with no mains drains, as well as about the lack of screen planting. Despite district councillors agreeing with village concerns, permission was granted because all but one councillor thought the developer might win on appeal. It took at least eight months to sell one property, almost a year to sell two more and at the end of 2004 only four of the 11 houses were occupied.

According to the voter's list there are 336 properties and 658 voters in Codford and, at the last count, there were about 130 children. In the early 1970s there was a significant number of farm cottages for rent; at the time of writing there are an estimated 20, most of which have long-term occupants.

There are six farms: East Farm, Manor Farm, Bury Farm, Mayflower Farm, Punchbowl Farm and Auckland Farm. The major employers are Lyons Seafoods, once The Flying Goose, along the Chitterne Road, and West Country Fine Foods at East Farm, while the New Road Service Station with workshops, coach hire, a general store and a Post Office, provides many local jobs. Codford has two antique shops, one pub (the George Inn), a car outlet, The Sound Post (a facility for storing and shipping musical instruments), an industrial area on the old piggery and, in Station

Listed farm cottages and Old Police Station, looking west from the tower of St Mary's Church.

Nos 52, 53 and 54 High Street. (PHOTO BRIAN MARSHALL)

St Mary's graveyard from the church roof.

French Horn Cottages. (PHOTO BRIAN MARSHALL)

St Mary's Church and St Mary's Cottage along Beanis Path leading to Church Lane, c.2003. The ANZAC hut is on the far right. The luxuriant wild flowers and grasses are on the old allotment site. (PHOTO BRIAN MARSHALL)

Landscaping around the new village hall, c.1994. Left to right: Mike Gibbens, Sue Mitchell, ? Pluess, John Gibbens, Kate Forbes, Colin Nunn, ?, Sue Poolman, ?, ? (child in front), Frank West senr, Frank West junr, Shelagh Boyd, actor Niven Boyd, John Wyeth, ?, Louise McDonald with Corrie (?), ?, Caroline Crossman, Karen Barnard, Julie Barnard holding Ruth with oldest daughter Faye (in front), Gary Poole, David Delius.

September 2004 at the Guards Armoured Division commemoration in the Woolstore. Left to right: Godfrey Cole, Ruby Otterwell, Iris and Walt Conduit. The bearded man in the mirror is Major Richard Carr-Gomm of the Coldstream Guards. (PHOTO DAVID PETERS)

Maurice Cole and Doreen Szeliga (née Cole) at the Guards Armoured commemoration in 2004. (PHOTO DAVID PETERS)

The late Peter Leonard, c.1995.

Above: *Louise McDonald with Kelsey and Corrie, c.2000. The girls have been transported in this way since they were very young.*

Above: *The mother and toddler group join in with the 50th anniversary of VE Day parade, passing Overton House and St Peter's Church with their pushchairs turned into Spitfires. From the back: Louise McDonald, Karen Barnard, Julie Barnard, Caroline Crossman, Colleen Gower and Bertha Pluess.*

Left: *Major Mike (Spike) Cotterill at the Bypass Party in 1990.*

Alan Nash at the Jubilee Parade in 2003. The bier was in use between Corton and Boyton for a century from 1900.

The opening of the new telecottage in the new village hall, c.1993–94. Left to right: Stan Bissell, Sue Mitchell, John Wood, John Nuth and telecottage chairman Dr Jack Barrow.

Looking down Church Lane towards the High Street in 2003. (PHOTO BRIAN MARSHALL)

Janet Lavery with Gordon (with teddy bear) *and John, as a factory girl and evacuees. They were part of the parade to celebrate the 50th anniversary of VE Day in 1995.*

Road, the Country Gentleman's Association buildings include office space to let.

The village can boast the only village theatre owned by its own company in the country, an excellent doctors' practice with a dispensary, a veterinary surgery and a popular primary school. There is a purpose-built village hall that also houses a sports and social club, with the opportunity to play skittles, badminton, short-mat bowls or use the computer centre, and a huge playing-field with a youth chill-out centre and a children's playground. The recycling centre on village hall land with paper, metal, cloth, plastic, clear, green and brown bottle banks is consistently one of the best used in West Wiltshire. Villagers have a range of clubs, societies and groups: football, cricket, tennis, gardening, Scottish country dancing, keep fit, Brownies, theatre, history, WI, Royal British Legion, pre-school and the pensioner's Evergreen Club. At Hillside there is the White Horse Trekking Centre for equestrian activities and Hillside Café providing all-day dining facilities.

Living in a rural community with the opportunity to walk, cycle, fish, shoot, ride, follow the local beagles or explore the country pubs is a delight.

Locally, shopping, theatrical and railway access are within easy reach – there are regular trains to London, with Salisbury and Warminster close by and Bath and Southampton about an hour away.

Villagers have regular opportunities to take part in communal activities, local organisations regularly hold fund-raising lunches in the village hall – for between £3–£4 a three-course lunch with a choice of soups, meat and cheese ploughman's, an impressive array of desserts and coffee; every November the Codford fireworkers put on the most spectacular display for miles around; for special celebrations there are parades and street parties; and, in early summer, the Codford Country Show fills the playing-field with stalls and attractions for every taste.

Codford lies in a beautiful setting; it has a fascinating history and a place in the hearts of those who have been transplanted, however briefly, within its environs. The story of any settlement is the story of its people; inextricably the village has links to the military and an agricultural past, while at the same time it moves forward with confidence to face the challenges of the future.

15 High Street. (PHOTO BRIAN MARSHALL)

West Country Fine Foods looking north-east from St Mary's tower.

Left: *The cottage by the bridge sometime in the early-twentieth century.*

Below: *A pair of listed farm cottages along Beanis Path, 2003.*

Subscribers

Dr Michael J. Allen, FLS, FSA, Codford

Mr Timothy Anderson, Codford, Wiltshire

Kenneth V. Axtell, Codford, Wiltshire

D. Bailey and C. Poolman (née Bailey)

The Barnard Family, St Mary's Cottage, Codford

Emily L. and Jessica J. Beagley, Codford, Wiltshire

Peter and Jenny Beales, Codford, Wiltshire

Lynne Benson, Codford, Wiltshire

Michael and Paula Bremridge

John Budden, Salisbury

Ellis and Tabitha Butcher, Summerbrook Cottage, Codford (Master Thatcher)

Brigadier and Mrs Iain Cameron, Codford, Wiltshire

Elaine Cantwell, Gunnislake, Cornwall

M. Carey, Corton, Wiltshire

Paul and Jill Cawse

Rita Chapman, Codford

Mrs I. Chivers, Codford, Wiltshire

Margaret D. Chivers, Sherrington, Wiltshire

Karl and Sirene Cleife, Codford, Wiltshire

Godfrey D. Cole, Wiltshire

Maurice Cole

Major John Corder

Major Geoffrey Cottrill MBE

Jack Davis, Codford, Wiltshire

Wg Cdr Crispin C. Edmonds Rtd

Earl Norton Fidler, Quebec, Canada

Andrew and Helen Forsyth, Corton, Wiltshire

Dorothy and Eddie Freak, West Moors, Dorset

Paul and Jane Freak

Dr Julie Gardiner, FSA, Codford

William G. Grace, Heytesbury, Wiltshire

Mrs Joyce Green, Codford, Wiltshire

Stewart N. Green, Westbury, Wiltshire

Wayne K. Green, Bishopstrow, Wiltshire

Mrs Barbara E. Gregory, Codford, Wiltshire

5 Hardings, Stockton

Janet Hill (née Davis), Amesbury, Wiltshire

Colonel Jerry Hunter, Codford St Mary

Keith and Diane Huntley, Ashton Gifford, Codford

Robert and Caroline Huntley, Codford, Wiltshire

Euan Hutchings, Codford St Mary

Alexander S. Jamieson, Bramley Cottage, Codford St Mary
Duncan A.R. Jamieson, Bramley Cottage, Codford St Mary
Ann Jessey (née Lush), Edmonton, Alberta, Canada
Lily E. Kitley, Heytesbury
David Last, descendent of the Coopers of Codford
Carol and Keith Martin, Tatworth, Somerset
Andrew and Anne Neish, Codford, Wiltshire
John Palmer, born Codford 1943
Owen D. Pearce, Codford, Wiltshire
Susan Poolman
Philip Rabbetts, Dinton
Mr and Mrs M.J. Redford, Salisbury, Wiltshire
Jill Richards (née Dear), Southampton, Hampshire
Mr Donald P.F. Stacey, Codford, Wiltshire
Mr Peter F. Stacey, Wembley, Middlesex
Mr P. Stacey-Cox, Codford, Wiltshire
Phyllida Stratton, Stockton
Doreen Szeliga
Gwen Thorne, Codford, Wiltshire
Richard Thorne
John E. Tilbury, Old Coulsdon, Surrey
Gwen Twist
Mrs Heather Uwins, Grouville, Jersey, Channel Islands
John F.W. Walling, Newton Abbot, Devon
Louise Waltham, Ashcombe
Francis Charles Watts, High Street, Codford
Ms Sue Williams and Mr David Woodland, Codford, Wiltshire
The Williams Family, Greenhill Place, Codford
Lew and Brenda Willmore (née Ford)
Gill Withington, Codford, Wiltshire
Mrs J. Wood

✦ FURTHER TITLES ✦

Community Histories

The Book of Addiscombe • Canning and Clyde Road
Residents Association and Friends

The Book of Addiscombe, Vol. II • Canning and Clyde Road
Residents Association and Friends

The Book of Ashburton • Stuart Hands and Pete Webb

The Book of Axminster with Kilmington • Les Berry
and Gerald Gosling

The Book of Bakewell • Trevor Brighton

The Book of Bampton • Caroline Seward

The Book of Barnstaple • Avril Stone

The Book of Barnstaple, Vol. II • Avril Stone

The Book of The Bedwyns • Bedwyn History Society

The Book of Bergh Apton • Geoffrey I. Kelly

The Book of Bickington • Stuart Hands

The Book of Bideford • Peter Christie and Alison Grant

Blandford Forum: A Millennium Portrait • Blandford Forum
Town Council

The Book of Boscastle • Rod and Anne Knight

The Book of Bourton-on-the-Hill, Batsford and Sezincote •
Allen Firth

The Book of Bramford • Bramford Local History Group

The Book of Breage & Germoe • Stephen Polglase

The Book of Bridestowe • D. Richard Cann

The Book of Bridport • Rodney Legg

The Book of Brixham • Frank Pearce

The Book of Buckfastleigh • Sandra Coleman

The Book of Buckland Monachorum & Yelverton •
Pauline Hamilton-Leggett

The Book of Budleigh Salterton • D. Richard Cann

The Book of Carharrack • Carharrack Old
Cornwall Society

The Book of Carshalton • Stella Wilks and Gordon
Rookledge

The Parish Book of Cerne Abbas • Vivian and
Patricia Vale

The Book of Chagford • Iain Rice

The Book of Chapel-en-le-Frith • Mike Smith

*The Book of Chittlehamholt with
Warkleigh & Satterleigh* • Richard Lethbridge

The Book of Chittlehampton • Various

The Book of Codford • Romy Wyeth

The Book of Colney Heath • Bryan Lilley

The Book of Constantine • Moore and Trethowan

The Book of Cornwood and Lutton • Compiled by
the People of the Parish

The Book of Crediton • John Heal

The Book of Creech St Michael • June Small

The Book of Crowcombe, Bicknoller and Sampford Brett •
Maurice and Joyce Chidgey

The Book of Crudwell • Tony Pain

The Book of Cullompton • Compiled by the People
of the Parish

The Book of Dawlish • Frank Pearce

*The Book of Dulverton, Brushford,
Bury & Exebridge* • Dulverton and District Civic Society

The Book of Dunster • Hilary Binding

The Book of Easton • Easton Village History Project

The Book of Edale • Gordon Miller

The Ellacombe Book • Sydney R. Langmead

The Book of Exmouth • W.H. Pascoe

The Book of Grampound with Creed • Bane and Oliver

The Book of Gosport • Lesley Burton and
Brian Musselwhite

The Book of Haughley • Howard Stephens

The Book of Hayle • Harry Pascoe

The Book of Hayling Island & Langstone • Peter Rogers

The Book of Helston • Jenkin with Carter

The Book of Hemyock • Clist and Dracott

The Book of Herne Hill • Patricia Jenkyns

The Book of Hethersett • Hethersett Society
Research Group

The Book of High Bickington • Avril Stone

The Book of Honiton • Gerald Gosling

The Book of Ilsington • Dick Wills

The Book of Kingskerswell • Carsewella Local
History Group

The Book of Lamerton • Ann Cole and Friends

Lanner, A Cornish Mining Parish • Sharron
Schwartz and Roger Parker

The Book of Leigh & Bransford • Malcolm Scott

The Second Book of Leigh & Bransford • Malcolm Scott

The Book of Litcham with Lexham & Mileham • Litcham
Historical and Amenity Society

The Book of Llangain • Haydyn Williams

The Book of Loddiswell • Loddiswell Parish History Group

The New Book of Lostwithiel • Barbara Fraser

The Book of Lulworth • Rodney Legg

The Book of Lustleigh • Joe Crowdy

The Book of Lydford • Compiled by Barbara Weeks

The Book of Lyme Regis • Rodney Legg

The Book of Manaton • Compiled by the People
of the Parish

159

For details of any of the above titles or if you are interested in writing your own history, please contact: Commissioning Editor, Community Histories, Halsgrove House, Lower Moor Way, Tiverton, Devon EX16 6SS, England; email: katyc@halsgrove.com.